Psychosis and Emotion

There is increasing recognition that emotional distress plays a significant part in the onset of psychosis, the experience of psychosis itself and in the unfolding of recovery that follows. This book brings together leading international experts to explore the role of emotion and emotion regulation in the development of and recovery from psychosis.

Psychosis and Emotion offers extensive clinical material and cutting-edge research with a focus on:

- the diverse theoretical perspectives on the importance of emotion in psychosis;
- the interpersonal, systemic and organisational context of recovery from psychosis and the implications for emotional distress;
- the implications of specific perspectives for promoting recovery from psychosis.

With thorough coverage of contemporary thinking, including psychoanalytic, cognitive, developmental, evolutionary and neurobiological, this book will be a valuable resource to clinicians and psychological therapists working in the field.

Andrew Gumley is Professor of Psychological Therapy in the Institute of Health and Wellbeing, University of Glasgow.

Alf Gillham is a retired Consultant Clinical Psychologist and an Honorary Senior Lecturer in the Institute of Health and Wellbeing, University of Glasgow.

Kathy Taylor is a psychoanalyst working in private practice and a Consultant Clinical Psychologist working in homelessness and psychosis services in South London and Maudsley NHS Foundation Trust.

Matthias Schwannauer is Professor of Clinical Psychology at the University of Edinburgh.

The International Society for Psychological and Social Approaches to Psychosis Book Series

Series editors: Brian Martindale and Alison Summers

ISPS (The International Society for Psychological and Social Approaches to Psychosis) has a history stretching back more than fifty years during which it has witnessed the relentless pursuit of biological explanations for psychosis. The tide has been turning in recent years and there is a welcome international resurgence of interest in a range of psychological factors that have considerable explanatory power and therapeutic possibilities. Governments, professional groups, people with personal experience of psychosis and family members are increasingly expecting interventions that involve more talking and listening. Many now regard practitioners skilled in psychological therapies as an essential component of the care of people with psychosis.

ISPS is a global society. It aims to promote psychological and social approaches both to understanding and to treating psychosis. It also aims to bring together different perspectives on these issues. ISPS is composed of individuals, networks and institutional members from a wide range of backgrounds and is especially concerned that those with personal experience of psychosis and their family members are fully involved in our activities alongside practitioners and researchers, and that all benefit from this. Our members recognise the potential humanitarian and therapeutic potential of skilled psychological understanding and therapy in the field of psychosis and ISPS embraces a wide spectrum of approaches from psychodynamic, systemic, cognitive and arts therapies to the need-adapted approaches, family and group therapies and residential therapeutic communities.

We are also most interested in establishing meaningful dialogue with those practitioners and researchers who are more familiar with biological-based approaches. There is increasing empirical evidence for the interaction of genes and biology with the emotional and social environment, and there are important examples of such interactions in the fields of trauma, attachment relationships in the family and in social settings and with professionals.

ISPS activities include regular international and national conferences, newsletters and email discussion groups. Routledge has recognised the importance of our field in publishing both the book series and the ISPS journal: *Psychosis – Psychological, Social and Integrative Approaches* with the two complementing one another. The book series started in 2004 and by 2012 had 13 volumes with several more in preparation. A wide range of topics are covered and we hope this reflects some success in our aim of bringing together a rich range of perspectives.

The book series is intended as a resource for a broad range of mental health professionals as well as those developing and implementing policy and people whose interest in psychosis is at a personal level. We aim for rigorous academic standards and at the same time accessibility to a wide range of readers, and for the books to promote the ideas of clinicians and researchers who may be well known in some countries but not so familiar in others. Our overall intention is to encourage the dissemination of existing knowledge and ideas, promote productive debate and encourage more research in a most important field whose secrets certainly do not all reside in the neurosciences.

For more information about ISPS, email isps@isps.org or visit our website, www.isps.org.

For more information about the journal *Psychosis* visit www.isps.org/index.php/publications/journal.

Models of Madness: Psychological, Social and Biological Approaches to Schizophrenia
Edited by John Read, Loren R. Mosher and Richard P. Bentall

Psychoses: An Integrative Perspective
Edited by Johan Cullberg

Evolving Psychosis: Different Stages, Different Treatments
Edited by Jan Olav Johanessen, Brian V. Martindale and Johan Cullberg

Family and Multi-Family Work with Psychosis
Gerd-Ragna Block Thorsen, Trond Gronnestad and Anne Lise Oxenvad

Experiences of Mental Health In-Patient Care: Narratives from Service Users, Carers and Professionals
Edited by Mark Hardcastle, David Kennard, Sheila Grandison and Leonard Fagin

Psychotherapies for the Psychoses: Theoretical, Cultural, and Clinical Integration
Edited by John Gleeson, Eión Killackey and Helen Krstev

Therapeutic Communities for Psychosis: Philosophy, History and Clinical Practice
Edited by John Gale, Alba Realpe and Enrico Pedriali

Beyond Medication: Therapeutic Engagement and the Recovery from Psychosis
Edited by David Garfield and Daniel Mackler

Making Sense of Madness: Contesting the Meaning of Schizophrenia
Jim Geekie and John Read

Psychotherapeutic Approaches to Schizophrenia Psychosis
Edited by Yrjö O. Alanen, Manuel González de Chávez, Ann-Louise S. Silver and Brian Martindale

CBT for Psychosis: A Symptom-based Approach
Edited by Roger Hagen, Douglas Turkington, Torkil Berge and Rolf W. Gråwe

Psychosis as a Personal Crisis: An Experience-Based Approach
Edited by Marius Romme and Sandra Escher

Psychosis and Emotion: The Role of Emotions in Understanding Psychosis, Therapy and Recovery
Edited by Andrew Gumley, Alf Gillham, Kathy Taylor and Matthias Schwannauer

Experiencing Psychosis: Personal and Professional Perspectives
Edited by Jim Geekie, Patte Randal, Debra Lampshire and John Read

Insanity and Divinity: Studies in Psychosis and Spirituality
Edited by John Gale, Michael Robson and Georgia Rapsomatioti

Surviving, Existing, or Living: Phase-specific Therapy for Severe Psychosis
Pamela Fuller

Psychosis and Emotion

The role of emotions in understanding psychosis, therapy and recovery

Edited by Andrew Gumley,
Alf Gillham, Kathy Taylor and
Matthias Schwannauer

Routledge
Taylor & Francis Group
LONDON AND NEW YORK

First published 2013
by Routledge
4 Park Square, Milton Park, Abingdon, Oxon OX14 4RN
605 Third Avenue, New York, NY 10017

Routledge is an imprint of the Taylor and Francis Group, an informa business

British Library Cataloguing in Publication Data
A catalogue record for this book is available from the British Library

Library of Congress Cataloging in Publication Data
A catalog record for this book has been requested

ISBN: 978-0-415-57040-4 (hbk)
ISBN: 978-0-415-57042-8 (pbk)
ISBN: 978-0-203-75976-9 (ebk)

Typeset in Garamond
by RefineCatch Limited, Bungay, Suffolk

Contents

List of illustrations

Figures

Tables

About the editors

Andrew Gumley, Professor of Psychological Therapy, BA(Hons), M.App. Sci., PhD, CPsychol, AFBPsS graduated in clinical psychology from the University of Glasgow in 1993. His first position as a Clinical Psychologist was within a north Glasgow Community Mental Health Team. In that team he was able to develop his interests in the psychological treatment of individuals with psychosis. He moved to Ayrshire and Arran Community Care NHS Trust in 1996. During this time he was able to carry out his PhD research into psychological aspects of relapse in schizophrenia. This research involved the implementation of a randomised controlled trial of cognitive therapy for relapse and an investigation of the role of cognitive factors in the vulnerability and transition to relapse. He is currently Professor of Psychological Therapy and Head of Mental Health and Wellbeing within the Institute of Health and Wellbeing. He is a Consultant Clinical Psychologist at ESTEEM: North Glasgow First Episode Psychosis Service. His current research interests include the application of attachment theory to understanding development, adaptation to and recovery from psychosis.

Alf Gillham, BSc(Hons), MSc, CPsychol is a retired Consultant Clinical Psychologist whose last post was at Leverndale Hospital, South Glasgow, where he worked in a specialist Psychiatric Rehabilitation setting. He is an Honorary Senior Lecturer at the Department of Psychological Medicine, Glasgow University where he has taught for the past 25 years. He was a committee member of the Psychosis and Complex Mental Health Faculty of the Division of Clinical Psychology UK. He is a committee member of the International Society for Psychological and Social Approaches to Psychosis UK (Treasurer). He has a longstanding interest and experience in working with severe and enduring mental illness. A particular area or interest has been in the overlap between cognitive and psychoanalytic approaches to psychosis.

Kathy Taylor, BSc(Hons), MSc, CPsychol is a psychoanalyst of the British Society of Psychoanalysis working in private practice, and a Consultant

Clinical Psychologist working in Homelessness and Psychosis services in South London and Maudsley NHS Foundation Trust. She trained as a Clinical Psychologist in 1989 and has worked in Adult Mental Health across a broad range of services in the south east of England since then, with a growing interest and specialisation in working with psychosis. She led the establishment of an Early Psychosis service in East Surrey in 2002 and now leads a psychology service to people experiencing psychosis in conjunction with complex social needs, especially homelessness. Since training as a psychoanalyst she is committed to developing the use and understanding of psychoanalytic concepts in NHS work with psychosis and other complex mental health needs. She offers psychoanalytic consultation and supervision to Psychosis teams and has taught on the Psychoanalytic Module of the Clinical Psychology Doctorate course at University College London. She is also a member of the Complex Mental Health Faculty of the Division of Clinical Psychology of the BPS, an Associate Member of ISPS-UK and a member of the Association for Psychoanalytic Psychotherapy in the NHS.

Matthias Schwannauer, Professor of Clinical Psychology, MA, MSc, DPsych, PhD, CPsychol, AFBPsS graduated in clinical and applied psychology from the University of Marburg in 1998. His first position as a clinical psychologist was in the Adolescent Mental Health Services in Glasgow. He moved to NHS Lothian and the University of Edinburgh in 2000. During this time he was able to carry out his PhD research into psychological interventions for bipolar disorders. This research involved the implementation of a randomised controlled trial of cognitive interpersonal therapy and an investigation of the role of interpersonal and cognitive factors in the recovery process. He is currently Head of the Section of Clinical and Health Psychology and Programme Director for the Doctorate in Clinical Psychology training programme at the University of Edinburgh. He is a Consultant Clinical Psychologist in the Early Psychosis Support Service at CAMHS Lothian. His current research interests include the application of attachment theory and affect regulation to understanding development, adaptation to and recovery from psychosis and recurrent mood disorders.

About the contributors

Max Birchwood is Clinical Director of Youthspace mental health services in Birmingham and Professor of Psychology at the University of Birmingham. He is well known for his research on the place of emotion in psychosis and presented his '3 pathways to emotional dysfunction model' in 2003. He introduced the social evolutionary model of affective dysfunction in psychosis undertaking work on depression and social anxiety disorder in first episode psychosis. He pioneered the development of early intervention in psychosis services in the UK and developed a distinctive approach to CBT for psychosis, focusing on what makes psychotic symptoms distressing and dysfunctional for the individual.

Frank R. Burbach is a Consultant Clinical Psychologist with the Somerset Partnership NHS Foundation Trust. He is the Head of Psychology and lead for Early Intervention in Psychosis services. As a Systemic and Cognitive-Behavioural therapist he has been developing integrated family interventions services in Somerset since 1995. He is a member of the Triangle of Care national steering group, chairs the Family Interventions Network within the Division of Clinical Psychology Psychosis and Complex Mental Health Faculty, is joint IRIS South West Early Intervention lead and is also a member of the Editorial Board of the *Journal of Family Therapy.*

Rory Byrne is a postgraduate researcher based in Manchester, UK. His main focus is user-led qualitative research into psychosis-spectrum experiences, and psychological therapies for treating or preventing psychosis (e.g. CBT). He is also interested in evaluating service users' priorities and preferences for treatment, and the promotion of choice in treatment delivery.

Michelle Campbell is a Clinical Psychologist currently working for the NHS in a community mental health team in Bolton, Lancashire. She is part of a multidisciplinary team providing support for adults who experience severe and enduring mental health problems. Her PhD explored some of the cognitive processes implicated in psychotic experiences with a particular focus on the impact of trauma upon these in both clinical and non-clinical groups. She has published articles in these areas along with a paper examining the effectiveness of a workshop for teenagers in reducing stigma about psychosis. She is generally interested in the cognitive processes involved in the development and maintenance of psychological distress in the context of a person's attachment and coping style.

Sarah Dilks, PhD is a Consultant Clinical Psychologist and Lead Psychologist for the Promoting Recovery care pathway at South London and Maudsley NHS Foundation Trust, London. She has maintained an interest in the links between the individual and the social in therapy in psychosis, beginning from the experience of closing large UK psychiatric hospitals in the move to community-based care.

David Garfield, MD is Professor, Associate Chair and Program Director, Department of Psychiatry and Behavioral Sciences, RFUMS/The Chicago Medical School, North Chicago. Faculty, Institute for Psychoanalysis, Chicago.

Paul Gilbert is the head of the Mental Health Research Unit as well as Professor of Clinical Psychology at the University of Derby. He has a degree in Economics (Wolverhampton, 1973), Masters in Experimental Psychology (Sussex, 1975), PhD in Clinical Psychology (Edinburgh, 1980) and a diploma in Clinical Psychology awarded by the British Psychological Society (1980). He is a Fellow of the British Psychological Society for contributions to psychological knowledge in 1993 and was president of the British Association for Cognitive and Behavioural Psychotherapy in 2003. He also served on the government depression NICE guideline committee. In 2011 he was awarded an OBE. Professor Gilbert has published and edited 21 books, over 100 academic papers and 39 book chapters. He is currently a series editor for a 'compassionate approaches to life difficulties' series. After years of exploring the processes underpinning shame and its role in a variety of psychopathologies, Professor Gilbert's research is exploring the neurophysiology and therapeutic effectiveness of compassion focused therapy.

Susanne Harder, PHD is Associate Professor in Clinical Psychology at Copenhagen University. Her research focuses on applying developmental psychopathology to the prevention and treatment of psychosis, with special interests in risk processes in early mother–infant interaction and change processes in psychotherapy.

Gerhard Heim, born in Munich, Germany, Diploma and Doctorate in Psychology (schizophrenia research) at the University of Konstanz (Germany), is a Clinical Psychologist at the Psychiatric Department of the Free University of Berlin and practising Psychotherapist and Supervisor (CBT) in Berlin. He is President of the Pierre Janet Society, Berlin.

Robert D. Hinshelwood is Professor in the Centre for Psychoanalytic Studies, University of Essex, and previously Clinical Director, the Cassel Hospital, London. He is a Fellow of the British Psychoanalytical Society, and a Fellow of the Royal College of Psychiatrists. He has authored *A Dictionary of Kleinian Thought* (1989) and other books and articles on Kleinian psychoanalysis. *Observing Organisations* (2000) was edited with Wilhelm Skogstad and is among a number of texts on psychoanalytic applications to social science. In 2004, he published *Suffering Insanity*, a book on schizophrenia in psychiatric institutions. He founded the *British Journal of Psychotherapy* and *Psychoanalysis and History*. Currently he is completing *Research on the Couch: Single Case Studies, Subjectivity and Psychoanalytic Knowledge* to be published 2013.

Heather Laithwaite is a Consultant Forensic Clinical Psychologist working in the Directorate of Forensic Mental Health and Learning Disabilities in NHS Greater Glasgow and Clyde. Her research and clinical interests are in promoting recovery and compassion-focused approaches to treatment in individuals with psychosis residing in forensic clinical settings.

Paul Lysaker, PhD is a Clinical Psychologist at the Roudebush VA Medical Center and Professor of Clinical Psychology in the department of Psychiatry at the Indiana University School of Medicine. He is an author of more than 250 published articles. His research interests include understanding the psychological factors that are involved in wellness and dysfunction in schizophrenia and the development of psychotherapy that promotes recovery.

Anthony P. Morrison is a Professor of Clinical Psychology at the University of Manchester and is also Associate Director for Early Intervention for Bolton, Salford and Trafford Mental Health NHS Trust. He has published a number of articles on cognitive therapy for psychosis and experimental studies of cognitive processes in psychosis, has been involved in a number of treatment trials for cognitive therapy for psychosis and has a special interest in the cognitive theory of and therapy for hearing voices. More recently, he has developed a research interest in people at high risk of developing psychosis, the links between trauma and psychosis and the facilitation of user-led research into psychosis and mental health services.

Andrew Moskowitz, PhD is Professor of Clinical Psychology at Aarhus University in Denmark, where he teaches and supervises graduate and undergraduate students, and leads a research unit on attachment, dissociation and psychological trauma. His core research areas involve understanding psychotic symptoms and schizophrenia from a trauma/dissociation perspective, and developing intervention approaches, informed by this perspective, for working with persons who hear voices.

Paul Patterson is currently Research Manager and Public Mental Health lead for the Youthspace programme within Birmingham and Solihull Mental Health Foundation Trust and Honorary Senior Research Fellow with the School of Psychology, University of Birmingham. He has previously been involved in developing and evaluating early detection of psychosis initiatives and has a strong interest in developmental and preventative approaches to improving youth mental health including educational and web-based interventions (see youthspace.me).

Anil Ramachandran, MD is Senior Resident in Psychiatry, Department of Psychiatry and Behavioral Sciences, RFUMS/The Chicago Medical School.

Michael Robbins is a psychoanalyst and former Professor of Clinical Psychology on the faculties of Harvard Medical School and University of California, San Francisco. In addition to numerous articles and book chapters he has written three books: *Experiences of Schizophrenia*, *Conceiving of Personality*, and most recently (2011) *The Primordial Mind in Health and Illness: A Cross-Cultural Perspective.*

Edwin K. Simon, MD is Assistant Professor of Psychiatry, Department of Psychiatry and Behavioral Sciences, RFUMS/The Chicago Medical School.

Ross White is a university teacher and Clinical Psychologist working in Mental Health and Wellbeing at the University of Glasgow. He completed a PhD at the Queen's University of Belfast that focused on depression and hopelessness experienced by individuals diagnosed with schizophrenia. Ross's subsequent research has continued to investigate emotional adaptation following psychosis. He has a particular interest in the use of Acceptance and Commitment Therapy to facilitate recovery from psychosis. Ross has an honorary contract with NHS Greater Glasgow and Clyde.

Acknowledgements

We would like to thank the many colleagues and our contributors who have influenced our work. These include many researchers, clinicians and psychotherapists from the field of psychosis. In particular we would like to acknowledge the support of the following services: ESTEEM NHS Greater Glasgow & Clyde and the EPSS team in NHS Lothian; and the support of Suzy Clark, Susanne Harder and David Kennard. We are also greatly indebted to Brian Martindale, Alison Summers and all at Routledge for their continuing and invaluable support throughout the process of proposing, editing and completing this book. Our thanks also go to Dr Laurence Errington for indexing our book. Most importantly we would like to thank our clients and their families, who have taught us, inspired us, moved us and most of all energised us towards a shared goal of promoting the central importance of emotion in understanding the expression of psychosis, adaptation to the demands of psychosis and recovery from these experiences.

Andrew Gumley, Alf Gillham, Kathy Taylor and Matthias Schwannauer

For Lee-Anne. **AGu**

For Janet. **AGi**

For Pete. **KT**

For Claire. **MS**

Chapter 1

Psychosis and emotion

The role of emotions in understanding psychosis, therapy and recovery

Andrew Gumley, Alf Gillham, Kathy Taylor and Matthias Schwannauer

Introduction

This book aims to bring together a collection of current, fresh and original perspectives on contemporary international work with psychosis, under the aegis of the International Society for the Psychological Treatments of the Schizophrenias and Other Psychoses (ISPS), which has a long and distinguished history of building bridges between differing approaches to psychosis. As editors, all practitioners of psychotherapeutic work with psychosis in the UK, we share a passionate interest in broadening the base of theory considered relevant to our clinical work.[1] Recently the dominant psychotherapeutic model has been a cognitive-behavioural approach to working with psychosis, particularly as a variety of convincing randomised controlled trials (RCT) have demonstrated the effectiveness of cognitive-behavioural therapy (CBT) for reducing distress and improving coping with psychotic symptoms. However, in clinical practice a wide range of concepts and ideas is drawn upon with increasing importance being placed on developmental processes, emotional processing, trauma, early experiences, close interpersonal relationships, family and organisational systems in the evolution and expression of psychosis.

We have approached a range of authors from different theoretical backgrounds to provide a rich, varied and distinctive range of perspectives on the importance of emotion in understanding and helping people with psychosis. In doing this, it is our expressed aim to give voice to this range, which we believe can introduce richness and complexity into our growing understanding of this challenging area. We do not attempt to integrate these different perspectives; some are really quite different in essential ways.

1 In 2006, a successful conference 'Working with Emotion in Psychosis' was convened by Kathy Taylor and Alf Gillham, linking ISPS-UK and the Faculty for Complex Mental Health and Psychosis, a specialist interest group in psychosis within the Division of Clinical Psychology, British Psychological Society. This conference brought together a range of alternative theoretical approaches to psychological work with psychosis in the UK.

We hope that this collection will inspire a discourse on the role of affect and distress in psychosis, which is driven by different theoretical and psychotherapeutic perspectives. However, this introduction to the text aims to provide some commentary on and linking between the chapters contained within the book, without losing the diversity we are presenting here.

Since the concept of schizophrenia was introduced in 1911, emotion has been at the heart of understanding psychosis. Over the years this emphasis on emotion and affect as an essential aspect of the disorder has been replaced with increasingly biological and neurophysiological paradigms and a disproportionate focus on positive symptoms of psychosis. A revitalisation of concepts and theories of emotion and psychosis, especially in the context of psychological and psychotherapeutic treatments, is long overdue and we have chosen this portal with which to make an entry into publishing some emerging and stimulating therapeutic treatment models. In this volume we emphasise the importance of emotion in psychosis and explore how thinking about affect can contribute to care, psychotherapeutic intervention and recovery. We will now aim to highlight how each of the authors has approached the complex relationship between emotion and psychosis from their own perspective.

In Chapter 2, Andrew Moskowitz and Gerhard Heim give an important and essential insight into the role of emotion in schizophrenia, returning to the essential components of Bleuler's historical concept. Moskowitz and Heim's chapter reminds us that the original conception of schizophrenia was closely linked to the development of psychoanalytic thought. Eugen Bleuler and Carl Jung collaborated on the further development and refinement of Wundt's word association test at the Burghölzli as a means of revealing the psychological and emotional significance of individuals' responses to word stimuli. It is through this association with Jung that we can understand the psychological roots of Bleuler's concepts of 'loosening of associations' and 'emotionally-charged complexes'. Moskowitz and Heim argue that Bleuler's concepts of 'splitting' and 'complexes', central to his concept of schizophrenia, are interestingly quite close to the contemporary concepts of dissociation and dissociative identities. Later psychoanalytic theorists working to understand psychosis, especially the post-Kleinians, Segal and Bion (see Lucas, 2009), saw this extreme separation, or splitting, as a particular feature of psychotic symptoms where immediate perceptual experience becomes divorced from its emotional significance and meaning, and then further fundamental disturbance of psychic functions might also occur, as Bleuler originally proposed. Moskowitz and Heim's chapter is important because it enables us to revisit these original conceptualisations that have all too easily become lost through time.

Emotion and the therapeutic relationship

As an important aspect of our book, Chapters 3, 4 and 5 focus our attention on the expression of emotion in the context of the therapeutic relationship.

Garfield (1995) has previously argued that unbearable and unintegrated affect lies at the core of psychosis and that repair following psychosis involves the processes of acknowledging, bearing and putting in perspective the intolerable emotions, which often have their origins in early development. In Chapter 3, David Garfield and his colleagues argue that it is the reworking of emotion and psychosis, the expanding of the individual's emotional subjective life that becomes the primary goal of treatment. Key to this reworking of emotion and psychosis is the centrality of affective attunement as a core process in bringing about an integration and understanding of psychotic experiences. This can be a painful process since emotional experiences and meanings have their roots in often difficult experiences containing powerful affects which are not necessarily readily accessible verbally. Simultaneously Garfield reminds us powerfully that this is also a challenge for the psychotherapist – to be emotionally available and to be able to respond to and create a safe context for recovery to unfold, making a link with Bion's notion of 'container-contained'. This introduces an important and crucial theme in the book, which is the central importance of the therapeutic relationship. This theme is particularly exemplified in the following two chapters.

In Chapter 4, Sarah Dilks provides a dialogical view of change processes in psychological therapy. Dilks shows how the co-construction of a narrative provides a context for understanding how processes of managing painful emotions and developing new insights and perspectives unfold within psychological therapy. The core process of 'building bridges to observational perspectives' provides a means of conceptualising conversational processes in therapy, where new perspectives are continually and *jointly* created by the client and therapist as a means of opening up new possibilities for thoughts, emotions and coping. This does not happen by accident: rather the therapist provides the emotional containment and scaffolding to create opportunities for the processing of emotional distress and the development of activities focused on managing and mastering difficult emotions. Dilks's chapter wonderfully illustrates these concepts through detailed and vivid accounts taken from clients describing their experiences of different psychological therapies.

Building on the role of the therapist scaffolding the unfolding of a conversational process enabling the emergence of new perspectives, Susanne Harder and Paul Lysaker explore this further in Chapter 5. They show how the formation of the early therapeutic relationship shares basic principles of interpersonal attachment similar to how mothers and infants form the initial relationship prior to language acquisition. They show how findings on optimal interpersonal interactions between mothers and infants are understood within a balanced model of self and interactive regulation. This is crucial to the development of a secure attachment that can be utilised to develop strong working alliances, which often require a complex and lengthy process of therapeutic engagement. This illustrates how for some individuals and their therapists the development of a therapeutic relationship can be difficult, complex and challenging. Together, Chapters 3, 4 and 5 show us from differing perspectives the verbal and non-verbal processes which enable regulation of internal states and experiences, and how these states manifest in the context of an emotionally attuned therapeutic relationship, and the transformation of these into productive and meaningful forms of language that co-create and release new understandings, perspectives and reactions to promote recovery.

The wider context of emotion

Moving from the context of the therapeutic relationship, the book turns its focus to give consideration to the attachment context of affect and affect regulation (Chapter 6); how this manifests from the perspective of wider organisational and professional caregiving considerations (Chapter 7); the cultural and societal (Chapter 8) and the systemic and familial (Chapters 9 and 10) contexts and experiences of psychosis. Building on the emergent themes concerning past and current relationships and the concept of attachment, in Chapter 6, Matthias Schwannauer describes an attachment-based understanding of mentalisation and reflective functioning. Psychosis involves the disruption of social relationships and the understanding of self in relation to others. In this context psychotherapy can directly address the development of a mentalising capacity to enable the clarification of sensitisation to and tolerance of complex affects. Enhancement of capacities to recognise and relate to emotional and mental states in self and others is key to the development of a coherent sense of self.

In Chapter 7, Robert D. Hinshelwood explores, in a thought-provoking way, the professional caregiving context of psychosis. He argues that psychiatric culture can struggle to enable staff to develop meaningful understandings of psychosis and to deal with the emotional impact that the care for individuals with psychosis can have on them. As highlighted by Garfield and colleagues (Chapter 3), Dilks (Chapter 4) and Harder and Lysaker (Chapter 5), the development of attuned understandings of psychosis and capacities to tolerate painful, sometimes unbearable, affects, coupled with the development of helpful forms of conversation, is a skilled activity necessitating a safe organisational and caring environment that can permit and enable these skills and activities. Organisations that often lack these capacities to contain and explore difficult emotions and experiences therefore foster greater feelings of anxiety, threat and helplessness amongst staff in relation to supporting individuals with psychosis. In response to this, organisations can then react in ways which dehumanise, stereotype, scapegoat or depersonalise service users. This can be through processes of disembodying the person from their symptomatic experiences (for example, focusing on unidimensional understandings of psychosis) or seeing individuals as not being capable of or motivated for recovery. Hinshelwood succeeds in creating a sense of discomfort at becoming aware of our own unwanted feelings that can occur in relation to working with psychosis, but importantly this chapter is an important call for developing compassionate understandings of why organisations and care staff may act in ways that disempower individuals.

Michelle Campbell, Rory Byrne and Anthony P. Morrison also explore the dehumanisation of individuals with psychosis in Chapter 8. They focus on the importance of discrimination against individuals with psychosis and the presence of stigmatising attitudes. Campbell and colleagues show the importance of recognising stigmatising representations against people with psychosis and their implications for public mental health and the design of clinical services. Such attitudes have important implications for individuals with psychosis in terms of acting as an external barrier to recovery, where external stigma generate actual experiences of discrimination and social exclusion. In addition, stigmatising attitudes are also internalised, leading to reduced help seeking and prolonging the duration of untreated psychosis. These factors can create a vicious cycle leading to feelings of social anxiety, depression and social isolation yet further reducing self-esteem. Issues of stigma have important implications for the design of public health and community-based strategies aimed at enhancing mental health literacy and enhancing access to user-focused services.

Since its original conception, expressed emotion (EE) has been a major construct in understanding the importance of family context in shaping the expression of recovery in people with psychosis (Brown *et al.*, 1972). In Chapter 9, Frank R. Burbach has provided an excellent review of the current status of the EE construct and a systemic formulation of the role of the affective environment of the family system. He argues elegantly that any understanding of the family emotional climate and outcome of psychosis must incorporate an interactional understanding of how the language people use shapes and defines the unfolding of appraisals and the expression of affect. This formulation of the role of interpersonal processes in the formation and development of attributions which underpin expressions of criticism, hostility and warmth opens up new systemically based family interventions. Complementing Burbach's analysis, Paul Patterson (Chapter 10) offers a developmentally based analysis of the role of attachment and loss in the evolution of expressed emotion. Psychosis can be understood as a highly distressing life event, which acts on the family attachment system. In Bowlby's (1980) formulation of attachment theory, illness was understood as a key life event acting on the attachment system. Through the development of internal working models (IWMs) the attachment system organises individuals' affectional and affiliative bonds, providing an adaptive context to regulate painful emotions and experiences. Patterson argues that in the context of psychosis, individuals' and carers' internal working models are activated and trigger potentially disorientated or disorganised attachment behaviours through feelings of threat, separation and loss. It is out of these fundamental experiences of the threat of loss, separation and harm that painful and difficult emotions emerge, which often remain unintegrated. Patterson's model helps us understand the developmental and attachment based roots of criticism and hostility as an adaptive response to the threat of loss.

Theoretical perspectives and new horizons

We now turn our attention to a series of chapters that offer new and developing theoretical insights from psychoanalytic theory (see Chapter 11), and evolutionary psychology (Chapters 12 and 13). In Chapter 11, Michael Robbins makes the important distinction between affect on the one hand referring to fundamental somatosensory experiences, and emotion on the other referring to the thoughtful awareness and mental representation of feeling states. In making this distinction Robbins helps us understand his psychoanalytic perspective on psychosis where unregulated sensations, perceptions and affects express themselves in psychotic experiences. In common with other chapter authors, he also makes us aware, through his use of a clinical illustration, that the process of becoming conscious of the emotional meaning of the underlying affect can be a painful experience for both patients and therapists, requiring considerable tolerance and capacity.

In Chapter 12, Andrew Gumley and Max Birchwood outline the key role of shame in the evolution of emotional distress after psychosis. They particularly focus on the experience of depression and social anxiety, both of which are underpinned by a sensitivity to social identity threat and stigma. They propose that, as a means of coping with social identity threats, individuals submit or subordinate to externalised negative stereotypes of mental illness. As a consequence of these processes of subordination, experiences of depression, hopelessness, fear and social anxiety emerge as unintended consequences of the person's best attempts to cope with externalised and internalised shame and stigma of mental illness.

Finally in Chapter 13, Ross White, Heather Laithwaite and Paul Gilbert outline an evolutionary based understanding of negative symptoms as expressions of experiences of chronic social defeat. This thought-provoking chapter makes links to the underlying biology of social defeat. White and his colleagues argue that negative symptoms represent a particular organisation of affect regulation, where efforts to avoid experiences of threat result in the attenuation and minimisation of the expression of both positive and negative affect. This approach opens up new opportunities for therapeutic work with negative symptoms based on the focus on developing self-compassion in individuals recovering from psychosis.

Taken together this group of chapters draws on a wide range of theoretical perspectives and disciplines including evolutionary theory, psychoanalytic theory, attachment theory, developmental psychopathology and anthropology.

One of the important contributions that ISPS makes is the presentation of ideas and perspectives in one volume that would not normally be found together.

Conclusions

We hope that it becomes very clear how psychological understandings of emotion and psychosis have a long and distinguished history and that the separation of affect and psychosis in theoretical models of psychosis and schizophrenia is highly problematical. The separation of affect from experience and meaning by researchers and service providers fails to recognise how these processes together are central to how we can understand and respond to the needs of individuals with psychosis. In fact the separation of affect from experience and meaning potentially mirrors these mechanisms in an anti-therapeutic and anti-collaborative way. At its extreme, the focus of services on the removal of psychotic experiences without understanding their developmental, interpersonal and psycho-affective context risks alienating service users, families and staff.

Emotions are closely entwined in our understandings of the interpersonal context of psychosis. From a psychotherapeutic point of view, this relational framework begins with understanding emotional experiences in the context of the therapeutic relationship and in particular the way in which the affect underpinning psychotic experiences expresses itself subjectively and intersubjectively. This leads to our understanding of the importance of developing a relationship that can tolerate, bear, acknowledge and compassionately respond to the unfolding pattern of reconstructed experiences. Language and communication provides a crucial medium through which to co-construct narratives, stories and understandings that enlighten new perspectives and methods of coping and adapting. These complex patterns of affect and emotional expression can be further understood in their organisational, cultural and societal and systemic contexts. Organisational culture and insecurity can create barriers to developing attuned understandings of the needs of individuals with psychosis. Societal stereotypes can lead to experiences of actual discrimination and internalised feelings of shame and stigma. As individuals can struggle to develop new understandings as part of their recovery after psychosis, families also face important struggles to understand and respond to the needs of their loved one. It is crucial not to conceive of these struggles as separate and independent of each other but rather to understand and attend to the developmentally based processes of adaptation to and coping with feelings of threat, illness, separation and loss. An interactional and systemically based understanding provides a compelling insight into the further role of discourse, language and narrative in the evolution of individuals' appraisals and in their expressions of positive and negative affect.

A particularly strong theoretical thread has emerged through the collection of authors in this book: that of attachment theory. This body of work offers models currently of strong interest, not only within psychosis work. It perhaps enables a particularly accessible way of thinking about developmental issues in the experience of psychosis and emotion. As a developmental theory of adaptation and control, attachment theory offers a non-pathologising stance that allows for the understanding and integration of adaptive and protective behaviour, emotion regulation, and interpersonal functioning in close relationships with significant others and more generally help seeking. However, there are also important differing emphases and nuances represented here, even within the attachment field itself. It is hoped the collection in this text will spark off further thought and work to facilitate a necessary discourse to integrate these ideas.

In revisiting emotions in psychosis, particularly through recognising the emotional effect on the individual, their family, the therapist, groups and services, we hope that the importance of emotion in psychosis, irrespective of epistemological or theoretical orientation, has been demonstrated. The introduction of diverse perspectives and experiences brought by each of our contributors illustrates how these understandings can converge without losing their unique contributions.

References

Bowlby, J. (1980) *Attachment and Loss, Vol. 3: Loss, Sadness and Depression*, London: Hogarth Press.

Brown, G.W., Birley, J.L.T. and Wing, J.K. (1972) Influence of family life on course of schizophrenic disorders: a replication, *British Journal of Psychiatry* 121: 241–258.

Garfield, D.A.S. (1995) *Unbearable Affect: A Guide to the Psychotherapy of Psychosis*, New York: Wiley.

Lucas, R. (2009) T*he Psychotic Wavelength: A Psychoanalytic Perspective for Psychiatry*, Abingdon: Routledge.

Chapter 2

Affect, dissociation, psychosis

Essential components of the historical concept of schizophrenia

Andrew Moskowitz and Gerhard Heim

> It has been known since the early years of modern psychiatry that an 'acute curable' psychosis became 'chronic' when the affects began to disappear.
>
> (Bleuler, 1911/1950, p. 40)

> The stronger the affects, the less pronounced the dissociative tendencies need to be in order to produce the emotional desolation. Thus, in many cases of severe disease, we find that only quite ordinary everyday conflicts of life have caused the marked mental impairment; but in milder cases, the acute episodes may have been released by powerful affects. And not infrequently, after a careful analysis, we had to pose the question whether we are not merely dealing with the effect of a particularly powerful psychological trauma on a very sensitive person rather than with a disease in the narrow sense of the word.[1]
>
> (Bleuler, 1911/1950, p. 300)

Eugen Bleuler's seminal text (1911/1950), *Dementia Praecox or the Group of Schizophrenias*, was published 100 years ago, the term 'schizophrenia' having been introduced a few years earlier. As these quotes illustrate, Bleuler – unlike subsequent interpreters of schizophrenia such as Kurt Schneider (1959) who emphasised a disorder of thinking – believed that powerful affective experiences, in conjunction with tendencies toward 'splitting', were central to the genesis and development of schizophrenia. He also argued that the absence of affect in schizophrenia was only apparent, a secondary response to some sort of a dissociative or repressive process.

Though we will primarily be focusing on Bleuler's 1911 book, the title of this chapter harks back to Bleuler's first book, published in 1906 before the term schizophrenia was coined and translated into English six years later. In *Affectivity, Suggestibility, Subjectivity, Paranoia* (Bleuler, 1906/1912), a slim volume just a quarter the length of his 1911 tome, Bleuler sets out his broad

1 Translation by Suenje Matthiesen.

concept of affectivity relative to the disorder of paranoia, and hints at its importance for the developing concept of schizophrenia. He also highlights 'suggestibility', a concept linked to hypnosis and thus to dissociation. Accordingly, 'Affect, Dissociation, Psychosis', our title, seems an appropriate modern analogy to Bleuler's 'Affectivity, suggestibility, paranoia'.

While Bleuler is well known today for introducing the term and diagnosis of schizophrenia, his ideas remain poorly understood. His central concept of 'splitting', which drove his choice of term to replace Emil Kraepelin's *Dementia Praecox*, has been narrowly interpreted as an extreme separation of thinking and emotion; in actuality, it is much broader than this. Bleuler used it most often to refer to a split between 'affectively-charged complexes' which included a modicum of consciousness, notions close to contemporary conceptions of 'dissociation' and dissociative disorders. Further, he considered affect to be of central importance to the development of symptoms such as hallucinations and delusions, and only apparently lacking in schizophrenia, the result of the 'splitting off' of affectively charged complexes. As we shall see, this notion of 'complexes', along with Bleuler's concepts of 'splitting' and 'affectivity', was of great importance to his theory of schizophrenia, second only to the biologically based deficit he assumed to underlie the disorder – a 'loosening of associations'. We will discuss these concepts of Bleuler's in detail in this chapter, followed by some speculation as to the twentieth-century professional and political forces that minimised and distorted these ideas.

Biographical sketch

Eugen Bleuler was born in Zollikon, a small village outside Zurich. As he was growing up, there was much discontent among the local Swiss on behalf of family members who were mentally ill. It was believed that they were not being well treated in the asylum – Burghölzli – primarily because the German doctors in charge did not speak the regional dialect. Bleuler grew up with the desire to fulfil this need – to deal humanely and with understanding with villagers and locals who required psychiatric care. In addition, his motivation may have been strongly personal. Eugen Bleuler's eldest sister was hospitalised at Burghölzli for the first time when he was a teenager; his family's experience of her treatment, as well as his direct contact with her, were likely decisive in determining his choice of career.

After completing his medical training in the early 1880s, Bleuler worked in psychiatric hospitals in Switzerland and travelled for a couple of years in Germany, France and England, studying under Von Gudden and Charcot in the process. He had already developed a strong interest in association psychology and in hypnosis, which was likely extended during his several months stay with Charcot in Paris, and by August Forel, with whom he worked at Burghölzli. Then in 1886, Bleuler was chosen to head an asylum in Rheinau, in the Swiss countryside some distance from Zurich. It was during these 12 years, when he spent all of his time with his patients (dining with them, working with them – even attending social events with them), that Bleuler began to formulate his ideas on what he later came to call 'schizophrenia'.

Bleuler became convinced during these years that there was, in his chronically psychotic patients, some sort of underlying disturbance in their association network. After accepting the directorial and professorial position at Burghölzli in 1898 (as an administrative position it allowed him significantly less contact with patients but placed him closer to his ailing mother and mentally disturbed sister), Bleuler decided that he could best clarify the nature of the associational disturbance he posited to underlie dementia praecox/schizophrenia by means of Wundt's word association test, which Kraepelin had been using in his Heidelberg laboratory. So, in 1900, Bleuler dispatched Franz Riklin, a young psychiatrist, to Heidelberg to learn the association task at Kraepelin's feet. Riklin returned in 1901, a few months after Carl Jung arrived at Burghölzli, and together they began to develop the word association test, initially using it on non-psychiatric patients to establish norms, before turning to psychiatric patients for investigation.

The word association test

As Kraepelin and others had used it, the word association test involved reading out a list of words one at a time to a participant who was instructed to respond with the first word that came to mind. The response and the length of time before responding were recorded. Before Riklin and Jung adapted the test, it had been used primarily to record the impact of various conditions, such as fatigue and alcohol use, on the accuracy of a person's responses. But Riklin and Jung came to believe that response 'errors' could be psychologically significant, and paid particular attention to long pauses before responding, odd responses, and the apparent forgetting of prior responses. They concluded that these errors typically resulted from the triggering of some issue of personal significance. In essence, they had created the first *projective* psychological test – in which a neutral stimulus triggered idiosyncratic, and personally meaningful, responses. Jung proposed that these responses indicated the presence of what he called an 'emotionally charged' or 'feeling toned' *complex of representations*, or 'complex' for short. Jung argued that such a complex, when triggered, commanded an individual's attention, distracting from the task at hand (word association) and leading to 'errors'. He also noted that it often took some time for this 'inner distraction' to wane, leading to more superficial associations (including 'clang' associations, such as 'fish/dish') for some time. This concept of emotionally charged complexes came to be of significant importance for Bleuler's developing ideas on schizophrenia.

The development of the concept of schizophrenia

While Bleuler had previously believed that dementia praecox was characterised by a disturbance of association and noted that emotions appeared to be lacking or were inappropriately expressed, his ideas were vague and ill formed prior to Jung and Riklin's experiments. For example, in an English language publication, Bleuler said only that dementia praecox was characterised by a 'stunting' of the emotions and a 'definite alteration' not only of the emotions but also of the 'association of ideas'[2] (Bleuler, 1902–1903, p. 115). Through Bleuler's and Jung's publications from 1904 to 1908, one can see the concept of schizophrenia taking form, with increasing emphasis on the importance of powerful affects and dissociation, along with the development of Bleuler's ideas about the specific nature of the association disturbance he had long assumed.[3]

Bleuler's ideas on schizophrenia have often been summarised under the rubric 'four A's' – representing 'affect' (flat or inappropriate), 'associations', 'autism' and 'ambivalence', as though these characteristics were fundamental to his concept of schizophrenia. This, however, is inaccurate, as has most recently been pointed out by McNally (2009). In his 1911 book, Bleuler differentiated the symptoms or signs present in schizophrenia in two ways: (1) *fundamental* (i.e. particularly characteristic of schizophrenia) or *accessory* (shared with other disorders); and (2) *primary* (directly due to an assumed organic deficit) or *secondary* (developing *as a result of* the primary disturbance). While all of the 'four A's' were considered *fundamental* symptoms, only *loosening of associations* was also considered *primary*, making it the core deficit underlying schizophrenia. With regard to other symptoms of schizophrenia, Bleuler appeared to emphasise 'affectivity' over 'autism' and 'ambivalence',[4]

2 It is important to recognise that the terms 'association' and 'ideas' were used much more broadly in the nineteenth and early twentieth century than they are now. 'Associations' with their corresponding 'laws' were assumed by Bleuler, following Hume, Hartley and Wundt, to be the basic building blocks for *all* mental activities – not only thoughts – and 'ideas' were synonymous with mental or psychological 'elements', which could also include behaviour.

3 It is abundantly clear that Bleuler and Jung felt they were building on each other's work. Bleuler references Jung's not yet published *The Psychology of Dementia Praecox* several times in his 1906 book, and refers readers of his 1911 book back to Jung's book for a review of popular theories of schizophrenia. Jung, for his part, extensively refers to Bleuler's *Affectivity, Suggestibility, Paranoia* (1906/1912) in *The Psychology of Dementia Praecox* (1907/1960), which he claims developed out of 'almost daily conversations' with Bleuler (p. 3). It was also during these years that Jung contacted, and began his significant relationship with, Sigmund Freud. Both Jung and Bleuler were powerfully influenced by Freud and his ideas, but there is evidence the concept of schizophrenia is more indebted to Pierre Janet – the father of dissociation theory – than Sigmund Freud (see Moskowitz, 2006, 2008, for further discussion).

4 For example, noting that 'autism' could only be understood in relation to affectivity and loosening of associations, and was thus a 'secondary manifestation' phenomenon (Bleuler, 1911/1950, p. 354).

particularly focusing on 'affectively charged' complexes as central to the genesis of schizophrenia.

Bleuler posited a fundamental, organically based psychological deficit – a 'loosening of associations' – as central to schizophrenia because he was reluctant to give up his decades-long commitment to association psychology and unwilling to believe that schizophrenia could be psychologically caused. His colleague Carl Jung had no difficulties in this regard, and consistently argued that schizophrenia itself could be caused by the intense affective experiences that triggered its symptoms (though he sometimes also posited a secondary toxic effect of the emotions on the brain). For his part, Bleuler seemed to vacillate between emphasising this core 'association disturbance' and giving precedence to splitting and complexes. For example, when introducing the term 'schizophrenia', Bleuler makes no mention of any association disturbance. So, in April 1908, in his first public comment on the term, Bleuler justified its introduction by saying: 'I believe that the tearing apart or splitting of the psychic functions is a prominent symptom of the whole group' (Bleuler, 1908/1987, p. 59). In his 1911 book, Bleuler says: 'I call dementia praecox "schizophrenia" because (as I hope to demonstrate) the "splitting" of the different psychic functions is one of its most important characteristics' (Bleuler, 1911/1950, p. 8). In the next section, entitled, 'The Definition of the Disease', he continues:

> In every case, we are confronted with a more or less clear-cut *splitting of the psychic functions.* If the disease is marked, the personality loses its unity; at different times different psychic complexes seem to represent the personality . . . one set of complexes dominates the personality for a time, while other groups of ideas or drives are 'split off' and seem either partly or completely impotent.
>
> (Bleuler, 1911/1950, p. 9, emphasis in original)

Loosening of associations

Though, as noted above, Bleuler had long felt that a disturbance in associations underlay the symptoms of dementia praecox, he did not characterise this disturbance in any particular way until he coined the term 'loosening' ('Lockerung') of associations in 1908. Bleuler's emphasis on 'associations' has often been equated with 'thought disorder'; thus, many have argued that Bleuler considered 'thought disorder' to be the most important symptom of schizophrenia. But he never said this. While he did often discuss disturbances of thought in schizophrenia, it is clear that his concept of 'loosening of associations' was much broader than this.

First of all, Bleuler's concept arose out of the 'association' psychology of the nineteenth century, the dominant psychological paradigm of the time. From this perspective, 'associations' were viewed as the psychological force which held mental contents together: 'Every psychical activity rests upon the interchange of material derived from sensation and from memory traces, upon *associations*' (Bleuler, 1904/1918, p. 1, italics in original), and 'Perception, thinking, doing, cease as soon as association is impeded' (p. 3). Note that 'thinking' is only one of the activities affected by an impairment in associations. Second and significantly, Bleuler never used the term 'loose associations', a phrase that is often attributed to him and refers narrowly to a disturbance of speech or thought. Rather, he saw in the frequent disturbances of thought and speech in schizophrenia evidence for 'loosening of associations', an underlying psychological deficit or a predisposition of sorts, which explained the exaggerated impact of the emotions in schizophrenia on the psychological functions: 'The affective sway over the associations is far stronger [in schizophrenia] than in the healthy' (Bleuler, 1911/1950, p. 364). This erroneous attribution of the term 'loose associations' to Bleuler, a form of thought disorder considered to be characteristic of schizophrenia (as opposed to the manic 'flight of ideas', in which ideas are tangentially connected but can, with effort, be followed), is one of the main reasons Bleuler is inaccurately viewed as arguing for schizophrenia as a primary disorder of thinking.

Affectivity

Of great importance to Bleuler's view of schizophrenia was his concept of 'affectivity'. Bleuler developed this concept most fully in his 1906 book *Affectivity, Suggestibility, Paranoia*, which was translated into English a few years later. In this brief monograph of about 120 pages, Bleuler sets out his ideas, coining the neologism 'affectivity' ('Affektivität') after rejecting other existing terms as either too narrow or too broad ('feelings', for example). Bleuler defined 'affectivity' in his 1906 text as including 'affect' in the traditional sense of the word, but also 'the slight feelings or feeling tones of pleasure and displeasure which accompany all sorts of experiences' (Bleuler, 1906/1912, p. 4). He felt that it was closely linked to 'will' and to 'action'; 'affectivity', according to Bleuler (1906/1912), 'far more than reflection, is the determining factor in our acts and omissions' (p. 13) and 'determines the direction of our endeavours' (p. 14).

While Bleuler's (1906) book was primarily about paranoia, not dementia praecox, he did make some comments about the role of the affects in the latter disorder, which presaged his more detailed comments in his schizophrenia book written two years later:

> There is a disease in which the suppression of the emotions may be said to occupy the foreground of the picture, viz. dementia praecox . . . The affectivity, however, in the majority of cases, is hopelessly defective . . . (T)he question is, *what has become of the affects in dementia praecox?* The

> question is answerable, and I hope that the work of my colleague Jung will in the near future be so far along as to afford us at least a glimpse of the mechanisms which remove the affects from our observation.
>
> (Bleuler, 1906/1912, p. 37, italics in original)

> In dementia praecox affective experiences are transformed into hallucinations, delusions, stereotypies, all generally having some obscure symbolism, while the original affect cannot be demonstrated or is rudimentary.[5]
>
> (Bleuler, 1906/1912, p. 23)

Importantly, Bleuler noted that a strong affect not only powerfully draws associations to it (becoming an 'affectively charged complex' in the process) but also *inhibits* opposing associations. In 1911, he used this idea to propose an answer to the question he posed in 1906:

> Since in schizophrenia the associative linkings are weakened and loosened, the result is that those very affects, which have the tendency to split off, very often become latent (unconscious) either after a very brief time or *in statu nascendi*. Since they still partly retain their influence, and in many ways are developed with less restraint, they exercise a repressive influence on the rise of other affects: on the whole, the patient seems without affect, indifferent.
>
> (Bleuler, 1911/1950, pp. 367–368)

In a striking footnote, Bleuler then adds: 'The "purpose" of the whole arrangement, the erection of defenses against unpleasant affects, is attained in this way. The patient suffers no more; he has established a kind of *nirvana*' (p. 368, italics in original).

Affectively charged complexes

Jung developed the notion of complexes from his work on the word association task, adapting Theodore Ziehen's *Gefühlsbetonter Vorstellungskomplex* or 'emotionally-charged complex of representations' (Ellenberger, 1970). Similar concepts have been proposed since Herbart (1818, 1824; see Scharfetter, 2001). He described them (Jung, 1907/1960) as clusters of ideas 'cemented' together by a powerful affect (p. 28) and accompanied by 'somatic innervations' (p. 41). Bleuler firmly embraced Jung's concept, discussing it in detail

5 These comments bear some similarity to certain contemporary models of psychosis, such as Freeman and Garety (2003), which emphasise affect as a causative agent in the development of delusions and hallucinations.

in his 1905 paper, 'Consciousness and Associations'. Here, he makes statements such as:

> Independently of the conscious personality, wishes and fears regulate ideas to their liking and combine them in a compact complex, whose expressions emerge as 'hallucinations'; these appear to be so consequential and deliberate that they simulate a third person . . . But it is merely a piece of the split-off personality; it represents aspirations of this personality which would otherwise be suppressed.
>
> (Bleuler, 1905/1918, p. 279)

Bleuler also focused on complexes in his 1906 book on affectivity and paranoia and suggested that Jung's forthcoming book would provide 'proof' of their importance to dementia praecox. Jung did, indeed, focus extensively on complexes in his dementia praecox book; at one point he, somewhat metaphorically, described a complex as a 'being, living its own life and hindering and disturbing the development of the ego-complex' (Jung, 1907/1960, p. 47).

There is little reason to believe that Jung's and Bleuler's definition of complexes differed. Echoing Jung's ideas, Bleuler defined complexes in his 1911 book (1950) as 'a shortened term for a complex of ideas which are strongly affectively charged so that it permanently influences the content of the psychic process . . . (and) strives to obtain a kind of independence' (p. 24). Further, Bleuler and Jung co-authored a paper in 1908 entitled, 'Complexes and Aetiology in Dementia Praecox'. In it they expressed broad agreement with each other's positions, arguing only about the extent to which dementia praecox itself (and not just its symptoms) might be psychological in nature; Jung thought it could be; Bleuler disagreed. However, Bleuler did not suggest that his concept of complexes was in any way different from Jung's; had he wanted to, this would have been the obvious place to do so.

Splitting

The concept of 'splitting' was central to Bleuler's theory of schizophrenia, driving – more than anything else – his choice of name for the disorder. While the 'splitting of psychic functions' has been interpreted in contemporary circles as an 'extreme separation of thought and affect', this was not typically how Bleuler used the term.[6] While he most often refers to the

6 That this is not an accurate interpretation of Bleuler's 'splitting' can be seen in his criticism of Stransky's theory of dementia praecox as a 'partial dissociation' of the 'thymo' (feeling) and 'noo' (thinking) psyches. Bleuler (1911/1950) comments that Stransky's concept has the 'disadvantage' of implying that the intellect and affectivity are independent functions when they are actually 'different aspects of the same psychic process' (p. 364).

splitting of 'idea-' or 'affect-laden' complexes, at other times he refers to 'association-splitting' or simply the 'splitting of psychic functions'. Indeed, he appears to use these terms interchangeably at times, as in: 'the affectively charged complex of ideas continues to become isolated and obtains an ever increasing independence (splitting of the psychic functions)' (Bleuler, 1911/1950, p. 359).

While Bleuler regularly used the term 'dissociation' in his important 1905 paper 'Consciousness and Association', and in his 1906 book *Affectivity, Suggestibility, Paranoia* (as did Jung in his 1907 *Psychology of Dementia Praecox*), the term 'splitting' ('Spaltung') was introduced in Bleuler's and Jung's April 1908 lectures and described in Bleuler's 1911 book. Similar terms had been used for almost 90 years previously (Scharfetter, 2001), some of which Bleuler (1911/1950) contrasts with 'splitting':

> What Gross understands by his term 'fragmentation' (or disintegration) of consciousness corresponds to what we call 'splitting' . . . The term 'dissociation' has already been in use for a long time to designate similar observations and findings. But dissociation also designates more: for example, the constriction of the content of consciousness . . . [and] may thus give rise to misunderstandings.
>
> (Bleuler, 1911/1950, p. 363)

Jung, in his April 1908 talk at the Salzburg Congress of Psychoanalysis, also compared 'dissociation' to 'splitting':

> We have taken over from French psychology a similar concept which initially was true for hysteria – namely, 'dissociation'. Today, the name means a 'splitting of the self' . . . Hysteria is primarily characterised by dissociation and because dementia praecox also shows splitting ('Spaltung'), the concept of dissociation seems to 'run into' the concept of Schizophrenia.[7]
>
> (Jung, 1908)

Pruyser (1975), in an important discussion of the historical concept of splitting, notes that Bleuler's 'splitting' and Janet's 'dissociation' 'just happens . . . without a causative agent' (p. 28) and concludes that Bleuler's 'splitting' was closer in meaning to 'dissociation' than to Freud's 'repression' (which requires an agent which *represses*). Indeed, it is noteworthy that Bleuler's eldest son, Manfred, who was the Head of Burghölzli Hospital for many years after his father's death and the foremost Bleuler scholar, often uses the term

7 'On Dementia Praecox'. This paper has not been published, but was reviewed in the Jung Archives at ETH Zurich in September 2006, and parts of it translated into English (by Suenje Matthiesen).

'dissociation' interchangeably with 'splitting' in describing his father's ideas. For example, in a 1986 English language summary of Bleuler's 1911 book, Manfred Bleuler stated: 'He believed that the splitting (the dissociation of thoughts, of emotions, of attitudes and of acting) were close to "primary symptoms" (Bleuler and Bleuler, 1986, p. 663). Even more strikingly Manfred Bleuler, in commenting on his father's concept of 'ambivalence' states: 'the patient thinks, feels, and acts in many respects as if there were different souls in him, as if he consisted of different personalities, that he becomes "split" to a psychotic degree' (p. 663).

Splitting and complexes, dissociation and dissociative identities

Bleuler's historical notions of 'splitting' and 'complexes', central to his concept of schizophrenia, are quite close to the contemporary concepts of dissociation and dissociative identities. In some ways this is not surprising, as there was considerable interest at the turn of the twentieth century in hypnosis, alternate states of consciousness and unusual personality states. Bleuler was trained in hypnosis and many of his early writings relate to this topic. Jung's medical thesis, supervised by Bleuler and considered by both to be relevant to the topic of schizophrenia (Jung, 1956/1960), was on the possession states of a medium, which Jung concluded were alternate personalities. And proposed names for dementia praecox which emphasised some form of splitting or dissociation abounded around this time, and included Wernicke's *Sejunktionspsychosis*, Zweig's *Dementia dissecans* and Otto Gross's *Dementia sejunctiva* (Scharfetter, 2001).

In addition, Bleuler's concept of 'splitting', particularly with regard to 'affective complexes', demonstrates strong similarity with the current *DSM-IV* definition of dissociation: 'a disruption in the usually integrated functions of consciousness, memory, identity, or perception of the environment' (American Psychiatric Association, 2000, p. 822). Likewise, 'independent' or 'autonomous' affectively charged complexes appear somewhat similar to dissociative identities, as defined in the *DSM-IV-TR*: 'two or more distinct identities or personality states (each with its own relatively enduring pattern of perceiving, relating to, and thinking about the environment and self)'[8] (APA, 2000, p. 529).

Bleuler's very broad concept of schizophrenia co-opted much of the clinical phenomena that had previously been described as multiple personality (then

8 The proposed *DSM-V* criteria veer even closer to Bleuler's concept, as dissociative identities now require only *discontinuities* in the 'sense of self, cognition, behavior, affect, perceptions, and/or memories' (retrieved from the APA *DSM-V* website www.dsm5.org/Proposed Revisions/Pages/proposedrevision.aspx?rid=57, 12 August 2010). Of course, a diagnosis of dissociative identity disorder requires other criteria, including amnesia, which are relatively uncommon in schizophrenia.

considered a form of hysteria) or hysterical psychosis.[9] Some have gone so far as to propose that Bleuler's concept of schizophrenia was one of the key reasons for the loss of interest in multiple personality in the twentieth century (Rosenbaum, 1980). Certainly, in the public's mind, schizophrenia has long been associated with split personality and as such confused with multiple personality disorder. Psychiatric professionals have been at great pains to 'correct' this public misconception, and in doing so frequently distort Bleuler's term schizophrenia to mean only a splitting of affect and thought. But as we have seen, this is largely inaccurate, and has led to a significant minimisation of the important links between dissociation and psychosis (particularly auditory hallucinations), which are only now being rediscovered (Moskowitz and Corstens, 2007; Moskowitz *et al.*, 2008).

Schizophrenia, affect and the 'neo-Kraepelinians'

While there are several reasons for the distortion that Bleuler's ideas received in the second half of the twentieth century, of greatest importance to contemporary nosology are the changes implemented by the so-called 'neo-Kraepelinians' in the 1960s and 1970s (Blashfield, 1984). The 'neo-Kraepelinians' were a group of prominent, overwhelmingly North American psychiatrists and researchers who advocated a return to Kraepelin's ideas (Klerman, 1978). These were argued to include the belief that mental illnesses were discrete from one another and were discontinuous with normal behaviour (Klerman, 1978).

The fundamental task of the neo-Kraepelinians in developing the *DSM-III* (American Psychiatric Association, 1980) and subsequent manuals was to reinforce a medical paradigm of mental disorders (Blashfield, 1984). To do this, they needed to fortify the fundamental Kraepelinian distinction between schizophrenia (*dementia praecox*) and manic-depression, clearly seen as the twin pillars supporting the foundation of a biologically based nosology. This motivation, distinguishing schizophrenia – narrowly viewed as a disorder of *thought* – from manic-depression (renamed bipolar disorder), defined as an *affective* or *mood* disorder, can be seen in three ways: (1) changes in the schizophrenia criteria; (2) the treatment of schizoaffective disorder; and (3) the allowance of *mood-incongruent* psychotic symptoms in affective disorders.

9 Indeed, Bleuler (1911/1950) explicitly states that all hysterical symptoms can originate 'on a schizophrenic basis' (p. 269). And leaving no doubt as to his position on the differential diagnosis of hysterical psychosis and schizophrenia, he says: 'I have never yet had any reason for making a diagnosis of "hysterical psychosis". All cases so diagnosed by others differed in no wise from other schizophrenics. When a supposed hysteric becomes psychotic or deteriorates, he is, in my experience, not a hysteric at all, but a schizophrenic' (p. 289).

Under the guise of improving reliability, the editors of the *DSM-III* emphasised schizophrenia as a disorder of thought in two ways: (1) by limiting the extent of allowable affective symptoms; and (2) more importantly, by emphasising specific symptoms proposed by Kurt Schneider as typical or indicative of schizophrenia (symptoms which Bleuler considered only *secondary* for schizophrenia). These symptoms were overwhelmingly related to disorders of thinking, and included specific delusions or hallucinations.[10]

However, the most significant challenge to the neo-Kraepelinian paradigm was (and continues to be) the category of schizoaffective disorder. The editors of the *DSM-III* reluctantly removed schizoaffective disorder from its placement as a subtype of schizophrenia after an influential review (Procci, 1976) found evidence of links both to affective disorders and to schizophrenia. However, the editors significantly limited the utility of the category by not including any specific diagnostic criteria, and explicitly discouraging its use. In addition, the expansion of the affective disorders categories to include the presence of mood-incongruent psychotic symptoms (i.e. inconsistent with the prevailing mood) also significantly limited the utility of the schizoaffective disorder category. Previously, patients manifesting significant affective symptoms along with mood-incongruent psychotic symptoms (such as delusions of control) would have been called schizoaffective. But once again, research has undermined these politically based distinctions – the schizoaffective disorder category now includes diagnostic criteria and recent research strongly supports its validity (Marneros and Akiskal, 2007).

Conclusion

When Emil Kraepelin codified dementia praecox and contrasted it with manic-depressive insanity, he was setting the stage for the calcification of the latter as a disorder of emotion and the former as a disorder of thinking. Eugen Bleuler's contribution has frequently been viewed as extending this vision of schizophrenia as a primary disorder of thought, in contradistinction to affective disorders. This perspective was particularly championed by the neo-Kraepelinians, whose motivation in the development of the *DSM-III* was to solidify Kraepelin's fundamental distinction between schizophrenia and manic-depression to buttress the biological view of these disorders. As a consequence of this agenda, the important role of emotion in schizophrenia, recognised by Bleuler, was forgotten. And likewise, because of discomfort over the true meaning of Bleuler's choice of term, schizophrenia ('split mind'),

10 Interestingly, the *DSM-V* schizophrenia committee has recommended that these Schneiderian symptoms be eliminated from the schizophrenia diagnostic criteria, acknowledging that there is no evidence that these symptoms are unique to schizophrenia (www.dsm5.org/ProposedRevisions/Pages/proposedrevision.aspx?rid=411#, retrieved 13 August 2010).

links between schizophrenia, dissociation and the dissociative disorders have long been minimised.

However, if one looks closely at Bleuler's writings on schizophrenia, as we have done here, the concepts of affect and dissociation/splitting appear essential. Bleuler's central concept of 'loosening of associations' cannot be equated with a narrowly defined thought disorder, and he believed that affective capacity in schizophrenia was not essentially disturbed, but only submerged by the activity of one or more 'emotionally charged complexes' which drove the psychotic symptoms.

After decades of neglect, publications such as this one indicate that Bleuler's view of affect disturbances and dissociative processes as central to the nature of schizophrenia is finally getting the attention it deserves. It is hoped that the implications of these ideas for contemporary conceptions of schizophrenia will be further drawn out in the years to come.

References

American Psychiatric Association (APA, 1980) *Diagnostic and Statistical Manual of Mental Disorders*, third edn (DSM-III). Washington, DC: American Psychiatric Association.

American Psychiatric Association (APA, 2000) *Diagnostic and Statistical Manual of Mental Disorders*, fourth edn, text revision (DSM-IV-TR). Washington, DC: American Psychiatric Association.

Blashfield, R.K. (1984) *The Classification of Psychopathology: Neo-Kraepelinian and Quantitative Approaches*, New York: Plenum.

Bleuler, E. (1902–1903) Dementia praecox, *Journal of Mental Pathology* III(4–5): 113–120.

Bleuler, E. (1904/1918) Upon the significance of association experiments (Trans. M.D. Eder), in C.G. Jung (ed.) *Studies in Word-Association*, London: William Heinemann, 266–296.

Bleuler, E. (1905/1918) Consciousness and association (Trans. M.D. Eder), in C.G. Jung (ed.) *Studies in Word-Association*, London: William Heinemann, 266–296.

Bleuler, E. (1906/1912) *Affectivity, Suggestibility, Paranoia* (Trans. C. Ricksher), Utica, NY: State Hospitals Press.

Bleuler, E. (1908/1987) The prognosis of dementia praecox: the group of schizophrenias, in J. Cutting and M. Shepherd (eds) *The Clinical Roots of the Schizophrenia Concept: Translations of Seminal European Contributions on Schizophrenia*, Cambridge: Cambridge University Press, 59–74.

Bleuler, E. (1911) *Dementia Praecox oder Gruppe der Schizoprenien*, Leipzig: Deuticke.

Bleuler, E. (1911/1950) *Dementia Praecox or the Group of Schizophrenias* (Trans. J. Zinkin), New York: International Universities Press.

Bleuler, M. and Bleuler, R. (1986) Dementia Praecox oder die Gruppe der Schizophrenien: Eugen Bleuler, *British Journal of Psychiatry* 149: 661–664.

Bleuler, E. and Jung, C.G. (1908) Komplexe und Krankheitsursachen bei Dementia praecox, *Zentralblatt für Nervenheilkunde und Psychiatrie*, XIX: 220–227.

Ellenberger, H.F. (1970) *The Discovery of the Unconscious: The History and Evolution of Dynamic Psychiatry*, New York: Basic Books.
Freeman, D. and Garety, P.A. (2003) Connecting neurosis and psychosis: the direct influence of emotion on delusions and hallucinations, *Behaviour Research and Therapy* 41(8): 923–947.
Jung, C.G. (ed.) (1906/1918) *Studies in Word-Association*, London: William Heinemann.
Jung, C.G. (1907/1960) The psychology of dementia praecox (Trans. R.F.C. Hull), in *The Psychogenesis of Mental Disease*, London: Routledge and Kegan Paul, 3–151.
Jung, C.G. (1956/1960) Recent thoughts on schizophrenia, in *The Psychogenesis of Mental Disease*, London: Routledge and Kegan Paul, 250–255.
Klerman, G.L. (1978) The evolution of a scientific nosology, in J.C. Shersow (ed.) *Schizophrenia: Science and Practice*, Cambridge, MA: Harvard University Press.
McNally, K. (2009) Eugen Bleuler's four A's, *History of Psychology* 12(2): 43–59.
Marneros, A. and Akiskal, H.S. (2007) *The Overlap of Affective and Schizophrenic Spectra*, Cambridge: Cambridge University Press.
Moskowitz, A. (2006) Pierre Janet's influence on Bleuler's concept of schizophrenia, in P. Fiedler (ed.) *Trauma, Dissoziation, Persönlichkeit: Über Pierre Janets Beiträge zur modernen Psychiatrie, Psychologie und Psychotherapie*, Lengerich: Pabst Science Publishers, 158–179.
Moskowitz, A. (2008) Association and dissociation in the historical concept of schizophrenia, in A. Moskowitz, I. Schäfer and M.J. Dorahy (eds) *Psychosis, Trauma and Dissociation: Emerging Perspectives on Severe Psychopathology*, Chichester: Wiley, 35–49.
Moskowitz, A. and Corstens, D. (2007) Auditory hallucinations: psychotic symptom or dissociative experience?, in S.N. Gold and J.D. Elhai (eds) *Trauma and Serious Mental Illness*, Binghamton, NY: Haworth Press, 35–63.
Moskowitz, A., Schäfer, I. and Dorahy, M.J. (eds) (2008) *Psychosis, Trauma and Dissociation: Emerging Perspectives on Severe Psychopathology*, Chichester: Wiley.
Procci, W.R. (1976) Schizo-affective psychosis: fact or fiction, *Archives of General Psychiatry* 33: 1167–1178.
Pruyser, P. (1975) What splits in 'splitting'? A scrutiny of the concept of splitting in psychoanalysis and psychiatry, *Bulletin of the Menninger Clinic* 39(1): 1–46.
Rosenbaum, M. (1980) The role of the term schizophrenia in the decline of the diagnosis of multiple personality, *Archives of General Psychiatry* 37: 1383–1385.
Scharfetter, C. (2001) Eugen Bleuler's schizophrenias – synthesis of various concepts, *Schweizer Archiv für Neurologie und Psychiatrie* 152: 34–37.
Schneider, K. (1959) *Clinical Psychopathology*, New York: Grune and Stratton.

Chapter 3

Psychosis and the human affective environment

David Garfield, Edwin K. Simon and Anil Ramachandran

Introduction

Separated by a mere 60 miles, the great descriptive psychiatrist of Zurich, Eugen Bleuler, struggled to understand the mysteries of the universe within, while a brilliant young patent office clerk in Bern, Albert Einstein, struggled to understand the laws of the mysterious universe that surrounds us all. By formulating that $E=MC^2$, Einstein opened the world to the idea that energy and structure may transform one into the other. Concurrently, through his discovery of the four A's of schizophrenia, Bleuler[1] (1905) concluded that "affectivity is the basis of life." As a kind of foreshadowing of this confluence of inner and outer mystery, John Keats (1817), the renowned British poet, 50 years earlier set the tone for both scientists by proclaiming "I believe in the holiness of the heart's affections and the truth of imagination."

The inner and outer human universe

This chapter looks at the great discoveries of the inside and the outside in a linked fashion. With Einstein, at one end of the spectrum, there is the objective world as it is known by science. With Bleuler, there is the other end of the spectrum, the subjective world as human beings understand it. This continuum is the topic of this exploration and how it applies to the psychotherapy of psychosis is the task at hand.

The preliminary thesis

The thesis here is that the objective world and the subjective world are on a continuum and are governed by two separate principles at each pole. At one end, the objective world conforms to the laws of motion. At the subjective end of the spectrum, the experiential, subjective world is governed by the

1 See Chapter 2, Moskowitz and Heim, for an extended discussion of Bleuler's conceptualization of schizophrenia.

laws of emotion. In addition, the supposition is that affect is psychic energy and that it too forms and transforms psychic structure in a parallel fashion to the way that the energy of physics forms and transforms the structure of matter.

Wendy's spatial rearrangements

Wendy Alice McMann[2] was a 32-year-old single Irish Catholic greenhouse/nursery saleswoman who came for a consultation for "spatial rearrangements." The history of the present illness dated back to one month prior to the consultation when she had been walking toward the lakeshore in downtown Chicago and "I lost grip on reality in terms of basic spatial arrangements. I was going West to East and East rotated into West." She continued, "At another time, I was trying to walk up Ontario Street from the lake to get to the train station and where I was on Ontario seemed 'compacted' closer to downtown than it should have been."

Wendy recounted that she had been diagnosed with schizophrenia at the age of 23 after having heard voices and "having thought intrusions" about witchcraft. "I saw things, smelled things and felt things." She noted that the doctors at the local hospital did two EEGs and an overnight EEG looking for temporal lobe epilepsy and did an MRI but found nothing. "The thought intrusions were not exactly language, they were kind of 'pre-language'—an unarticulated message which can be articulated . . . what was most striking was that it was 'out of place'." She knew what she needed: "I need grounding influences."

Developmental history

Wendy was intellectually gifted. Both her mother and her father were quite accomplished physicists although her mother wasn't working any more. She casually remarked that her mom had taught her to read before going to kindergarten. "I felt like the people at school thought I was trying to be too smart." She had wanted to move on to calculus in junior high school but they didn't have it. Although Wendy did not relate with ease to kids at school, she did have a friend from time to time. She excelled at the public high school with advanced classes in Latin and Math. "One of the field hockey stars, Madeline, took a liking to me and she celebrated when I won the regional science fair with balloons and cards. But some other kids tore them down. But I only really felt comfortable with peers when I went to a Math and Science Academy. I actually dated a few guys there. It was easier to socialize away from home. The honors program at the state university also was OK and

2 Pseudonym used to protect the person's anonymity.

I had friends there who were 'weird or smart like me'." The "extraneous voices and thought answers" that started at the age of eight for Wendy became more frightening when she graduated from the university honors program and she returned home. She had two suicide attempts. She started to travel a bit. As she traveled, the voices didn't bother her but the spatial rearrangements did scare her.

Family history

She later revealed that her mother was difficult. "Janet" (as she refers to her mother) "has a dissociative disorder and repressed memories. She was abused by her mother. I can't deal with her. Her repressed stuff is hard. She has a very distorted view of reality. My dad doesn't have such a great view on reality either but he is not difficult." Wendy has one younger sibling, Jonathan. "He stays away from all of us. He's kind of abrasive. His friends are OK though." She didn't want to talk much about her mother but later noted that her mother had two dominant personalities (of multiple personalities). "One was nice and helpful. She would show me how to plant tomatoes in the garden. But then the other personality was mean and nasty, she would reverse and play war games on the computer and she would play solitaire and I was not to be near her. That has gone on my entire life."

Wendy only stayed in treatment for a few months. From the beginning, it seemed that she had a certain "mask" on; that she was presenting only a given amount of her distressed self, a "surface layer," but that she was keeping the rest of herself out of reach. She engaged at that surface level and might have gotten deeper and further but the analyst's office was close to her home where she had been living with her parents and she quickly decided that she could not stay in town and she moved near to the state university. The analyst would not have the opportunity to be a "grounding influence."

Through the years, the analyst thought quite a bit about Wendy, wondering where she was and how she was doing and what was happening with her spatial rearrangements. In many years of working with psychosis, Ms McCann's presentation of these spatial rearrangements was somewhat unique to the analyst (DG). When she stepped into talking about her relationship with her mother, it was as if both analyst and patient knew that the source of her perceptual distortion was in the disorientation that had become embedded through her engagement with her mother's two distinct emotional personalities. Although she liked the analyst and although being at home was disorienting for her, the father of the analyst was dying during the months that Wendy was in treatment and it is a good guess that the patient could tell that the analyst did not have the emotional wherewithal to engage her, to help ground her, as she needed. The analyst wasn't surprised by her moving back near the university where she had a few relational connections that might help her get her feet back on the ground.

What would the analyst do differently today? If he had been more emotionally available back then, what would he have done to engage her more? Before turning to the topic of engaging the affective life of the patient, let's look at another brief example of the distortions of subjective time and space that sometimes confront those in psychosis.

One of the authors (DG) has recently had the enormous good fortune to edit with Daniel Mackler the first ISPS-US (International Society for Psychological and Social Approaches to Psychosis – United States) book (2008) – *Beyond Medication: Therapeutic Engagement and the Recovery from Psychosis*. Catherine Penny contributed a compelling chapter recounting her recovery from psychosis via her work with Dr. Dan Dorman. After two or three years of five times a week psychotherapy, Dr. Dorman was finishing residency at UCLA and was going into private practice. Through much of her time in psychosis, Cathy Penny had little hope of living and when she heard of Dorman's leaving she became despairing and suicidal. She figured she would be transferred to the state hospital. Of course, Dr. Dorman had no intention of stopping with her and made arrangements for her to be transferred to Westwood Hospital near his office. Would her new direction be upended?

> During our sessions Dr. Dorman and I exposed and gently peeled away more and more layers of trauma and repressed underground "stuff." I began to feel the reemergence of feelings that had been split off long ago and replaced by voices. I started showing interest in my environment and began going to Group. And with my growing awareness came the dawning of insight. My recovery and letting go of the schizophrenia was done in little steps. My improvement externally – the decreasing of my delusions and hallucinations – was just the beginning. For the first couple of weeks after I initially opened my eyes – as they had been literally closed for two years (except for when I needed to get around, at which point I would crack them open a little) – my visual perceptions were distorted. I experienced objects in my environment as being upside-down and in slow motion.

Here was a woman in psychosis, emotionally engaged. Feelings are reemerging. Her whole world was now being turned emotionally around. And with one eye on our brilliant Einstein and one now turning to our brilliant student of Bleuler's, Eugene Minkowski, somehow we are not surprised to hear not only of subjective spatial distortions in psychosis but also of subjective distortions of time. There is an objective time/space continuum and there is a subjective time/space continuum. One is configured by the laws of motion, while the other is governed by the laws of emotion.

The laws of emotion govern psychosis

In his incisive account *Lived Time*, the psychiatrist/phenomenologist Minkowski (1970) noted that: "In all psychopathologic cases some distortion of lived time or lived space has occurred, regardless of whether the disorder has an organic or a psychic origin" (p. xxii). Inside humans and between humans, distortions of lived time and space are common. Whether it is in the unique human capacity to fall in love or whether it is in the terror of an imminent car crash, one can either find oneself in a lived time where "the hours seem like minutes" or where one is frozen in a lived time that has slowed down to almost nothing.

The above patient accounts and Minkowski's observations lead to one of our main points which is that the perceptual apparatus has been "hijacked" in psychosis and therefore, it is probably not a surprise that the patient's subjective experience of time and space is distorted. But hijacked by what? In his in-depth thinking about psychosis, in "The Loss of Reality in Psychosis and Neurosis" (1924) Freud believed that the repression barrier cannot hold and that the ego is overwhelmed by the unconscious contents of the Id. Here is the classic formulation of "the return of the repressed" in psychosis. From his study of dreams (1900) and from the conclusion that the timelessness is a fundamental characteristic of the unconscious, Freud concluded that patients in the throes of psychosis are, in essence, "prisoners of the present" with no subjective sense of the past or the future; that is, the perceptual apparatus has been "hijacked" by the unconscious. This chapter sees it differently.

William Meissner has written a comprehensive account (2008) on subjective time and space and the self. He notes: "The subjective meaning of time may have nothing to do with motion and its measurement—suggesting a perspective somewhat different from that of physical science" (p. 7). He goes on to highlight the emotional influences that give subjective time its flavor: "This inner sense of time, time as subjectively experienced, time as a facet of the experience of the self, (is) influenced by dynamic and affective influences" (p. 7).

Freud (1900), in "The Interpretation of Dreams," also noted how dream activity did not conform to the laws of movement and motion. Gravity and time, two of Einstein's most essential ingredients in his theory of relativity, were noted to be completely obviated in the subjective venue of the dream state.

In psychosis, as Bleuler's other famous student Carl Jung (1907) so elegantly described, perception is governed by emotion. This view has been supported by Elvin Semrad at the Boston Psychopathic Hospital (Khantzian *et al.*, 1969) and Harold Searles (1965) at Chestnut Lodge, who documented the primary role that affect had in organizing subjectivity in psychosis. Semrad developed an affect-centered psychotherapy of psychosis, described in *Unbearable Affect: A Guide to the Psychotherapy of Psychosis* (Garfield, 2009) and Searles (1965, 1979) extensively privileged affect throughout his writings on psychosis. In his volume *Collected Papers on Schizophrenia and Related Subjects*, Searles (1965) wrote an illustrative account of how in psychosis perception is organized by affective theme. He describes a young woman in a confessional as she sees the priest's ears elongate; the priest began to look like a mule or an "ass." In the analysis of her experience, Searles became aware that his patient had experienced the priest as being mean to her – "an ass." Here instead of the perception giving rise to a feeling state (I perceive you as a mean person who makes me feel disdain), it is the other way around – my feeling state of disdain makes me perceive you as an "ass"! In the human affective environment, subjectivity is governed by emotion rather than the laws of motion.

An exploration of the other side of the spectrum

Moving back to the patent office in Zurich with the young Albert Einstein and the objective side of human experience, one can see how Einstein was ever-determined to discover the fundamental laws of this external universe. Einstein pushed and poked at the conventionally established Newtonian laws of physics. His discovery of the general theory of relativity evolved out of his grappling with the speed of light. Through his famous "thought experiments," Einstein was able to undermine the very nature of our understanding of external reality – time and space were not constant, they varied with respect to one another. Going faster on a train while looking out the window at the length of a field yielded a shorter length than if you were measuring the field while riding on a horse. There was no separating time and space. "Standing still" was never really standing still. Some kind of movement was always involved with external reality.

Genius as he was, the man in the patent office also realized that a perspectival approach to external reality extended into the subjective affective realm even though this was not his primary focus. Asked about how love and pain impact on time, Einstein presaged *West Side Story* in noting that when in love "the hours seem like minutes and yet, when in pain, time becomes interminable."

Movement in the physical world

The laws of physics not only predict the behavior of celestial bodies but also that of smaller objects like a ball thrown in a tight arc during a game of baseball. These laws hold well in different conditions and make it possible for us to launch a space ship or predict the trajectory of a boomerang.

The living world, from prions to vertebrates, vividly illustrates the central role of motion in life. Bacteria have the ability to move towards a source of nutrients through their use of flagellae. Kandel (1976), in his seminal studies of memory showed the ability of *Aplysia californica* (California sea slug) to move away from a squirt of water perceived as noxious. The same movement can be seen in the much-evolved *Homo sapiens*.

Movement and emotion

In the objective world, movement is the basis of life. No one has promulgated this idea more than Maxine Sheets-Johnstone, who in her ground-breaking work *The Primacy of Movement* (1999a) has collated massive amounts of evidence from anthropology, biology, psychology and evolution to support this thesis. Aristotle, she notes, "states in unmistakable terms that to understand nature is to understand motion, for nature—by its very nature—everywhere articulates a principle of motion. To understand the kinetic process by which we take in the sensible form of things without the matter and thereby experience qualities such as loud, sharp, soft" (Sheets-Johnstone, 1999b, pp. 259–277). She asserts that humans don't experience a world of objects per se, but rather a world of varied and changing physiognomies, a qualitatively dynamic world. Going back to Aristotle, she notes that his was an "essentially experiential, kinetic and qualitative explication of perception" which is drawn on an understanding of perception as sensorially localized. "We perceive at the site of our senses." That sensation is "a change of quality, and of change of quality as a matter of movement" (1999b, pp. 259–277).

Sheets-Johnstone goes on to establish the fact that language and all it achieves is post-kinetic. The newborn moves, cries but does not speak like an adult. All its efforts are movements. The first breath, the first cry, the first gulp of milk, the first caress it enjoys are all movements. The emotions exhibited by the baby and the affection showered on the baby is through motion. As a newborn grows, motion or movement is the basis for perceiving and understanding the world around it. The baby or child shows its independence by moving away from mother only to come running back, needing comfort if hurt or afraid. Sheets-Johnstone asserts that these behaviors form the underpinning of emotions and further the evolution of language.

She emphasizes the use of words in day-to-day language that has a basis in motion. She posits that the ideas we have are formed by what we perceive through movement. She notes that motion leads to emotion, just as it leads to language. In addition, she posits that movement is the mother of all cognitions and that it is the foundation of our sense of agency.

Sheets-Johnstone (1999a) extrapolates how emotion and movement are intertwined. She draws on Jacobson's (1974) work on "auto-sensory observation," to show that in a fundamental sense the brain and musculature work in unison. In one of his observations, Jacobson maintains that "when a trained observer relaxes the neuromuscular elements apparently specific in any activity, the mental activity as such disappears." He also says that "the muscle and brain proceed together in one effort-circuit, active or relaxed."

Sheets-Johnstone follows up on Jacobson's observations with Nina Bulls's notation that emotions are shaped by motor attitudes and that a basic neuromuscular sequence is essential in the production of affect. Her observations with hypnotized subjects show that when hypnotized and locked in a certain feeling state denoting one emotion (e.g. anger), the subjects were unable to experience an opposing emotion (e.g. joy) when they were instructed to, as they were still in a posture denoting the previous emotion. Sheets-Johnstone goes on to comment that affective feelings and tactile-kinaesthetic feelings are experientially intertwined.

There is one indivisible tactile-kinaesthetic body and movement is the foundation upon which the rest of human faculties are built; emotion and movement are inexorably linked and one inextricably influences the other and vice versa. This is Sheets-Johnstone's fundamental assertion.

The continuum between motion and emotion

On the continuum between the objective world and the subjective world, one now comes to understand that the objective world is governed by the laws of motion and the subjective world is governed by the workings of emotion. But what does it mean that it is a continuum? Is there a clear demarcation between the objective and subjective world? The physiologist Benjamin Libet answers in the affirmative: "One can only describe relationships between subjective phenomena and neuronal events, not how one gets from one to the other" (Libet, 1985). Sheets-Johnstone (1999a) concurs: "the reduction of the mental to the physical—or the identification of the former with the latter—is thus evidentially ungrounded."

Emotion holds the upper hand in configuring subjective experience. It can structure time and space according to its own dictates. This is the vital aspect in understanding and working with psychosis. As noted above, Carl Jung was perhaps the most significant contributor to this understanding. In his detailed work with the word association experiment with patients in the throes of psychosis at the Burghölzli, Jung derived the notion of the "feeling toned complex." In his "Psychogenesis of Mental Disease" Jung time and time again comes back to how normal psychic operations are overtaken by one or more feeling tones fused with an associational complex. These feeling tones are responsible for the "laws of association" which he enumerated as: (1) clang associations; (2) verbal-motor combination; (3) similarity; (4) co-existence; (5) sound combination.

Vitality affects and the objective subjective midpoint

The fact that the objective and subjective world live on a continuum between motion and emotion is further clarified by Daniel Stern (1985, 2004), who has best explored this in-between land. Before he became a psychoanalyst, Stern was a developmental infant researcher. A prolific writer, he has written many books that progressively outline the human continuum between movement and emotion. *The First Relationship*, *The Interpersonal World of the Infant*, and more recently *The Present Moment in Psychotherapy and Everyday Life* (2004). All depict how "forms of feeling" hold sway in both objective and subjective human experience. Stern first happened upon the notion of vitality affects to explain the mother's affective attunement to her infant as an early form of intersubjectivity. He has nicely expanded it since then. There is the motion aspect of vitality affects and then there is the emotional aspect of vitality affects. The first concerns stimulation that imprints on the nervous system from within or from without. Most stimulation, as Stern notes, is contoured in real time by intensity, rhythm – e.g. form of the stimulus. He gives a nice example of a "smile" that is seen on another's face. It takes time to form. It grows – crescendo in perhaps a second or so, reaches its high point of fullness of display which may be held for a moment with small modulations and then decomposes over a second or so. The decomposition might be rapid like a "shutdown" or slow as in a "fade-out" or somewhere in between. The whole performance flows together as one uninterrupted, several second stimulus. And there are, as he notes, a million kinds of smiles due to the difference in their temporal contours and these are not trivial in terms of their communication impact. It can indicate spontaneous pleasure or surprise or even guilt. Stern comments:

> Everything we do, see, feel and hear from people has a temporal contour. . . . By temporal contour, I mean the objective changes (even small) over time (even short) of intensity or quality of the stimulation (internal or external). By vitality affect, I mean the subjectively experienced shifts in internal feeling states that accompany the temporal contour of the stimulus.
>
> (2004, pp. 62–63)

Notice the clear delineation between the objective and subjective world. Stern goes on:

> The feeling quality of vitality affects is best captured by kinetic terms such as, surging, fading away, fleeting, explosive, tentative, effortful, accelerating, decelerating, climaxing, bursting, drawn out, reaching, hesitating, leaning forward, leaning backward and so on.
>
> (2004, p. 64)

He posits that from the moment of birth, we all have daily exposure to these experiences in the form of breathing, sucking, moving, defecating, swallowing, having cramps, and so on – each has its own temporal contour and vitality affect. Furthermore, Stern correctly notes that vitality affects, in their dimensional character, can be differentiated from the categorical Darwinian affects of happy, sad, fear, shame/disgust and anger. One emphasizes trait and one focuses on state. In the illustrations above of the case of Wendy and with Cathy Penny, states of emotion and vitality traits of emotion both work to structure the subjective perception of time and space.

Another middle ground – metaphor

Non-verbal, prosodic methods of psychoanalysis and psychotherapy such as cross-modal attunement via vitality affects are one way of engaging the patient's emotional life. Another way of engaging the patient's emotional life is through metaphor. Metaphor is a semantic, verbal way of engaging affect. Here, one comes a bit closer to how metaphor relates to the human affective environment:

> There are always two terms in a metaphor, the thing to be described, the metaphrand and the thing or relation used to elucidate it, which can be called metaphier. A metaphor is always a known metaphier operating on a less known metaphrand.
>
> (Jaynes, 1982, p. 48)

Not surprisingly, "the human body is a particularly generative metaphier, creating an enormous number of distinctions in a throng of areas" (Jaynes, 1982, p. 49). In day-to-day language, the human body is often used to convey meanings. For example, one refers to "the head of an army, table, page, ship . . . All of these concrete body metaphors are used to increase the human perception of the outside world and one's understanding of it, and can, literally create new objects. Indeed language is an organ of perception, not simply a means of communication" (Jaynes, 1982, pp. 49–50). Yet, behind this language, one feels the body metaphier and the body metaphier is inspired by infrastructure of one's senses. The link to sensation/emotion as the agent of the form of perception, is, thus, one small step away from the way perception is structured.

A theory of metaphor

Lakoff and Johnson (1999), in their powerful explication of metaphor, note that the overall theory of primary metaphor has four parts: (1) Johnson's theory of conflation; (2) Grady's theory of primary metaphor; (3) Narayanan's neural theory of metaphor; and (4) Fauconnier and Turner's theory of conceptual blending (pp. 45–56).

The theory of conflation that Johnson has put forth notes that subjective experiences and sensory motor experiences are often merged. They are "undifferentiated in experience and children do not distinguish between the two when they occur together. For example, an infant's subjective experience of affection is typically correlated with the sensory experience of warmth, the warmth of being held. During the period of conflation, associations are automatically built between the two domains." As children develop and are then able to separate out these areas, the cross domain associations persist. These persisting associations are the mappings of conceptual metaphor that will lead the same infant later in life to speak of a "warm smile" and a "close friend" (Lakoff and Johnson, 1999, p. 46).

Grady (Lakoff and Johnson, 1999, p. 47) hypothesized that most metaphors are "molecular" and are composed of "atomic" elements which he called "primary metaphors." Each primary metaphor has a template structure and evolves "naturally, automatically, and unconsciously" through day-to-day experience by means of the persistent associations – Johnson's idea of conflation – such that a merger of associations takes place, and thus, complex metaphors are formed through a type of conceptual "blending." These early childhood common experiences lead to "universal conflations which then develop into universal (or widespread) conventional conceptual metaphors" (Lakoff and Johnson, 1999, pp. 46–49).

Narayanan's (Lakoff and Johnson, 1999, pp. 46–50) neural theory of metaphor states that the "associations" made during the period of conflation are instantiated in simultaneous neuronal activations that result in permanent links being made across the neural networks that define conceptual domains. "These connections form the anatomical basis of source to target activations that constitute metaphorical entailments."

Fauconnier and Turner (Lakoff and Johnson, 1999, p. 49) state that separate conceptual areas can be "co-activated" and under certain conditions connections across domains can be formed as a result of this co-activation which leads to new inferences. Such "conceptual blends" may be either conventional or wholly original.

Lakoff and Johnson stress that "it is this unique blend of hardware cross domain mapping from our sensory motor self to targets of subjective experience in the melting pot of culture which leads us to experience 'closeness' with 'intimacy,' affection with warmth and 'achieving purposes' with 'reaching destinations' (p. 59). Lakoff and Johnson note:

> Metaphor allows conventional mental imagery from sensory motor domains to be used for domains of subjective experience. For example, we may form an image of something going by us or over our heads (sensory motor experience) when we fail to understand (subjective experience) . . . a gesture tracing the path of something going past us, over our heads can indicate vividly a "failure to understand."
>
> (1999, p. 45)

If one takes the above ideas and applies them to the earlier case of Wendy, one can come closer to the kind of space and time difficulties that Wendy encountered; here, Lakoff and Johnson's ideas of metaphor may be useful. She herself metaphorically notes "I was turned around."

Psychoanalysis and body metaphors

Jaynes (1976, p. 50) states:

> This is language moving out synchronically (or without reference to time) into the space of the world to describe it and perceive it more and more definitively. Language also moves in another and more important way, diachronically, or through time, and behind our experiences on the basis of structures in our nervous system to create abstract concepts whose referents are not too observable, except in a metaphorical sense.

And these too are generated by metaphors. Here, the body itself becomes a "space" and parts of the body become "spaces" – Kleinians and neo-Kleinians are very familiar with thinking about the body and body parts as spaces (Meltzer, 1993). Indeed, Bion's (2004) whole way of working with psychosis was predicated on the container metaphor and many of the most affectively powerful metaphors are container based. As Jaynes (1976, pp. 55–56) asserts:

> The mind-space in which these metaphorical activities go on has its own group of adjectives . . . We can be "occupied"; we can "get something off our minds", put something out of mind or we can "get it", let something "penetrate" or "bear", have, keep or hold it in mind. As with real space, something can be at the "back" of our mind, in its inner recess or "beyond" our mind or out of our mind. In argument we try to "get things through" to someone to reach their understanding or find a common ground or point out.

The middle ground between motion and emotion

Looking even more closely as to how emotion and motion co-mingle in the realm of metaphor, one sees that "there are many phrases in English language that describe emotional experiences that involve verbs of motion – swept away, blown away, transported, carried away" and others (Kövecses, 2003, p. 57). Why? Emotions evoke human responses indicating inner transformations that the self undergoes. In this way, emotion itself becomes a cause relative to the responses it induces. Kövecses (2003, p. 37) continues:

> The container metaphors suggest among other things, that lack of agitation corresponds to lack of emotion and that intense emotion may

> lead to an explosion. Emotions are natural forces . . . metaphors also suggest that emotion characteristically is a state of agitation e.g. emotion swept her away, there was a ground swell of emotion, emotions were running high.

There is a great literature on metaphor in psychology and psychoanalysis and the point here is that we borrow from the objective world of movement terms what we hope will impact on the subjective emotional world of our patient.

Finding a middle ground and grounding in the physical resonance of metaphor in the case of Wendy

With respect to being disoriented, the analyst offered: "With your mother's multiple personalities, you didn't know whether you were coming or going." With respect to the therapist's failure to understand one of Wendy's references to her adoration for a high school friend, he noted: "With my recent screw up, you found yourself going nowhere" (referencing her feeling that she was "compacted" closer to Michigan Ave as she tried to head to the train station). These kinds of interventions that use vitality affects as well as those that utilize metaphor link the culturally shared objective world of human affective experience to the subjective, personally encoded world of human experience structured on emotion.

From motion to emotion

How does this all impact on our work in psychosis? In his earlier work *The Interpersonal World of the Infant* (1985), Stern presented information about the development of the core self and its reliance on the early infant's experience of "becoming organized." There is a process of an emergent sense of self in which invariants (breathing, stomach digesting, defecating, etc.) are experienced and this experience becomes progressively more organized. Stern categorizes these under topics of self-coherence, self agency, self affectivity and self history as "islands of consistency: are built up and integrated. On the subjective side of the equation, primary psychological experience is based around the developmental paradigms of differentiation and integration" (pp. 71–75). Thus, all these physical movements, from the autonomic aspects of basic bodily processes to the movements of primary mothering, become inextricably linked to the basic perceptual processes of the mind. Any effective psychotherapy of psychosis (Garfield, 2002, 2009) will make use of both vitality affects as well as metaphor in the daily affective restructuring that is part and parcel of the endeavor.

Levels of emotional awareness

A psychoanalytic framework for the human affective experience

How stimuli are differentiated and integrated brings one to the question of how emotion is embodied and directly back to Wendy. Formulated by Lane and Schwartz in 1987, the levels of emotional awareness theory states that there are implicit or unconscious levels of emotional activity starting with primitive Piaget-like sensory motor patterns which become more elaborated and integrated (it is a developmental model based on the developmental principle of progressive differentiation of the parts combined with hierarchic integration of the parts) as one moves up to the next level. The sensory motor "emotional" patterns move up and integrate into somatic visceral forms of emotion which then move up into implicit emotional action patterns (unconsciously assimilated from family patterns of processing and expressing emotion; that is, some families will model screaming when mad and others will teach the "silent treatment" – being passive aggressive when mad). These more elaborated and integrated implicit forms of emotion go on to "conscious forms" such as "background" feelings ("something is bothering me") to focal emotional feelings ("I'm annoyed") to "reflective awareness of feelings" ("I am annoyed because of this and that and I am also sad at the same time" – blends of emotions). Lane and Garfield (2005) discussed the neurobiological correlates and the psychoanalytic utility of this theory. In the case of Wendy, one could approach the treatment by thinking about her autonomic nervous system and her visceral experience and her pattern of emotional behavior. These are imprinted in the early caregiver–patient relationship. With the analyst, in an intensive-frequent treatment, she will express and expect certain kinds of emotional interactions that will be mediated by her autonomic nervous system and by the different somatic levels noted above. "Getting Wendy oriented" will mean using prosody (vitality affect attunement) and metaphors to help impact on these lower levels of processing. She will no doubt have experiences with the analyst where he does not seem "the same to her" and she will, at those times, become fearful and will literally re-orient herself at those emotional points and she will not be aware of the emotion (it is implicit). When he fails her, which is inevitable, in hopefully tolerable ways, she will fragment and experience these emotionally governed time and space distortions. She and the analyst would need, then, to repair these misunderstandings, process what happened and hopefully bring these earlier emotional forms into new, more integrated patterns. This will take time to install via the therapeutic relationship.

As mentioned above, central to this process will be the role of what Daniel Stern calls "vitality affects." These are bodily based experiences of emotionality that have specific activation contours. For example, one can "breathe a sigh of relief" – where, literally, the chest relaxes, air comes out and a specific affect of "relief" rides on top of the body movement. In treatment, if one is attentive to these processes, one can "mirror" or join the patient in such experiences in a kind of empathic attunement (Garfield, 2002). These become "integrating"/strengthening/cohering experiences for the patient. One can even practice what is called "cross modal attunement" such that if your patient is happy and excited and is bouncing on their seat with glee, you can cross modally attune with vocal "bouncing" by saying "GREAT! So Good! SO SO GOOD!" – with a vocal inflection that "bounces" along with the patient.

The net effect of this focus on levels of emotional experience and the use of tools to facilitate interventions at various impacted levels in the patient is to decrease psychotic fragmentation, strengthen the therapeutic alliance, allow the patient to feel "accompanied" and not alone in their experience and, in our model, to use motion to integrate emotion. Thus, vitality affects along with metaphor sit right in the center in our motion/emotion continuum or, better said, sit at the motion/emotion interface between the objective and subjective world.

Conclusion

A final note on the selfobject concept

In the reworking of emotion and psychosis, expanding and strengthening the patient's emotional subjective life becomes the primary goal of treatment. Perception, sensation and language are all engaged in this therapeutic process. The question arises: How does the analyst or therapist fit into this matrix of reassembly? Herein is the concept of the selfobject as elucidated by Kohut (1971). It is the way that the clinician is experienced subjectively by the patient. The therapist becomes a "selfobject" experience for the patient. As Stolorow and Lachmann (1980) point out, the function of the selfobject is to provide cohesion, temporal continuity and positive affective coloring to the patient's internal, moment-to-moment experience.

Kohut (1971) originally detailed two dominant forms of selfobject experience; one he termed "mirroring" and the other "idealizing." One primarily involved with the patient's experience of being recognized, affirmed and alive and the other primarily involved with the patient feeling supported, safe and belonging. Stolorow and Saccharides (1987) extended these ideas to the realm of affects and their foundational role in the selfobject experience. Wolf (2002) then pointed out that it was the breakdown of the therapist/patient selfobject experience that results in a traditional transference experience and resultant symptomatology such as one can see in the cases presented above. Wolf emphasized that it was the repair of that rupture that was the curative factor in the reorganization of emotion and the pathway out of illness. In this chapter, we can see how early disturbances in the selfobject milieu may predispose to extreme, psychotic experiences of time and space. In addition, as the patient recovers in the matrix of the selfobject milieu between analyst and patient, these distortions clear.

References

Bion, W.R. (2004) *Learning from Experience*, Lanham, MD: Rowan and Littlefield.

Bleuler, E. (1905) Consciousness and association (Trans. M.D. Elder), in C.J. Jung (ed.) *Studies in word association*, London: William Heinemann, 266–296.

Freud, S. (1900) The interpretation of dreams, in J. Strachey (ed.) *Standard Edition*, Vols 4 and 5, London: Hogarth Press, 1962.

Freud, S. (1924) The loss of reality in neurosis and psychosis, in J. Strachey (ed.) *Standard Edition*, Vol. 19, London: Hogarth Press, 1962.

Garfield, D. (2002) The use of vitality affects in the coalescence of self in psychosis, *Progress in Self Psychology* 19: 113–128.

Garfield, D. (2009) *Unbearable Affect: A Guide to the Psychotherapy of Psychosis*, 2nd edn, London: Karnac.

Garfield, D. and Mackler, D. (2008) *Beyond Medication: Therapeutic Engagement and the Recovery from Psychosis*, Abingdon: Routledge.

Jacobson, E. (1974) *Progressive Relaxation: A Physiological and Clinical Investigation of Muscular States and Their Significance in Psychology and Medical Practice*, Chicago: University of Chicago Press.

Jaynes, J. (1976) *The Origin of Consciousness in the Breakdown of the Bicameral Mind*, Boston: Houghton Mifflin, 48.

Jaynes, J. (1982) *The origin of consciousness in the breakdown of the bicameral mind*, Boston, MA: Houghton Mifflin.

Jung, C.G. (1907/1976) The psychogenesis of mental disease, in W. McGuiere (ed.) *The Collected Works of C.G. Jung*, Vol. 3, Princeton, NJ: Princeton University Press.

Kandel, E.R. (1976) *Cellular Basis of Behavior*, San Francisco: Freeman.

Keats, J. (1817) Letter to Benjamin Bailey, 22 November 1817.

Khantzian, E.J., Dalsimer, J.S. and Semrad, E. (1969) The use of interpretation in the psychotherapy of schizophrenia, *American Journal of Psychotherapy* 23: 182–188.

Kohut, H. (1971) *The Analysis of The Self*, Madison, WI: International Universities Press.

Kövecses, Z. (2003) *Metaphor and Emotion: Language, Culture and Body in Human Feeling*, New York: Cambridge University Press.

Lakoff, G. and Johnson, M. (1999) *Philosophy in the Flesh: The Embodied Mind and its Challenge to Western Thought*, New York: Basic Books.

Lane, R. and Garfield, D. (2005) Becoming aware of feelings: integration of cognitive-developmental, neuroscientific, and psychoanalytic perspectives, *Neuro-Psychoanalysis* 7: 1–26.

Lane, R.D. and Schwartz, G.E. (1987) Levels of emotional awareness: a cognitive-developmental theory and its application to psychopathology, *American Journal of Psychiatry* 144: 133–143.

Libet, B. (1985) Unconscious cerebral intiative and the role of conscious will in voluntary action, *Behavioral and Brain Sciences* 8: 529–566.

Meissner, W.W. (2008) Self and time, *Journal of the American Academy of Psychoanalysis* 36: 707–736.
Meltzer, D. (1993) *The Claustrum: An Investigation of Claustrophobic Phenomena*, Strath Tay: Clunie Press.
Minkowski, E. (1970) *Lived Time: Phenomenological and Pathological Studies*, Evanston, IL: Northwestern University Press.
Searles, H. (1965) *Collected Papers on Schizophrenia and Related Subjects*, New York: International Universities Press.
Searles, H. (1979) *Countertransference and Related Subjects*, New York: International Universities Press.
Sheets-Johnstone, M. (1999a) *The Primacy of Movement*, Amsterdam: John Benjamins Press.
Sheets-Johnstone, M. (1999b) Emotion and movement: a beginning empirical-phenomenological analysis of their relationship, *Journal of Consciousness Studies* 6(11–12): 259–277.
Stern, D. (1977) *The First Relationship: Mother and Infant*, Cambridge, MA: Harvard University Press.
Stern, D. (1985) *The Interpersonal World of the Infant*, New York: Basic Books.
Stern, D. (2004) *The Present Moment in Psychotherapy and Everyday Life*, New York: Norton.
Stolorow, R. and Lachmann, F. (1980) *Psychoanalysis of Developmental Arrests*, New York: International Universities Press.
Stolorow, R.D. and Saccharides, D. (1987) in R.D. Stolorow, B. Brandchaft and G.E. Atwood (eds) *Psychoanalytic Treatment: An Intersubjective Approach*, Hillsdale, NJ: Analytic Press.
Wolf, E. (2002) *Treating the Self*, New York: Guilford Press.

Chapter 4

Linking dialogue and emotion in therapy in psychosis

Sarah Dilks

Social contexts and psychosis: implications

The importance of social context in shaping outcome for those experiencing psychosis is suggested by the World Health Organisation's long-term follow-up studies of people diagnosed with schizophrenia (Hopper *et al.*, 2007). In discussing the findings of good outcome for more than 50 per cent of the International Study of Schizophrenia participants and a pattern of better outcomes in the developing world, Warner (2007) concludes that 'bad outcome is not a necessary component of the natural history of schizophrenia; it is a consequence of the interaction between the individual and his or her social and economic world' (p. 1445). This point is underlined when one considers published personal accounts describing the experience of psychosis and recovery. For instance, Veronica Dewan (2001) concluded that a significant element of her recovery was finding other people with similar experiences and developing mutually supportive relationships:

> As our journeys converge we are gradually working out different ways to support each other without getting overwhelmed. This has been a starting point for me to learn what it feels like to belong and draw strength from being part of a community.
>
> (Dewan, 2001, p. 48)

In addition, I would argue it seems increasingly clear that processes of personal and social meaning making influence both the experience of psychosis and how it is managed by the individual. For instance, in terms of personal meaning making, the interpretations or attributions used to explain unexpected experiences like hearing voices affect the individual's emotional response and how they cope (see, for example, Peters *et al.*, 1999; Morrison, 2001; Birchwood *et al.*, 2002; Bentall, 2003). Larsen (2004) specifically considered the importance of social meanings in an anthropological study of the Danish OPUS early intervention service in which he conducted qualitative examinations of participants' experience of the service. He concluded that individuals engaged in a constant process of theory building about the experience of psychosis drawing on the range of explanations that were culturally available both within and outside of mental health services. Larsen (2007) suggested that the variety of ways in which mental health staff applied different understandings of psychosis impacted on the clients' experience of the early intervention service and their coping. So, one client Claus said of his relationship with his case manager, 'I think I have been guided in the right direction [. . .] having healthy thoughts and . . . well, and . . . also this about that there is a life after the psychosis' (p. 341).

So how might we understand what happens in psychological therapy in psychosis if we recognise the links between the individual and the social? This chapter draws on findings from a specific grounded theory study to explore the contribution of a dialogical perspective to understanding therapy processes in psychosis, with a particular emphasis on the place of emotion in therapy.

Exploring therapy processes in psychosis from a dialogical perspective

Therapy processes in psychosis are comparatively unexamined in psychotherapy process research in contrast to therapy with other forms of distress (for example, see reviews by Roth and Fonagy, 1996; Llewelyn and Hardy, 2001). Although some psychoanalytic considerations of therapy in psychosis (e.g. Garfield, 2003) and Lysaker and colleagues' work on the role of narrative in recovery from psychosis undertake systematic examinations of therapy processes in psychosis (e.g. Lysaker *et al.*, 2001, 2003; Lysaker and Buck, 2006), studies have mainly concentrated on specific examples of therapy in psychosis based on existing therapy models (e.g. Rhodes and Jakes, 2002; Lombardi, 2003; Grazebrook *et al.*, 2004). As a consequence of my own experience as a UK clinical psychologist working with people experiencing psychosis, I became interested in the therapy processes that might contribute to the subjective awareness and explicit articulation of private mental experience. While there is a variety of ways in which one might conceptualise this activity including, for example, metacognition (e.g. Teasdale, 1999; Morrison, 2001), mentalising (e.g. Langdon *et al.*, 2001), theory of mind (Frith, 1994), and reflective function (Fonagy *et al.*, 1998, 2004), I was curious about the role of language in shaping experience. This led to a consideration of ideas stemming from dialogical and narrative approaches to selfhood and therapy.

In common with attachment theory and psychoanalytic theory more generally, dialogical and narrative approaches regard the experience of self as being shaped by interaction with others (for considerations of attachment see also Chapter 6, Schwannauer, this volume). However, rather than seeing this as a developmental process where the endpoint is an internalised capacity to mentally represent one's own and others' experience, these approaches regard the individual as being engaged in a continual process of constructing the experience of being themselves in the social world. Dialogical and narrative approaches share a common emphasis on the conversational process of therapy and the importance of meaning construction in affecting the experience of distress. In particular though, dialogical approaches to therapy (e.g. Stiles, 1999; Georgaca, 2001; Dimaggio, 2006) draw on Hermans' conceptualisation of selfhood as multi-voiced; regarding selfhood as the product of an ongoing dialogue both within the individual and between the individual and others rather than seeing 'the self' as a single, unitary entity (Hermans *et al.*, 1993; Hermans, 1996; Hermans and Dimaggio, 2004). Hermans' conceptualisation of a dialogical self also builds on Vygotsky's (1978) work. Centrally, Vygotsky suggested that language is created socially and is used as a tool by the individual in relation to both their social and internal worlds. He suggested that language takes on an *intra*personal as well as an interpersonal function in proposing that children turn 'social speech' inwards to direct their own activity, first as 'egocentric speech' and then as 'inner speech' (Vygotsky, 1978, p. 27).

Dialogical approaches, in common with narrative approaches and social constructionism more generally, see language as both shaping private experience and as a kind of action (Shotter, 1993). That is, the dialogues that people engage in both privately and publicly about themselves and their experiences are understood to shape both the experience of being oneself and the actions possible for the individual in the social world. Stiles (1999) suggests that multiple 'I-positions' are used deliberately in therapy to facilitate reflective thinking by encouraging dialogue between different positions and the different perspectives they bring. Stiles (1999, p. 3) and Brinegar *et al.* (2006, p. 165) refer to creating 'meaning bridges' between different self positions/voices in both internal, private conversations and external conversations with a therapist in order to realise this.

There has been some interest in using narrative and dialogical approaches specifically in working with people experiencing psychosis. Michael White and colleagues in Australia (White, 1987, 1995; White and Epston, 1990) developed narrative therapy in working with families facing a variety of difficulties, including psychosis. Narrative therapy emphasises how certain 'stories' told about the self come to unhelpfully dominate others and concentrates on helping people to develop alternative stories or to enrich existing stories into more complex narratives. Lysaker and colleagues in the US have specifically investigated the role of narrative in therapy in psychosis (Lysaker and Lysaker, 2001; Lysaker *et al.*, 2001; Lysaker and Buck, 2006). Lysaker suggests that difficulties in psychosis might arise from the breakdown of a dialogically based self and that therapy might help via restoring this. He further suggests that therapy for people diagnosed with schizophrenia might help via the increased self awareness and sense of agency that can arise from narrative enrichment in dialogues of the self (Lysaker *et al.*, 2001). Part of this process according to Lysaker *et al.* is that 'processing affect to reduce distress' (2001, p. 259) happens alongside the development of more elaborate stories about being a person experiencing psychosis. Similarly, Seikkula and colleagues in Finland (Seikkula, 2003; Seikkula *et al.*, 2003, 2006) stress the importance of 'emotional regulation' (Seikkula and Trimble, 2005, p. 471) occurring in parallel with the opening up of new understandings in their Open Dialogue work with individuals experiencing psychosis and their families. Seikkula (2002) also notes that, similarly to the manner in which Vygotsky (1978) proposed an adult's more advanced functioning scaffolds a child's emerging abilities in order for development to progress, therapeutic conversations might support the development of new understandings for difficult experiences.

A grounded theory study of therapy processes in psychosis

I will describe a specific qualitative study exploring therapy processes in psychosis (Dilks *et al.*, 2008, 2010) in order to consider in more detail how emotional processing and meaning making may be linked in therapy in psychosis. The description of the study will necessarily be limited here but Table 4.1 gives an overview of the study's data set. Full details of the study's methodology and sampling are reported in Dilks *et al.* (2008) and Dilks *et al.* (2010). Grounded theory categories are indicated by quotation marks in this chapter.

Leiman's (2000) dialogical definition of reflexivity was chosen as a specific starting point for the study because it focuses on an active and ongoing relationship to subjective experience demonstrated publicly through the use of language and because it implies that this objectifying of subjective experience can change through relationships with others (including, it is assumed, a therapist). We focused on a dialogical approach rather than seeking to build on Lysaker's work on the role of narrative in psychosis because this appeared to allow a clearer focus on the *joint* activity of constructing experience in therapy. However, as Leiman's definition does not operationalise reflexivity, the qualitative methodology grounded theory was chosen to conduct the study; allowing as it does the exploration of an area as well as further conceptual development (Glaser and Strauss, 1967; Charmaz, 2003; Willig, 2001):

> To reflect requires the ability to create and use signs that refer to one's own activity, whether external or internal. To be the 'author of one's thoughts and feelings' means that the person is able to establish an internal subject-object relation (i.e. he or she can objectify personal experience and mental processes, and use some semiotic means to make sense of those complex phenomena as objects of reflective actions). To objectify one's own actions, experiences, thoughts and feelings is an

Table 4.1 Overview of grounded theory study of therapy processes in psychosis

Initial data set	**Extended data set (theoretical sampling)**
19 tapes of therapy sessions (three session tapes supplied by six psychologists and their clients spaced out over therapy course). 23 separate interviews with six psychologists and their clients (first set asking about experience of therapy and second set asking their views on the grounded theory model developed). See Dilks *et al.* (2008) for full details.	31 published personal accounts of psychosis and recovery. See Dilks *et al.* (2010) for complete reference list of personal accounts examined.

Psychologist (name changed)	*Gender*	*Age*	*Ethnicity (self identified)*	*Therapeutic orientation*	*Years qualified*	*Client (name changed)*	*Gender*	*Age*	*Ethnicity (self identified)*	*Diagnosis*[b]	*Years in contact with services*
Mark	m	37	white	integrative[a]	5	Colin	m	33	white British	schizophrenia	25
Lee	f	30	mixed	integrative	2	Anna	f	36	black African	schizophrenia	5
Charlotte	f	37	white British	CBT	9	Andrew	m	35	white British	depression with psychotic episodes[c]	3
Sue	f	33	white British	integrative	2	Isabel	f	34	white European	schizo-affective disorder	14
Louise	f	37	white British	CBT	10	Juliet	f	37	Nigerian	schizo-affective disorder	5
Liz	f	46	white British	integrative	9	Tanya	f	36	black British	schizophrenia	18

Source
Adapted with permission from Dilks *et al.* (2008) *Psychology and Psychotherapy: Theory, Research and Practice* © British Psychological Society.

Notes
a The term 'integrative' refers to the specifying of multiple models used to inform therapy. Those named by therapists included cognitive behavioural therapy (CBT), psychoanalytic approaches and systemic approaches.
b Diagnoses refer to the *DSM-IV* psychiatric classification system (American Psychiatric Association, 1994).
c Andrew was included with the initial sample due to concerns about the appropriateness of using psychiatric diagnoses to distinguish between clients' experiences (see Boyle, 2002; Bentall, 2003, for a discussion), and because the analysis of the therapy tapes suggested the activities of Andrew and Charlotte were not qualitatively different to the rest of the sample.

advanced task developed through a number of transformative stages and modes of 'joint subjectness'.

(Leiman, 2000, pp. 391–392)

The experience of psychosis: what the client brings to therapy

It is important to remember that therapy in psychosis begins with an individual who is going through unexpected, intense and often distressing experiences. One of the therapy sample clients, Colin, tried to explain what this was like: 'You're walking down the street and colour changes . . . lights, the sky, everything, the walls, everything just changes shape and you're just like "huh", you know, you realise *afterwards* but *in it* you don't' (Colin, Time 1 interview, 388–391, emphasis in original). Similarly, the following extract from Tanya's therapy tape suggested that the experience of psychosis was one of feeling out of control of your own experience:

> Tanya
> 'The girl came up, said if it happens again you're going to {locked ward} but I couldn't control myself, I just flipped {louder, plaintive} (Liz yeah). And that's what happens {louder}. (Liz I) When I get ill I (Liz yeah) I don't really, perhaps I don't really know I'm getting ill (Liz yeah). I should tell someone that I don't feel well (Liz yes), it would be better for me to say I don't feel well than let it all pile up inside and then lash out, all, all of it in one go.'
>
> (Liz and Tanya, 1st therapy tape, 786–796, emphasis in original)

Our analysis suggested that the experience of psychosis was one of 'getting caught up in experience' where the individual gets stuck in the immediacy of distress so that they are unable *at that point* to stand back from their own feelings or thoughts. 'Getting caught up in experience' appeared to follow unexpected perceptual changes associated for these clients with psychosis. However, in addition it also seemed to occur when they were talking about *any* area of distress, implying an overwhelming of observational perspectives by emotion. The extract below illustrates how this could happen in the therapy session itself as Colin was trying to describe the pressures of studying shortly after leaving hospital, following a general opening question from his psychologist Mark about how his week had been.

> Colin
> 'How it's been? Um .. k.. very tired (Mark mm) I've been very like, I've been studying a lot (Mark mm mm) .. um .. but I've been kind of .. feeling kind of *really* tired out, my eyes are burning up and .. stuff but

that's about it, you know, that's like that side of it, you know, cos that's taking up a *lot* of my time, mental time, thinking time, the lot, I mean all the days I'm not in there (Mark yeah) I'm just ff, because we get tested every two weeks it's, I *feel* the strain. But I'm *pushing* myself through that strain (Mark mm) you know what I mean? (Mark yeah) Some people in the class, which I've noticed, are just sort of skipping through it, you know. Like "oh it's no problem, bl, bl, bl", you know. I mean I'm reading notes, I mean I, in the first part I got nine out of nine I passed the .. the thing, you know (Mark that's great yeah) completely but .. that's cos I really pushed through it and now I'm going through that again, you know, now Friday's coming up and it's another test and then we've got another two weeks after that (Mark mm mm), *again* , er it was gonna be harder than for the last two weeks [. . .] So I just hope, *really* touch w'wood, that you know .. it's [the course] not going to send me under water, you know what I mean? (Mark mm .. mm) Cos that's all I'm worrying about.'

(Mark and Colin, 1st therapy tape, 16–32, emphasis in original)

Colin used the analogy of drowning to summarise his fear that the stress of the course might cause psychosis to return; in common with other therapy clients, something that he thought was out of his control:

Colin
'Falling down and picking myself up, falling down and picking myself up, it's become a routine. It's not like as if .. you know, *I can't plan*, I wish I could *plan* it, if I knew I had to be ill I would choose in the year when the best month to be ill in.'

(Mark and Colin, 2nd therapy tape, 1104–1110, emphasis in original)

Building bridges to observational perspectives: defining the core process in therapy in psychosis

The central activity in therapy in psychosis was defined as one of 'building bridges to observational perspectives'. This was understood as a conversational process where new perspectives on the client's distress were continually and jointly created in the ongoing dialogue between client and therapist. The process of continually moving between alternative perspectives appeared to 'open up new possibilities' for thought, action and feeling, to enable the 'processing of distress', and to 'enhance agency and self worth'. As Colin said:

'It's like finding the answers together. Do you see what I mean? Resolving it together. Like he'll help you, he'll come up with an idea, you say "well not really, that doesn't work for me, [but] that might do", and he somehow channels it in. You don't actually have the answer but it takes two of you to find it.'

(Colin, Time 2 interview, 299–302)

However, although 'building bridges' was conceptualised as a jointly negotiated process occurring in the therapeutic conversation between therapist and client, it appeared to be built on the therapist's strategic use of their own observational activities and their structuring of dialogue.

Importantly, the aim of the 'building bridges' process seemed to be one of enhancing the client's 'functioning in the social world' rather than one of developing reflexivity (Leiman, 2000) per se: 'that's what's important, not necessarily what's in your head but . . . how you're relating to other people. Basically can you get on in the world or can you not?' (Mark, Time 2 interview, 191–193). 'Functioning in the social world' was defined as individuals aspiring to participate in the roles, activities and relationships regarded by them as representing ordinary life without experiencing distress:

'I want to get back into work, I want to get back into a normal, stable life. And looking after my own well being in the best way I can manage it. And once I've got those things in place then seeing Mark [psychologist] will be less [important]. Because they're my goals to get to.'

(Colin, Time 2 interview, 341–344)

Engaging in reflexivity therefore appeared to be a means to an end rather than an end in itself: 'with the people we see it is about functioning, it's about survival so it's not quite so much a reflective exercise. The reflective exercise is more just a tool in order to engender change' (Charlotte, Time 2 interview, 176–178). Table 4.2 provides extracts from the therapy session tapes illustrating the process of 'building bridges to observational perspectives'.

Specifying therapy processes and linking therapy to the social world

The conceptualisation of 'building bridges to observational perspectives' included specifying a number of integral subcomponents and linking therapy to the clients 'functioning in the social world'. Rather than describing all of these here I will concentrate on those aspects relating to the management of emotion in therapy.

Processing distress and managing emotion

'Processing distress' was defined as clients standing back from distressing experiences, memories or concerns so they were no longer getting overwhelmed

Table 4.2 Examples illustrating the process of 'building bridges to observational perspectives' taken from therapy session transcripts[a]

Psychologist Sue and client Isabel speaking in their 2nd taped therapy session.	*Psychologist Louise and client Juliet speaking in their 1st taped therapy session.*

Isabel
'Cos my mind's very active it feels likely it should be doing things all the time (*Sue* mm) it's like it's all go.
Sue
// Is that, is that fair to do things all the time do you think?//
Isabel
// It's not fair but, but it's not fair no // because I remember when I used to work .. I used to .. be all go and I made myself ill over it ..
Sue
.. So it is important to have time to yourself?
Isabel
So it is important, yeah so (*Sue* right) when I feel you know like I've had a rest and we have a good laugh, when the other days come I feel more energy to [look after myself] (*Sue* yeah). You know more, more energy for other things (*Sue* yes, yes) […]
Sue
So positive affirmation also looking at what you have achieved …. [6 sec] because it's that confidence which is actually you know .. helped you take lots of steps forward and it continues to help you take lots of steps forward (*Isabel* mm) .. without rushing it needs to be gradual when you're ready (*Isabel* mm).
Isabel
.. Yeah just take it slowly like, like I, all I just take it as it comes I mean naturally, it's naturally slowly becoming naturally each day (*Sue* mm, yes, yes) .. so it's, it's not like I should push myself I just wanted to [inaudible] like it just happened when I started work and going to church and cooking, all of a sudden it just happened, that's how the rest will come // hopefully. //
	Louise
	And since you've been back to work you haven't felt that people were talking about you // or mocking you at all?//
	Juliet
	// Not at all // not at all.
	Louise
	But it's the same people.//
	Juliet
	// I find it more loving, receptive people (*Louise* mm). That sometimes when I come out of the environment I see them and they, these are the same people that have been mocking and laughing and jesting about this (*Louise* mm), what had transpired within this past two months that I've been away. Could it have been *me* that has changed (*Louise* mm) or could it have been them that has become a bit more sensitive to *my* feelings. It's kind of like um not having really found the answer // [can't hear] //
	Louise
	// It's a puzzle isn't it? //
	Juliet
	Yeah.
	Louise
	It's, it's .. it sounds like it's everybody (*Juliet* yeah) at work's changed not just one person (*Juliet* yeah). They *all* seem different (*Juliet* yeah) to you (*Juliet* yeah) um ..
	Juliet
	But I found it more loving people .. (*Louise* mm) more caring people.

Sue // More naturally. // *Isabel* Yeah that's how I feel maybe the rest will come more naturally // in time, in time, yeah. // (994–1072)	*Louise* Do you think anything's different about *you*, between when you were at work before and now? *Juliet* Yeah because people say, people compliment now that I'm a bit cheerful (*Louise* right) .. even though I'm going through a situation at home I'm more cheerful .. at work um, probably [more] relaxed than I used to be (*Louise* yeah) probably they used to see how tense I were and [...] so I .. feel very good, before all I was, was desperate to get out of the place (*Louise* yeah). // *Louise* // It's a kind of a sort of vicious circle isn't it? (*Juliet* yeah) If you're feeling tense and stressed (*Juliet* yeah) then people .. (*Juliet* react) aren't being kind of warm and kind to you (*Juliet* yes) they're being a bit stand-offish, you gonna feel more .. more you know (*Juliet* yeah) uncomfortable in their presence aren't you (*Juliet* yeah, yeah) and then you're gonna feel more stressed (*Juliet* yes). (151–199, emphasis in original)

Transcription key
[text] explanatory note; [...] section omitted; // interruption; // // both speaking at the same time; .. pause (< 5 seconds)

Source
a Adapted with permission from Dilks *et al.* (2008) *Psychology and Psychotherapy: Theory, Research and Practice* © British Psychological Society.

by emotion in speaking about them (and by implication in thinking about them). 'Processing distress' appeared to be facilitated by the client and therapist structuring distressing experience in a conversational account, thereby allowing distress to become the *object* of observational activities. Juliet summarised her experience of this process in the interview extract below:

> '[She is] helping me to understand what the difficulties in my life were, helping me to come to terms with it and helping me to look for a way forward [. . .] But why personally I haven't *even thought* of that, 'cos I've been *preoccupied* with that over the period of time and, you know, wallowing in self-pity, "why me, why do I have to go through, why do, people don't understand?" *That's* how I've been looking at it. But I never asked myself, *how do you move on*? And that's where the difference comes with talking with her as a psychologist. That's where the turning point is . . .'
>
> (Juliet, Time 1 interview, 557–572, emphasis in original)

'Processing distress' appeared to be supported by therapy activities focused on 'managing emotion' in combination with activities centring on the development of new perspectives on distress. 'Managing emotion' was defined as the psychologist regulating the emotional pace of therapy through actively 'structuring the conversation' in order to minimise the client 'getting caught up in experience' (and therefore losing access to an observing position). Liz's actions in the extract below represent this type of therapist activity but also illustrate how 'managing emotion' is embedded in the dialogical process of 'building bridges to observational perspectives', as Liz not only encourages Tanya to reconsider her fears about becoming unwell ('opening up views'), but also infers and acknowledges Tanya's distress. Although the clients also engaged in 'managing emotion' at times, e.g. by using humour to distance themselves from a painful topic, it seemed that this was done in a less systematic way than by therapists. That is, it seemed therapists assumed a particular responsibility for the maintenance of dialogue, in part by regulating the emotional pace of therapy.

> Liz
>
> 'it sounds like you're thinking oh, you know, last time someone left, Kevin [staff member], you got really unwell but I think you were *already* in the middle of a really *awful* (Tanya mm) period and this time maybe you'll feel sad but it doesn't necessarily follow that you would get unwell (Tanya mm-hm) not necessarily. . . . [14 sec pause] Or am I wrong Tanya? And, and, I'm not suggesting that, am I underestimating that actually Richard [staff member] leaving does, does really feel, make you feel quite sad and it's, in a considerable way?'

Tanya
'In a way um but . . . the thing is about me Liz is that . . . how can I put it? I don't really show my emotions very easily (Liz uh-huh, yeah) and then probably I might sort of break down and cry but . . . things that I don't, I don't really let things get to me, do you know, I try not to (Liz yes) . . . to let, to let, not to let it worry me that Richard's *gone* (Liz yeah) but I gotta face the fact that he's gone but (Liz yeah), you know, there's nothing I can do that he's gone, he's just gone. Nothing I can do about it (Liz right). There's no point dwelling on the situation that he's gone because, you know, I'll probably end up ill as well in hospital.'
(Liz and Tanya, 1st therapy tape, 898–917, emphasis in original)

'Processing distress' seemed also to be facilitated by developing shared understandings of distress that were more complex than those already held by the client; minimised self-blame; emphasised the client's active attempts to cope; and could be shared socially with at least some people. So, for example, Mark and Colin appeared to be working together during a series of therapy conversations to develop a richer understanding of Colin's experiences, one recognising multiple influences leading to distress. This process was defined as one of 'negotiating shared understandings':

Mark
'I guess thinking about what's been going on for the past few weeks, then you've had the course, which is sort of stress that you, well pressure that you've invited into your life, right (?) (Colin mm) [you've] said, "I will do this, I know it's going to put me under pressure but I want to do this".'

Colin
'Positive stress (Mark positive stress) I call it positive stress [laughs].'

Mark
'[Laughs] Yeah, no that's good, and then you've got the negative stress, (Colin stress) the stress coming from the neighbours and more, and more from [Colin's brother].'
(Mark and Colin, 2nd therapy tape, 870–881)

Negotiating shared understandings and making sense

The conceptualisation of 'negotiating shared understandings' was elaborated by examining an additional data set consisting of 31 published personal accounts of psychosis. These suggested that this aspect of therapy activity contributed to a more general process of 'making sense' of psychosis that individuals could engage in via a variety of means, including but not exclusively through therapy (e.g. sharing experiences with others, attending hearing voices groups, reading, writing poetry). 'Making sense' was defined as a process of developing personally acceptable accounts of psychosis/distress that accommodated these experiences into a complex view of the self; preserved a sense of self worth and agency; allowed hope for the future; and were able to be shared socially with at least some other people. So Juliet was able to move away from blaming herself for her difficulties to a richer understanding of her situation:

> 'It's not the pressures of the job affecting me (Louise mm) in a way that contributed to my problems (Louise okay). But looking back at my life from the time I step into this country, to the relationship that I had, the people that I mixed with, the kind of job that I did (Louise mm) a combination of all these things.'
>
> (Louise and Juliet, 1st therapy tape, 338–342)

It is important to note that 'making sense' was also conceptualised as a dialogical process. In 'making sense' of psychosis individuals appeared to draw on a range of socially and personally available perspectives in an ongoing dialogical process of meaning construction; whether this was in or outside of therapy, in conversation with themselves, or with other people. For instance, in her personal account Pembroke (2000) described 'making sense' of intense and frightening experiences in a way that fitted with her existing view of a spiritual component to her life and how she looked for help consistent with this interpretation:

> I told him about the entity in me, and he performed the exorcism. [. . .] I was okay for a while, but then the entity came back. I now know why it came back. I have a hole in my aura, and it is located in my chest. I know the exact point. I have learned to recognise when that hole opens. So now, when it opens, it is very simple to cover it with my hands, or my partner covers it. If I do this, entities cannot get in. I can stop them. It is so simple.
>
> (Pembroke, 2000, p. 169)

Summary

In examples of what one might call conceptual convergence or triangulation (Strauss and Corbin, 1998), the work summarised here, Stiles's concept of meaning bridges, Seikkula and colleagues' Open Dialogue approach, and Lysaker's body of work all emphasise how developing new meanings, dialogues or narratives can have a transformative effect on distress. Similarly, in common with Dilks *et al.*, Seikkula and Lysaker propose that emotional regulation needs to happen *alongside* developing new narratives or understandings of psychosis in order for people to get on with their lives.

A dialogical view of therapy processes in psychosis would seem to allow greater clarity in understanding how processes of managing emotion and developing alternative perspectives on experience get woven together during therapy conversations in a way that helps people experiencing psychosis function in the social world. It helps make explicit how the explanations or meanings used to understand psychosis or distress more generally are not neutral. These explanations and meanings impact on an individual's sense of personal agency and self worth, as well as influencing what becomes possible in terms of action, thought or feeling in dealing with distress. Developing new meanings and dialogues about distressing experiences during a conversational process scaffolded by a therapist can therefore have a transformative effect on distress and recovery in psychosis.

Note

This chapter is adapted with permission from Dilks *et al.* (2008), *Psychology and Psychotherapy: Theory, Research and Practice* © British Psychological Society.

References

American Psychiatric Association. (1994) *Diagnostic and statistical manual of mental disorders (4th edn., text revision)*, Washington, DC: Author.

Bentall, R. (2003) *Madness Explained: Psychosis and Human Nature*, London: Penguin.

Birchwood, M., Meaden, A., Trower, P. and Gilbert, P. (2002) Shame, humiliation, and entrapment in psychosis: a social rank theory approach to cognitive intervention with voices and delusions, in A. Morrison (ed.) *A Casebook of Cognitive Therapy for Psychosis*, Hove, UK: Brunner-Routledge, 108–131.

Boyle, M. (2002) *Schizophrenia: A scientific delusion (2nd edn.)*, London: Routledge.

Brinegar, M.G., Salvi, L., Stiles, W. and Greenberg, L. (2006) Building a meaning bridge: therapeutic progress from problem formulation to understanding, *Journal of Counseling Psychology* 53(2): 165–180.

Charmaz, K. (2003) Grounded theory: objectivist and constructivist methods, in N. Denzin and Y. Lincoln (eds) *Strategies of Qualitative Inquiry*, 2nd edn, Thousand Oaks, CA: Sage, 249–291.

Dewan, V. (2001) Life support, in J. Read (ed.) *Something Inside So Strong: Strategies for Surviving Mental Distress*, London: Mental Health Foundation, 44–49.

Dilks, S., Tasker, F. and Wren, B. (2008) Building bridges to observational perspectives: a grounded theory of therapy processes in psychosis, *Psychology and Psychotherapy: Theory, Research and Practice* 81: 209–229.

Dilks, S., Tasker, F. and Wren, B. (2010) Managing the impact of psychosis: a grounded theory exploration of recovery processes in psychosis, *British Journal of Clinical Psychology* 49: 87–107.

Dimaggio, G. (2006) Changing the dialogue between self voices during psychotherapy, *Journal of Psychotherapy Integration* 16(3): 313–345.

Fonagy, P., Target, M., Steele, H. and Steele, M. (1998) *Reflective-Functioning Manual. Version 5. For Application to Adult Attachment Interviews*, London: University College London.

Fonagy, P., Gergely, G., Jurist, E. and Target, M. (2004) *Affect Regulation, Mentalization, and the Development of the Self*, London: Karnac.

Frith, C. (1994) Theory of mind in schizophrenia, in A. David and J. Cutting (eds) *The Neuropsychology of Schizophrenia*, Hove, UK: Lawrence Erlbaum Associates Ltd, 147–161.

Garfield, D. (2003) The mask of psychotic diagnoses, *Journal of the American Academy of Psychoanalysis and Dynamic Psychiatry* 31(1): 45–58.

Georgaca, E. (2001) Voices of the self in psychotherapy: a qualitative analysis, *British Journal of Medical Psychology* 74: 223–236.

Glaser, B. and Strauss, A. (1967) *The Discovery of Grounded Theory: Strategies for Qualitative Research*, Chicago: Aldine.

Grazebrook, K., Siddle, R., Leadley, K., Everitt, J., Benn, A., Haddock, G., *et al.* (2004) First episode psychosis: two cases to illustrate the role of cognitive behaviour therapy in making sense of unusual experiences, *Behavioural and Cognitive Psychotherapy*, 32: 331–345.

Hermans, H. (1996) Opposites in a dialogical self: constructs as characters, *Journal of Constructivist Psychology* 9: 1–26.

Hermans, H. and Dimaggio, G. (eds) (2004) *The Dialogical Self in Psychotherapy*, London: Brunner-Routledge.

Hermans, H., Rijks, T. and Kempen, H. (1993) Imaginal dialogues in the self: theory and method, *Journal of Personality* 61(2): 207–236.

Hopper, K., Harrison, G., Janca, A. and Sartorius, N. (eds) (2007) *Recovery from Schizophrenia: An International Perspective. A Report from the WHO Collaborative Project, The International Study of Schizophrenia*, Oxford: Oxford University Press.

Langdon, R., Coltheart, M., Ward, P. and Catts, S. (2001) Mentalising, executive planning and disengagement in schizophrenia, *Cognitive Neuropsychiatry* 6(2): 81–108.

Larsen, J.A. (2004) Finding meaning in first episode psychosis: experience, agency, and the cultural repertoire, *Medical Anthropology Quarterly* 18(4): 447–471.

Larsen, J.A. (2007) Understanding a complex intervention: person-centred ethnography in early psychosis, *Journal of Mental Health* 16(3): 333–345.

Leiman, M. (2000) Ogden's matrix of transference and the concept of sign, *British Journal of Medical Psychology* 73: 385–397.

Llewelyn, S. and Hardy, G. (2001) Process research in understanding and applying psychological therapies, *British Journal of Clinical Psychology* 40: 1–21.

Lombardi, R. (2003) Mental models and language registers in the psychoanalysis of psychosis: an overview of a thirteen year analysis, *International Journal of Psychoanalysis* 84: 843–863.

Lysaker, P., and Buck, K. (2006) Moving towards recovery within clients' personal narratives: directions for a recovery-focused therapy, *Journal of Psychosocial Nursing* 44(1): 28–35.

Lysaker, P. and Lysaker, J. (2001) Psychosis and the disintegration of dialogical self-structure: problems posed by schizophrenia for the maintenance of dialogue, *British Journal of Medical Psychology* 74: 23–33.

Lysaker, P., Lysaker, J. and Lysaker, J. (2001) Schizophrenia and the collapse of the dialogical self: recovery, narrative and psychotherapy, *Psychotherapy* 38(3): 252–261.

Lysaker, P., Lancaster, R. and Lysaker, J. (2003) Narrative transformation as an outcome in the psychotherapy of schizophrenia, *Psychology and Psychotherapy: Theory, Research and Practice* 76: 285–299.

Morrison, A. (2001) The interpretation of intrusions in psychosis: an integrative cognitive approach to hallucinations and delusions, *Behavioural and Cognitive Psychotherapy* 29: 257–276.

Pembroke, L. (2000) It helped that someone believed me, in J. Read and J. Reynolds (eds) *Speaking Our Minds: An Anthology*, Basingstoke: Palgrave, 168–174.

Peters, E., Day, S., McKenna, J. and Orbach, G. (1999) Delusional ideation in religious and psychotic populations, *British Journal of Clinical Psychology* 38: 83–96.

Rhodes, J. and Jakes, S. (2002) Using solution-focused therapy during a psychotic crisis: a case study, *Clinical Psychology and Psychotherapy* 9: 139–148.

Roth, A. and Fonagy, P. (1996) *What Works for Whom? A Critical Review of Psychotherapy Research*, New York: Guilford Press.

Seikkula, J. (2002) Open dialogues with good and poor outcomes for psychotic crises: examples from families with violence, *Journal of Marital and Family Therapy* 28(3): 263–274.

Seikkula, J. (2003) Open dialogue integrates individual and systemic approaches in serious psychiatric crises, *Smith College Studies in Social Work* 73(2): 227–245.

Seikkula, J. and Trimble, D. (2005) Healing elements of therapeutic conversation: dialogue as an embodiment of love, *Family Process* 44(4): 461–475.

Seikkula, J., Arnkil, T. and Eriksson, E. (2003) Postmodern society and social networks: open and anticipation dialogues in network meetings, *Family Process* 42(2): 185–203.

Seikkula, J., Aaltonen, J., Alakare, B., Haarakangas, K., Jyrki, K. and Lehtinen, K. (2006) Five-year experience of first-episode nonaffective psychosis in open-dialogue approach: treatment principles, follow-up outcomes, and two case studies, *Psychotherapy Research* 16(2): 214–228.

Shotter, J. (1993) *Cultural Politics of Everyday Life: Social Constructionism, Rhetoric and Knowing of the Third Kind*, Buffalo, NY: University of Toronto Press.

Stiles, W. (1999) Signs and voices in psychotherapy, *Psychotherapy Research* 9(1): 1–21.

Strauss, A. and Corbin, J. (1998) *Basics of Qualitative Research: Techniques and Procedures for Developing Grounded Theory*, 2nd edn, Thousand Oaks, CA: Sage.

Teasdale, J. (1999) Metacognition, mindfulness and the modification of mood disorders, *Clinical Psychology and Psychotherapy* 6: 146–155.

Vygotsky, L.S. (1978) *Mind in Society: The Development of Higher Psychological Processes*, Cambridge, MA: Harvard University Press.

Warner, R. (2007) Recovery from schizophrenia: an international perspective. A report from the WHO collaborative project, The International Study of Schizophrenia, *American Journal of Psychiatry* 164(9): 1444–1445.

White, M. (1987) Family therapy and schizophrenia: addressing the 'in-the-corner' lifestyle, *Dulwich Centre Newsletter*, Spring.

White, M. (1995) Psychotic experience and discourse, in M. White (ed.) *Re-authoring Lives: Interviews and Essays*, Adelaide: Dulwich Centre Publications, 112–154.

White, M. and Epston, D. (1990) *Narrative Means to Therapeutic Ends*, New York: Norton.

Willig, C. (2001) *Introducing Qualitative Research in Psychology: Adventures in Theory and Method*, Maidenhead: Open University Press.

Chapter 5

Narrative coherence and recovery of self-experience in integrative psychotherapy

Susanne Harder and Paul Lysaker

Introduction

Psychosis is widely accepted as involving not merely the experience of positive and negative symptoms but also alterations in how people experience themselves as being in the world. There may be both an experience of one's own being as fundamentally diminished and concurrently as unable to sustain interpersonal relationships and other forms of engagement in the world. From different perspectives interest has consequently grown in how psychotherapy might be able to address these difficulties (Gumley and Schwannauer, 2006; Rosenbaum and Harder, 2007; Lysaker and Lysaker, 2008). Psychotherapy as broadly considered after all has long been concerned with issues of how persons experience themselves and others. Yet it is unclear how to conceptualize the therapeutic processes when applied to disturbances in self-experience in psychosis.

In this chapter we explore the possibility that disturbances in subjectivity and social relationships are closely related to disturbance in affect regulation and that, consistent with work with individuals without psychosis (e.g. Fonagy *et al.*, 2002), the therapeutic relationship may offer qualities that are comparable to those of a secure attachment relationship. Within such a relationship, we examine whether affects, which when not modulated threaten sense of self, can be better regulated and thereby allow for the creation of a consensually valid narrative. The origins of self disturbance in psychosis are likely to be varied and certainly not well understood. However, based on evidence from, for example, studies of autism (Charman, 2009) we suggest that the interpersonal processes of a secure attachment relationship might be a vehicle for profound change toward more normal functioning even if the individual starts from a more severely disturbed position for any of a varied number of reasons. Accordingly, this chapter first presents a discussion of contributions from research on the nature of preverbal infant–caretaker interactions with the aim of understanding the formation of a therapeutic relationship in the psychotherapy of psychosis. We then return to the issue of disturbance in social and subjective functioning in psychosis suggesting some of the same issues exist in psychotherapy of psychosis as in the formation of early relationships. Finally, a case study is presented in which we attempt to explore the possibility that some of the observed therapeutic processes may be understood in terms of the processes involved in the formation of early relationships. We conclude with a discussion of how psychotherapy might result in the development of a coherent narrative and the recovery of self-experience.

The infant–caretaker relationship

The basic patterns for relating to others are generally considered to be established in early mother–infant communication, that is, in interactions that occur before the infant has developed symbolic language. In this preverbal period different modalities such as vocalizations, facial expressions, movements and touch are utilized, which are thought to be the scaffold for later patterns of verbal dialogue. These interactions have been linked to the later development of the dialogical structures of talking, pausing and turn taking (Jaffe and Feldstein, 1970). Once the infant's capacity for verbalization develops, these early procedural patterns of interacting continue to develop (Bucci, 1997) along the lines initially laid down, though it is assumed that they are amenable to change. The procedural level of interacting contributes to an array of important areas in the developmental process (Lyons-Ruth, 1998) such as the formation of an attachment relationship, including the developing affect modulation and self-experience.

Establishing a relationship through contingency

Research on mother–infant interaction has been preoccupied for decades with understanding what is happening in the earliest period. A growing amount of research suggests that contingency is a key process by which contact is established and maintained. Groundbreaking research by Meltzoff and Moore (1977) has shown that infants as early as one hour after birth are able to detect contingencies between behaviors of self and other. Contingency can occur in different ways including matching, different and opposing responses. Similar contingent interactions have been given a range of different labels: mutual influence, reciprocity, affect attunement, moments of meeting and intersubjectivity. The similar response contingency is a cross modal matching involving facial expression, movements, vocalization and touch featuring temporal structures such as rhythm and tempo (Lewkowitz and Lickliter, 1994), intensity and form of the expressions (Trevarthen, 1998). By contrast, an opposing contingency pattern has been described by Stern *et al.* (1977) as "chase and dodge," where a pattern of intensified avoidance-intensified attempts to engage might evolve. Traditionally a unidirectional view, focusing on the mother's contribution, has been dominated, but more and more research has now revealed the active participation of the infant from the very beginning in the forming of the interaction process (Tronick, 2005) starting from a limited set of behaviors such as, for example, avoiding by head turning (present from birth), or engaging by smiling (well established by six weeks), becoming more and more complex with time.

The importance and emotional powerfulness of these contingent interactions has been demonstrated in the "still-face paradigm," which asks mothers to exhibit a "still face" interrupting the contingent interaction with their infant for a few minutes. The experience of a halt in contingency and response caused a dramatic shift in the infant's mood and reactivity from positive to negative emotionality and finally looking away, with only a slow recovery when the mother starts interacting again (Tronick *et al.*, 1978). Several other studies (e.g. Murray and Trevarthen, 1985; Gergely and Watson, 1999) as well have demonstrated that contingent responses are vital in fostering engagement in a relationship.

While it was initially assumed that the more sensitivity and contingency the better, several studies have suggested that both very high and very low contingency were less optimal for the developmental process, where as a midrange level of contingent interaction is associated with later secure attachment (e.g. Isabella and Belsky, 1991; Jaffe *et al.*, 2001). Tronick and Cohn (1989) have found that only during 30 per cent of the time in face-to-face interaction in healthy mother infant dyads is the behavior of the infant and the mother matched. They suggest that a pattern of successful and unsuccessful matches reflects a normal and healthy process of rupture and repair of the communication between mother and infant. Stern (2001) has further described the need for a shift between repetition and novelty to create a mid-range level of engagement and the promotion of creativity and development in the interaction process. Extreme forms of difference or opposition such as severe chase and dodge patterns or hypervigilant, remote/disengaged, intrusive and disruptive maternal behavior have been found to predict disorganized attachment in infants at 12 months (Lyons-Ruth and Jacobvitz, 2008).

Affect modulation through interactive co-constructed proto narratives

A key aspect of early attachment is that not only is communication established but through the attachment system the development of capacity to modulate affects and construct proto narratives is initiated. Beebe *et al.* (2005) have proposed a "balance model of self- and interactive regulation" of attention, affect and arousal in the mother–infant interaction. She stresses the fact that inner states of activation and arousal are simultaneously regulated by the self, as well as through interaction with the other, each person being affected by his or her own behavior as well as by that of the other. She hypotheses that a flexible midrange balance of self and interactive regulation is optimal for development. An excessive monitoring of the other, at the expense of self-regulation, defines one pole of imbalance, which she named "interactive vigilance," whereas preoccupation with self-regulation, at the expense of interactive sensitivity, defines the other pole of imbalance leading to withdrawal or inhibition. Different imbalances may lead to different kinds of pathological attachment relationships, all characterized by difficulties in regulating emotion. In an avoidant attachment relationship the infant minimizes direct expression of emotional distress in the interaction and is preoccupied with self-regulation. In a resistant attachment relationship the infant tends to maximize expressions of distress and relies excessively on interactive regulation by the mother, and in the disorganized attachment there is conflicted, contradictory or disoriented behavior in an attempt to cope with distress in the presence of the mother.

Stern (1999, 2000) further suggests that within states of affect attunement of mother and infant there are dynamic micro-processes of changes over time, perceived as patterns of change that are similar in self and other. These instant-by-instant patterns that shift over time are labelled vitality contours and suggested to have a fundamental narrative structure. Moment-to-moment expressions are "composed" to produce a sequence of coherent proto-narratives with shared rhythms. The concept of narration, normally associated with verbal storytelling, has been applied to the interactive process in mother–infant interaction following the classical steps of opening, building up, climax and closing (Malloch, 1999).

Following Beebe's balance model of self- and interactive regulation, proto narratives are jointly constructed by individuals who are monitoring their arousal at the same time as interactively regulating the contour of the shared affective arousal from beginning to end of the interactive narrative. In this way affects are modulated within tolerable levels with a beginning and an end. This is in contrast to the opposing chase and dodge patterns or disruptive forms of interaction where the arousal levels are not kept within tolerable levels. Here reactions such as getting bodily limp, losing tonus or freezing are observed as efforts to escape intolerable levels of arousal.

The interactive narrative processes give the interaction coherence and form and thus give meaning to the interaction: "I can influence you and you can influence me and we can create a meaningful experience, a narration, together." This coherent process produces continuity from moment-to-moment and gives rise to a coherence experience of self-with-others. This experience of coherence of self-being-with-other may then lay the ground for the ability to engage and maintain in interpersonal interactions being confident that the interaction can be meaningful and kept within tolerable levels of arousal. Further these interactions experiences lay the ground for the forming of coherent thought, narration and self-representation as has been found in attachment research linking the behavioral and the representational level of attachment (Main *et al.*, 1985).

Disturbances in interpersonal interaction, affect regulation and narration in psychosis

In the previous section we suggested patterns of interaction between mothers and infants that are associated with the development of a secure attachment (see also Chapter 6, Schwannauer, this volume). A midrange level of contingent co-created interaction leaves space for a balance between self and other regulation and consists of a blend of narrative interactive sequences where coherence and meaning are created alternating with periods of less contingency, lack of engagement or mismatch kept within tolerable levels of negative arousal. Turning to psychosis we suggest that many of the processes described here are profoundly disturbed. First, authors from many different perspectives suggest that intimacy is often experienced by people with psychosis as both overstimulating and overwhelming (Searles, 1965; Laing, 1978; Lysaker *et al.*, 2005). It has been suggested, for instance, that those with psychosis are relatively unable to perceive self–other boundaries or to develop a theory of the thoughts and intentions of others (Staghellini, 2004).

In a study of attachment pattern in psychosis Tyrell *et al.* (1999) and Dozier *et al.* (2008) found that 89 per cent of individuals diagnosed with schizophrenia were classified as having a dismissing attachment style. Here the affect-regulation strategy is to withdraw and self-regulate outside the relationship. Harder (2000) has studied the relationship pattern of six individuals with first-episode psychosis as assessed with the Structural Analysis of Social Behavior coding system (Benjamin, 1974) applied to narratives about their social relationships. A pattern of unbalanced interpersonal regulation emerged where others were described as being active and positively inviting whereas they described themselves as passive reactive alternating with responses of negative avoidance and withdrawal. On a wish–fear dimension the most common fear was fear of rejection, combined with a wish for positive engagement and interpersonal closeness. Thus they failed to respond in a reciprocal manner not contributing to an affective co-regulation and co-creation of the interaction that allowed a sustained and meaningful interaction to emerge, even they wished for closeness. Their withdrawal strategy suggests an affect regulation strategy that resembles that of a dismissing attachment pattern as found in psychosis in the Dozier study and is also consistent with the suggestion of Berry *et al.* (2007) of the presence of a type of avoidance in psychosis, due to fear of rejection.

In additional to difficulties with relationships, research has suggested that individuals with psychosis experience difficulties regulating affect in general. Distressingly high levels of arousal are reported in the face of unexpected challenge. These disruptions in affective experience are also linked with difficulties in actively coping and may be a risk factor for relapse (Docherty, 1996; Lysaker and Taylor, 2007). Barrowclough and colleagues (2003) found that the relationship between expressed emotion and psychotic symptoms was mediated via changes in self appraisal demonstrating that disruptions in a self narrative are crucial aspect of recovery/relapse. Further, Harder (2006) found that people who were able to preserve some positive self-experience during episodes of acute psychosis were better able to recover from psychotic symptoms and improve their social functioning. Beyond this a range of other authors have also observed individuals with schizophrenia who have difficulties constructing coherent narratives not only about daily life events but also of their lives in general. There may, for instance, be difficulties with temporal connections, lack of details or generally implausible assertions made disrupting the abilities of others to engage with the person in a conversation about themselves and their lives (Lysaker and Lysaker, 2008).

Growth in psychotherapy and attachment research

A case illustration

The client, Clara, a woman in her thirties, has a diagnosis of schizophrenia. She was hospitalized for most of her twenties due to persistent hallucinations and delusions and an inability to care for herself. By her early thirties she had recovered to a level where it was possible for her to be discharged and to live in her own apartment and at that time she began psychotherapy with the first author (SH). Clara's goal was to learn how to live a normal life outside institutions, which had been her home for most of her adult life. Further she wanted help to handle painful feelings related to her identity as a unique person. At the time she entered therapy she had few relationships and experienced severe social anxiety and delusional ideations in relation to participating in group activities at educational courses, leading to a breakdown of a coherent sense of self. She was on a moderate dose of antipsychotic medication, which was decreased during the subsequent years.

The first recollections of Clara were of her entering the therapy office moving fast, restless, as if unable to decide where to sit. She spoke quickly in a loud, tense voice while tapping her foot on the floor. Her speech flowed in a monologue. If interrupted her emotional tone changed abruptly and she stopped talking. She only looked at the therapist with rapid glimpses. Now and then Clara's legs suddenly went limp and she lay down to rest in the middle of the session. Clara also appeared to react to the therapist's every move, while at the same time she had seemingly completely lost track of her own affects. This made the therapist feel trapped and hyperconscious of everything she said and did, taking care to move and speak in a way so as not to disturb Clara.

There was a sense that Clara's behaviors were an attempt at self-regulation during the therapy hour. The continuous talking seemed an attempt to keep the therapist from disturbing what limited self coherence she possessed. Her becoming limp seemed both an extreme form of self-regulation in the face of overarousal and a way to break any engagement that had formed with the therapist. Thus her behavior was conceptualized as extreme self-regulatory strategies for coping with emotional overarousal and for keeping the therapist's voice of the dialogue for fear it would result in Clara's losing what limited sense she had of herself. With the affective contour in the interaction rising and then abruptly closing there was little sense that a meaningful dialogue would be possible.

Therapeutic stance

The therapist operated with the assumption that it was essential to initially accept the client's self-regulation strategies, to be open to her own experiences of Clara's inner states and behaviors upon her emotional states and to regulate those states, and to be aware of how she influenced Clara. In the initial phase of therapy, the therapist attempted to be attuned to the patient's balance of self and other regulation going out of balance of her normal self and other regulation in interaction. She was more passive, responding, taking an active listening stance rather than taking initiatives. She tried to follow Clara to a degree where her anxiety was at a level that did not threaten her engagement in therapy. She sought to match Clara's tempo and intensity to a certain degree in order to "send on her channel" at the same time self-regulated trying to draw down the intensity contour during the process of interaction in an attempt to oppose her pattern of fast rising arousal and abruptly breaking off. This was done through active listening to Clara's stories, through bodily movements and tone of voice. Simultaneously the therapist tried to keep track of her own thoughts about what was going on, trying to let go of the sense of being attended to so hypervigilantly by Clara.

Therapeutic gains

Initially after a period in which it seemed no narrative work could proceed, slowly the actions noted above led to periods of co-regulation and narrative processing began with meaning making finally possible in the sessions. Two years later Clara and the therapist were working more on a symbolic level, combining what happens on the procedural level with Clara's thoughts and memories, in a process of disentangling some of the internal experiences that coincided with different procedural patterns of behavior. Further when she spoke about her experiences outside therapy the therapist recognized the same pattern as in the therapeutic relationship. Clara either told about how she had a very special exclusive relationship with the teacher – she spoke and he listened – making her feel competent and excluding all the other students – or she felt lost in the group. When lost in the group she felt she had no right to be there and was exhausted by trying to do the right thing, occupied by delusional thoughts about how the other students perceived her.

One day she drew a picture of her self-experience: her real self was behind a barrier and the she-in-the-world was split up in different separate fragments, her with the therapist, her at her job, her with her mother, and her in the bus. When moving from one context to another, she experienced herself as not the same person in the moment as she had been in the last context. Her self-experience was not connected to anything outside herself that could lend any coherence.

Another year later a more coherent understanding of her procedural pattern evolved, in parallel with herself becoming more coherent in the sessions, better able to be present in relationships to the therapist and to a recent boyfriend. Clara now drew another picture where her self-with-other fragments now were places within herself as parts of her identified self – but still disconnected to each other. Slowly Clara and the therapist were able to make sense of her sudden shifts in the sessions. She started to reveal abrupt shifts between feeling competent to handle her own life to feeling she had no right to be here in the normal world and that she was an ugly crazy nonhuman patient. She had the feeling she was a liar, a fraud, and felt convinced that other people including her boyfriend would reject her, if they knew who she really was. When that happened outside therapy sessions, Clara had the experience of disintegrating and losing any coherent sense of identity.

In the following period she began to remember her time at the hospitals, which she had not been talking about before. She still experienced her "patient self" in glimpses but slowly her identity as a "crazy nonhuman patient" became connected to experiences in the past and was modulated to a more nuanced picture of her self as patient, incorporating some of her present competencies, making her self-experience over time less fragmented. She gained self-confidence, becoming more confident in her present self as competent. At this point in time her social anxiety had diminished and she was able to pass exams in her educational process. One day she came and declared that she was beginning to think she had a future. She felt she had until now put all her energy into getting away from the past. Her present life had for a long period been "the end of the story." Succeeding in leaving her past behind her finally opened a whole new perspective for her. Clara could think of and make plans for a future, she could hope, dream of an education, a family and a job.

Discussion and conclusions

At the outset of this chapter we noted renewed interest in the potential of psychotherapy to assist people to recover a full sense of self, one that might have been lost with the onset of psychosis, but also recognized the lack of an articulated model of how this might happen. In response we have reviewed a range of literature regarding early attachment patterns and how from shortly after birth, prior to the formation of verbal language, infants and their caretakers form attachments out of which the template for relatedness, the regulation of affect and the creation of basic narrative structure are initially formed. Noting how psychosis may involve a range of difficulties which belong to the realm observed in the birth of consciousness, we have then presented a case study in which the fundamental therapeutic processes were seen as taking place on the same procedural level as has been empirically observed in the early mother–infant relationship.

On the basis of this we would suggest several possibilities that could be explored in further work. First, it may be that in cases in which persons are experiencing significant psychosis, the formation of the early therapeutic relationship shares some basic principles with how mothers and infants form relationships prior to language acquisition. Empirical mother–infant research has highlighted possible process patterns that are fundamental to interpersonal interaction conceptualized here in the balanced model of self and interactive regulation. This balance may be as essential in therapist–client interactions. In other words, the same kinds of matching, different and opposing responses from the therapist may be more important than the specific words said in establishing a secure attachment, making a therapeutic alliance possible.

As illustrated in the case above, unlike in healthy mother–infant dyads, Clara was unable to tolerate a self and interactive regulation that was a mid level. In fact instead there was a hypervigilance on her part to basic changes in the therapist's internal state, as if any failures on the part of the therapist to mirror or understand the internal experiences for which there were no words promised catastrophe. Clara did not expect any interactive regulation to be possible and turned off intersubjective experiences for vital self-regulatory purposes. This behavior could provoke different kinds of therapeutic reactions threatening the development of a helpful working alliance. Either the therapist might become a compensatory moment-to-moment soother of the patient, be very directive, controlling, reinforcing the patient's passive responsive state or reject the patient regarding her unsuitable for psychotherapy because of her inability to take part in a dialogue. Instead very subtle work was required of the therapist to become attuned to both the fluctuating internal state of the patient and her needs. By use of procedural interpersonal means the co-regulation of the affective interpersonal process was developed towards a more mid level balance, in this case by creating a space for the patient for taking initiatives asserting herself and to enable her to dare to regulate her emotions together with the therapist, not feeling forced to interrupt and withdraw from the intersubjective experience. Perhaps years could have been spent listening to Clara's monologues, but the therapist, given her faith in Clara's potential for recovery, interjected.

It also seems an important point that in order to be able to attune to the patients and thus make oneself vulnerable as a therapist a certain amount of psychological health is required. Beebe *et al.* (2005) proposed that operating outside the midrange level of co-regulation in mother–infant interaction may index an adaptive attempt to cope with a disturbance in the interaction. The importance of such procedural strategies in psychotherapy is supported by research on attachment in psychotherapy. Securely attached therapists are found to be able to respond in a flexible way, sometimes "in style" with the client's style of communication, mirroring the client's experience, and at other times challenging the client's state of mind, by responding out of style (Slade, 2008). A key point is that to go along with a client feels safer and the therapist's willingness to offer a kind of attachment that pulls for mid levels of contingent co-created interaction is more demanding and makes one more vulnerable as a therapist.

What seems then to emerge from the therapist's understanding and challenge is a pattern of understanding, rupture and repair which enables clients to accept and tolerate affects previously overwhelming and then to construct meaning. Indeed as in the case study, the tolerance of affects seems to require a healthy relation with the therapist in which an overly soothing, directive or rejecting position was not taken. It is then that delusional constructions of the world were able to be abandoned and genuine hope appeared. Most likely this level of communication was scaffolded by the experience of intersubjectivity and coherence of experience and by the modulation of affect within levels that are optimal for metacognitive functioning.

We wish to acknowledge that there are limitations to what can be learned from a single case study. We look forward to further qualitative and quantitative studies of these phenomena.

References

Barrowclough, C., Tarrier, N., Humphreys, L., Ward, J., Lynsey, G. and Andrews, B. (2003) Self-esteem in schizophrenia: relationships between self-evaluation, family attitudes, and symptomatology, *Journal of Abnormal Psychology* 112: 92–99.

Beebe, B., Knoblauch, S., Rustin, J. and Sorter, D. (2005) *Forms of Intersubjectivity in Infant Research and Adult Treatment*, New York: Other Press.

Benjamin, L.S. (1974) Structural analysis of social behavior (SASB), *Psychological Review* 81: 392–425.

Berry, K., Barrowclough, C. and Wearden, A. (2007) A review of the role of adult attachment style in psychosis. Unexplored issues and questions for further research, *Clinical Psychology Review* 27: 458–475.

Bucci, W. (1997) *Psychoanalysis and Cognitive Science: A Multiple Code Theory*, New York: Guilford Press.

Charman, J. (2009) Developmental approaches to understanding and treating autism. Paper presented at the 39th annual meeting of the Jean Piaget Society: Development at Risk. Typical and Atypical Developmental Pathways, Park City, Utah.

Docherty, N.M. (1996) Affective reactivity of symptoms as a process discriminator in schizophrenia, *Journal of Nervous and Mental Diseases* 184: 535–541.

Dozier, M., Stovall-McClough, K.C. and Albus, K.E. (2008) Attachment and psychopathology in adulthood, in J. Cassidy and P.R. Shaver (eds) *Handbook of*

Attachment. Theory, Research and Clinical Applications, 2nd edn, New York: Guilford Press.

Fonagy, P., Gergely, G., Jurist, E. and Target, M. (2002) *Affect Regulation, Mentalization and the Development of the Self*, New York: Other Press.

Gergely, G. and Watson, J. (1999) Early social-emotional development: contingency perception and the social biofeedback model, in P. Rochat (ed.) *Early Social Cognition: Understanding Others in the First Months of Life*, Hillsdale, NJ: Lawrence Erlbaum Associates, Inc., 101–137.

Gumley, A. and Schwannauer, M. (2006) *Staying Well After Psychosis. A Cognitive Interpersonal Approach to Recovery and Relapse Prevention*, Chichester: Wiley.

Harder, S. (2000) Relationship patterns in first episode psychosis. Unpublished dissertation, University of Copenhagen.

Harder, S. (2006) Self-image and outcome in first episode psychosis, *Clinical Psychology and Psychotherapy* 13: 285–296.

Isabella, R. and Belsky, J. (1991) Interactional synchrony and the origins of infant–mother attachment: a replication study, *Child Development* 62: 373–384.

Jaffe, J. and Feldstein, S. (1970) *Rhythms of Dialogue*, New York: Academic Press.

Jaffe, J., Beebe, B., Feldstein, S., Crown, C.L. and Jasnow, M.D. (2001) *Rhythms of Dialogue in Infancy*. Monographs of the Society for Research in Child Development. Chichester: Wiley 1–132.

Laing, R.D. (1978) *The Divided Self: An Existential Study in Sanity and Madness*, New York: Penguin.

Lewkowitz, D.J. and Lickliter, R. (eds) (1994) *The Development of Intersensory Perception: Comparative Perspectives*, Hillsdale, NJ: Lawrence Erlbaum Associates, Inc.

Lyons-Ruth, K. (1998) Implicit relational knowledge: its role in development and psychoanalytic treatment, *Infant Mental Health Journal* 19: 282–291.

Lyons-Ruth, K. and Jacobvitz, D. (2008) Attachment disorganization: genetic factors. Parenting context, and developmental transformation from infancy to adulthood, in J. Cassidy and P.R. Shaver (eds) *Handbook of Attachment. Theory, Research and Clinical Applications*, 2nd edn, New York: Guilford Press.

Lysaker, P.H. and Lysaker, J.T. (2008) *Schizophrenia and the Fate of the Self*, Oxford: Oxford University Press.

Lysaker, P.H. and Taylor, A. (2007) Personality dimensions in schizophrenia: associations with symptoms and coping concurrently and 12 months later, *Psychopathology* 40: 338–344.

Lysaker, P.H., Johnannesen, J.K. and Lysaker, J.T. (2005) Schizophrenia and the experience of intersubjectivity as threat, *Phenomenology and the Cognitive Sciences* 4: 335–352.

Main, M., Kaplan, N. and Cassidy, J. (1985) Security in infancy, childhood and adulthood: a move to the level of representation, in I. Bretherton and E. Waters (eds) *Growing Points of Attachment Theory and Research*. Monographs of the Society for Research in Child Development. Chichester: Wiley, 66–104.

Malloch, S.N. (1999) Mothers and infants and communicative musicality, *Musicae Scientiae*, Special Issue, 29–57.

Meltzoff, A. and Moore, M. (1977) Imitation of facial and manual gestures of human neonates, *Science* 178: 75–78.

Murray, L. and Trevarthen, C. (1985) Emotional regulation of interactions between two-month-olds and their mothers, in T.M. Field and N.A. Fox (eds) *Social Perception in Infants*, Norwood, NJ: Ablex.

Rosenbaum, B. and Harder, S. (2007) Psychosis and the dynamics of the psychotherapy process, *International Review of Psychiatry* 19: 13–23.

Searles, H. (1965) *Collected Papers on Schizophrenia and Related Subjects*, New York: International Universities Press.

Slade, A. (2008) The implications of attachment theory and research for adult psychotherapy, in J. Cassidy and P.R. Shaver (eds) *Handbook of Attachment. Theory, Research and Clinical Applications*, 2nd edn, New York: Guilford Press.

Staghellini, G. (2004) *Disembodied Spirits and Deanimated Bodies*, Oxford: Oxford University Press.

Stern, D.N. (1999) Vitality contours: the temporal contour of feelings as a basic unit for constructing the infant's social experience, in P. Rochat (ed.) *Early Social Cognition – Understanding Others in the First Months of Life*, Mahwah, NJ: Lawrence Erlbaum Associates, Inc., 67–90.

Stern, D.N. (2000) Putting time back into our considerations of infant experience: a micro diachronic view, *Infant Mental Health Journal* 21: 21–28.

Stern, D.N. (2001) Face-to-face play: its temporal structure as predictor of socioaffective development, in J. Jaffe, B. Beebe, S. Feldstein, C.L. Crown and M.D. Jasnow (eds) *Rhythms of Dialogue in Infancy*. Monographs of the Society for Research in Child Development. Chichester: Wiley, 144–150.

Stern, D.N., Beebe, B., Jaffe, J. and Bennet, S. (1977) The infant's stimulus world during social interaction, in H.R. Schaffer (ed.) *Studies in Mother–Infant Interaction*, New York: Academic Press.

Trevarthen, C. (1998) The concept and foundations of infant intersubjectivity, in S. Braten (ed.) *Intersubjective Communication and Emotion in Early Ontogeny*, Cambridge, MA: Cambridge University Press, 15–46.

Tronick, E.Z. (2005) Why is connection with others so critical? The formation of dyadic states of consciousness: coherence governed selection and the co-creation of meaning out of messy meaning making, in J. Nadel and D. Muir (eds) *Emotional Development*, Oxford: Oxford University Press, 293–315.

Tronick, E.Z. and Cohn, J. (1989) Infant–mother face to face interaction: age and gender differences in coordination and the occurrence of miscoordination, *Child Development* 60: 85–92.

Tronick, E.Z., Als, H., Adamson, L., Wise, S. and Brazelton, T.B. (1978) The infant's response to entrapment between contradictory messages in face-to-face interaction, *Journal of the American Academy of Child Psychiatry* 17: 1–13.

Tyrell, C.L., Dozier, M., Teague, G.B. and Fallot, R.D. (1999) Effective treatments relationship for person with serious psychiatric disorders: the importance of attachment states of mind, *Journal of Consulting and Clinical Psychology* 67: 725–733.

Chapter 6

Attachment, mentalisation and reflective functioning in psychosis

Matthias Schwannauer

Introduction

As outlined throughout this volume, the individual experience of psychosis is marked by intense emotional states and stressful interpersonal experiences. The advent and subsequent relapse of psychosis is characterised by extreme affective reactions including fear, helplessness, hopelessness, shame and depression. It is essential to develop a regulatory theory that provides a model of the affective distress underlying the experience of psychosis and its interpersonal context (Gumley and Schwannauer, 2006). Emotional recovery from psychosis is governed by an integration of the affective experience, interpersonal adaptation and constructive help seeking in the face of crisis. A central theory that has been developed to explain the link between emotional distress, adaptation and help seeking is attachment theory (Bowlby, 1969, 1973, 1980). This is in essence a regulatory theory which could form the basis for a developmental understanding of patterns of emotion regulation and proximity seeking.

Attachment theory offers an approach to understanding a range of key processes in the emotional recovery of individuals with psychosis: interpersonal functioning and coping; the individual's capacity to seek and utilise supports in times of emotional distress and to engage with services; variation in individuals' abilities to cope with the meaning making and the emotional distress associated with the experience of psychosis. This capacity for adaptive affect regulation is closely related to a person's attachment states of mind and their reflective functioning or mentalisation. Mentalisation (the ability to effectively understand behaviour in terms of the associated mental states of self and others) is essential for the individual to be able to integrate their experience of their own mental state with alternatives presented in their interaction with others. This is particularly relevant to psychological therapy and the individual's ability to utilise the interaction and so to generalise the emotional experiences to other interpersonal contexts.

Origins of attachment theory

John Bowlby (1969, 1973, 1980) posited that infants' behaviours had important evolutionary significance in that they increased the likelihood that caregivers would attend to infants' needs which would subsequently increase the chances of their survival. Based on his observations, Bowlby proposed an attachment motivational and behavioural system which would promote the survival of babies by ensuring that they maintain proximity to a caregiver (the attachment figure), especially under conditions of threat (Bowlby, 1973, 1980). Bowlby also hypothesised that how well the attachment motivational and behavioural system fulfilled its function of perceived proximity and exploration depended upon the mutually responsive quality of interactions between infants and caregivers (Bretherton and Munholland, 1999). Through interactions with their caregivers, babies developed internal working models, or representations, made up of beliefs, feelings and expectations of themselves and caregivers in the attachment relationship, which eventually generalise to other relationships. The function of internal working models is to help the individual interpret and anticipate others' behaviours in order to guide his or her own behaviours in relationships. Although certain life events may modify internal working models, they generally tend to show stability and resistance to change over time (Fraley, 2002).

Bowlby's (1969/1980, 1973) internal working models concept was also influenced by prominent psychoanalysts, including objects relations theorists, cognitive psychologists and developmental psychologists. The psychoanalytic influence originated with Freud (1933, pp. 158–184), who presupposed an 'inner world' that is essentially a representation created by one's senses and perceptions of connections and relationships in the external world, reproduced or reflected in an internal world, that enables one to understand, predict and alter future connections and relationships. Psychoanalytic object relations theorists also espoused a representational world or, more specifically, the concept of infants' internalisations of aspects of themselves and their parents. Individual differences in the quality of internal working models of early attachment appear to depend largely upon the quality of interactions between babies and their primary caregivers. In other words, healthy, secure attachment provides individuals with a sense of stability (a secure base) that enables them to explore their environments freely and develop interests and skills more readily than individuals whose relationships are troubled or threatening in some way (Morgan and Shaver, 1999). Based on early attachment patterns, Bowlby proposed that attachment representations are significantly stable across time yet amenable to change with important attachment-related experiences (Waters *et al.*, 2000).

Attachment classification and psychopathology

It is important to note that attachment experiences, attachment mental states and the related capacity of reflective function and mentalisation are not per se linked to psychopathology, but rather provide an indication of underlying *vulnerability*, in particular, in the context of emergent psychopathology and mental health, to interpersonal stressors and risk factors. It is generally well established that early adverse experiences such as early loss and trauma are strongly linked to significant emotional and psychological problems in adulthood (Brown *et al.*, 1986; Rutter, 2000; Hofstra *et al.*, 2002). However, this association between early loss and/or trauma and later adult psychopathology is no longer understood as arising from a direct causal link or relationship between early adverse events and later psychopathology.

There have been numerous studies describing the impact of early attachment experiences on individuals' interpersonal functioning and emotional regulation (summarised in Fonagy, 1998; Fonagy *et al.*, 2002), interpersonal relationships and trust, and identity formation (Cole and Putnam, 1992; Briere, 2002). The development of mentalisation, reflective function and affect regulation also becomes intrinsically linked to the development of self-regulation through the context of close attachment relationships (Fonagy *et al.*, 2002). Mentalisation is defined as the process by which we come to understand that having a mind mediates our experience of the world via the mental representation of psychological states. It refers to 'mind mindedness'. Reflective function describes the processes by which mind mindedness is acquired. For example, in infancy this function is provided by the caregiver's appropriate mirroring of the infant's intentional and emotional expressions (see Chapter 5, Harder and Lysaker, for a further discussion of infant–caregiver reciprocity). For instance, the capacity to perceive and understand oneself and others in terms of mental states (thoughts, feelings, desires) arises in the context of sensitive and attentive caregiving, where the child recognises their own wishes and intentions (the 'intentional stance') in the appropriately reflective behaviour of the caregiver. In adults this reflective functioning in interactions with close others is evidenced by an awareness of the nature, and opaqueness, of the mental states of others, where the individual shows the capacity and motivation to understand how mental and emotional states underpin the behaviour and reaction of others (Fonagy, 1998).

In adulthood several mental states of attachment crystallise which are summarised in the following attachment styles. First, secure attachment is associated with the development of a range of capacities that depend on interpretive skills, such as explorative play, language ability, resilience and control, frustration tolerance, communication and social cognition capacities. The caregiver's sensitivity towards the intentional and emotional states of the infant is one of the strongest predictors of secure attachment (e.g. Slade *et al.*, 1999). The positive impact of attachment security on cognitive competence, emotion regulation and communication style is not mediated through the child's general security and self-confidence but because attachment security allows capacity for reflective function. Furthermore, it is documented that children with secure attachment are better at understanding negative emotion (Laible and Thompson, 1998) and perform better at theory of mind tasks (Fonagy and Target, 1997; Meins *et al.*, 1998). Adults who have a secure or autonomous state of mind with respect to attachment are able to behave with flexibility and openness in relationships. They are able to reflect openly on and communicate information about their own state of mind without excessive distortions or censorship. They are more able to reflect on and attune to the mental states of others. Autonomous adults communicate an autobiographical narrative that is free flowing, fresh, reflective, sensitive to context and collaborative with another person. Early experiences may thus play a formative role in generating internal working models and later social functioning through their robustness, rather than their representation of secure infant/caregiver interactions per se. These relational schemata that are formed through experience have a marked impact on the individual's capacity to form and maintain meaningful relationships with others (Briere, 2002), and also the regulation of negative and unwanted emotions (Alexander, 1992).

In contrast, a devalued model of self can develop when caregivers are construed as having been rejecting, or disruptive of exploratory behaviour (Bretherton and Munholland, 1999). Indeed, long-term reliance on behavioural strategies associated with insecure attachment increases vulnerability to later adult psychopathology (Bowlby, 1988). In the context of attachment there are two key interpersonal strategies available to regulate affect and distress, which determine the development of two different organised insecure mental states of attachment: by minimising (dismissive strategies) affect or by exaggerating (preoccupied strategies) affect. Dismissing adults minimise and avoid attachment-related experiences and therefore autobiographical memories related to attachment experiences tend to be under-elaborated. The dismissing adult's ability to reflect on his or her own affective experience, and attune to the minds, intentions and mental states of others is diminished. In a preoccupied state of mind with respect to attachment, adults are valuing of attachment but are insecure, ruminative and distressed. They are often concerned with themes of abandonment and rejection.

Finally, disorganised (or unresolved) attachment status is not an attachment pattern as such. It refers to the absence of a coherent attachment strategy or the collapse of a pre-existing attachment strategy due to unresolved trauma and/or loss. The description refers to infants most often parented by carers who are either frightening, frightened or both. For example, carers who are abusive, hostile, under the influence of drugs or alcohol, or carers who are highly distressed often by unresolved losses and trauma would provide a disorganised and disorientating attachment base for an infant. The parenting strategies of those with unresolved and disorganised attachments include errors in mirroring and responding to affect, disorientated behaviour (e.g. confusion, panic and fear), negative intrusive behaviour (mocking and teasing of a child in distress), role confusion (where the parent seeks comfort from the child) and withdrawal (where the parent is distant and dissociated). In an effort to synchronise with a frightening and/or frightened parent, infant and child attachment strategies become disorganised and deregulated.

Adults with disorganised and unresolved attachments patterns will characteristically show disorganisation of affect regulation, behaviour and the monitoring of narrative and discourse. This is characteristic of the approach avoidance conflict that we often see in adults seeking help for past trauma and abuse.

Early attachment patterns are highly predictive of adult representational attachment styles, up to 77 per cent in the case of secure representations (Waters *et al.*, 2000) and 94 per cent in terms of insecure representations when associated with subsequent negative life events (Weinfeld *et al.*, 2000). Beyond that there is no clear prediction of adult psychopathology from insecure or disorganised attachment styles even though these seem to be overrepresented in certain clinical groups. Therefore, it again appears that the association between early attachment experiences and adult interpersonal functioning (and consequently psychopathology) is mediated by internal working models, underlying processes of affect regulation, behavioural adaptation and reflective functioning, hence contributing to vulnerability.

In particular, the mediation of insecure or disorganised attachment to later maladaptive or pathological outcomes arises specifically through the main variable of self-regulation and reflective functioning in combination with a number of external risk factors. In terms of known cognitive risk factors such as attentional processes, perceptual sensitivity and effortful control, it has been demonstrated that these are developmentally related to many of the sequelae of secure attachment including social competency, empathy and low levels of aggression (Rothbart *et al.*, 1994, 2000; Kochanska *et al.*, 2000).

In light of this, both avoidance and resistance (frequently observed as coping strategies in psychosis) can be alternatively construed as self-protective strategies in intense interpersonal contexts. If the individual's internal working model is insecure, to avoid instability he or she might either withdraw from others, strengthening his self-representation relative to other representations (dismissive style) or protectively emphasise representations of others (preoccupied). In a study linking adolescents' state of mind in relation to attachment to psychopathology, Rosenstein and Horowitz (1996) reported a strong link between attachment strategies and differential vulnerability to psychiatric symptoms. In their sample of 60 hospitalised adolescents a dismissing attachment organisation was linked to strategies minimising distress and a rejection of the attachment figures. Mental states associated with denial or a downplaying of distress occurred in the context of such dismissing attachment organisation. Adolescents using preoccupied attachment strategies relied on a maximising of the attachment system and within that activated mental states where negative affect was acknowledged and/or exaggerated. Harrop and Trower (2003) contend that a key aspect of adolescence is the struggle for autonomy from the parental base, and that the premature development of autonomy or inability to achieve autonomy is a potential risk factor for psychosis.

Attachment and psychosis

There are a limited number of studies investigating directly the link between attachment states of mind and psychosis. Generally samples of individuals with psychosis tend to report higher levels of insecure attachment styles than control groups. In a sample of individuals with a first episode of psychosis, Couture and colleagues (2007) investigated attachment styles in association with social functioning and found that in comparison with a healthy control group first episode participants showed higher levels of insecurity and had higher levels of preoccupation and discomfort with interpersonal closeness. Both attachment avoidance and attachment preoccupation were associated with lower quality of life. Ponizovsky and colleagues (2007) assessed attachment styles in a small sample of individuals with a diagnosis of schizophrenia. They found that three-quarters of participants reported higher anxious/avoidant and anxious/ambivalent attachments styles than healthy controls. Anxious/avoidant attachment styles were overrepresented in the schizophrenia group and linked to younger age at onset.

Utilising the Adult Attachment Interview (AAI), Dozier (1990) established in a small clinical sample of individuals suffering from schizophrenia and affective disorder respectively that the former demonstrated more dismissive attachment styles than individuals with an affective disorder. They also established that dismissive styles were associated with lower levels of perceived distress when compared to individuals with preoccupied styles. In individuals with psychosis this can often be observed in the apparent lack of emotional distress associated with their experience of psychosis. This tendency found replication in Dozier and Lee (1995) where in a sample consisting of participants with diagnoses of schizophrenia and bipolar disorders individuals with preponderance to dismissive and deactivating attachment styles reported less affective distress and lower symptoms than those with preoccupied and activating strategies. In a later study (Tyrrell and Dozier, 1997), attachment organisation was investigated in a further small mixed sample of participants with bipolar disorder, schizoaffective disorder and schizophrenia. In this study most (89 per cent) of these participants were classified as dismissing of attachment. Dozier and colleagues have argued that adult states of mind with respect to attachment in the context of schizophrenia and bipolar disorder have the potential to explain service engagement and treatment use.

Attachment to services

In relation to engagement with services Dozier (1990) examined attachment organisation and use of treatment; more secure attachment ratings were associated with greater compliance. Clients were more likely to show up for appointments and take medication. Individuals with avoidant attachment strategies were less likely to seek out treatment and more likely to reject treatment. Avoidance was inversely related to disclosure. Individuals with preoccupied attachment strategies were more likely to self-disclose and were more likely to seek help. In a later study, Dozier *et al.* (2001) found that clients with dismissing states of mind spent less time discussing problems and their solutions with their case managers and displayed more rejecting behaviour during problem solving, compared to those with more preoccupied attachment representations. Furthermore, individuals with dismissing representations reported being more confused by these interactions than those with preoccupied attachment representations, and family members of dismissing clients felt greater sadness following problem solving. Therefore, we can see from this study that interpersonal interaction is clearly mediated by the person's organisation of their attachment model.

Attachment to services and psychosis

Investigating attachment style and service engagement, Tait and others (2003, 2004) established in a clinical sample of individuals with a first episode of psychosis that poor engagement with services was predicted with a so-called sealing over recovery style (McGlashan and Carpenter, 1979) and that in turn a sealing over recovery style was associated with an insecure attachment style. Tait and colleagues further observed that individuals who demonstrated a sealing over recovery style also scored high on the Evaluative Beliefs Scale (Chadwick and Birchwood, 1994), indicating mentalisation deficits in terms of a belief that others see them negatively. Looking at recollection of parenting styles in individuals with psychosis, Drayton and others (1998) found that participants with a sealing over recovery style also reported their parents as less caring associated with higher self-negative evaluations. It appears therefore that diminished mentalising, dismissive attachment patterns and a sealing over attitude towards recovery indicate a minimisation and reduced acknowledgement of the affective impact of the experience of psychosis and poorer levels of service engagement and active help seeking.

Metacognition and regulation of emotion in psychosis

The capacity to construct and relate a consistent and coherent narrative of personal and interpersonal experiences and the explication of mental states is closely related to attachment security:

> Secure attachment is marked by coherent stories that convince and hang together, where detail and overall plot are congruent, and where the teller is not so detached that affect is absent, is not dissociated from the content of the story, nor is so overwhelmed that feelings flow formlessly into every crevice of the dialogue. Insecure attachment, by contrast, is

characterized either by stories that are overelaborated or enmeshed . . . or by dismissive, poorly fleshed out accounts.

(Holmes, 2001, p. 58)

Both in observational terms and in relation to attachment narratives, attachment styles or mental states are developed from individuals' attempts to regulate emotions within the context of infant–caregiver relationships. Affect is therefore central to attachment theory and vice versa the concept of attachment is an integral component of theories of affect regulation (Shaver and Mikulincer, 2007). It is within the early infant–caregiver interactions that these regulatory capacities develop through the emotional representation of physiological states and in the caregiver's sensitive reflection of their own emotional states and reactions to the infant. If responses are consistent then emotions become predictable, contained and regulated within representational systems or internal working models which are in turn associated with particular attachment styles and mentalising capacities (Zimmerman and Fassler, 2003). Secure attachment sustains the organisation of the self and the capacity to modulate difficult emotions (Fonagy and colleagues, 2007).

Metacognition

Metacognition is more narrowly defined as a specific form of thinking about thinking, including the awareness of one's own cognitions within the domain of mentalisation involving cognitive monitoring and cognitive regulation, inhibition and adaptation (Fernandez-Duque *et al.*, 2000). In the context of attachment theory, Mary Main (1991) introduced the term 'metacognitive monitoring'. She distinguishes between representational and metarepresentational processes or the difference between 'possessing a mental representation of an experience vs. being able to reflect on its validity, nature, and source' (Main, 1991, p. 128).

Moving on from the focus on the cognitive processes associated with mentalising activities, Fonagy *et al.* (2002) coined the term 'mentalising affectivity' and stressed its essential regulatory function in achieving clarity about emotional experiences and their intentional structure or meaning. In that sense mentalisation describes the process of mental elaboration (Lecours and Bouchard, 1997), or turning something non-mental or emotional into something mental. In his phenomenology of emotion, Jean-Paul Sartre describes emotional consciousness as a non-reflective consciousness of the world, or a way of understanding the world where the object and the subject of its understanding are essentially the same (Sartre, 1939, p. 57). Emotions are thus integrated with cognitions, and mentalisation therefore combines both emotional and cognitive appraisal and construction of meaning and intentionality, just as Fonagy and colleagues would espouse (2002). Many individuals with psychosis who experience apparently unintelligible cognitive and emotional states also often show a tendency to dismiss and overregulate emotions more generally, which may be a way to understand the disruption of the basic regulatory function of mentalising emotions as a way of self regulation (Allen *et al.*, 2006).

Metacognition and psychosis

Developmental processes of individual separation and individuation dominate adolescence, where processes of attachment organisation and affect regulation become more autonomous and enable individuals to perform these processes within their reflective capacity. As the sense of self develops in adolescence, so do the individuals' internal working models, and childhood representations become reorganised and updated not least through increased reflective capacity (Kobak and Cole, 1994). In the context of dysfunctional family environment and developmental interpersonal trauma as key risk factors, impairments in cognitive processes of accurate self and other awareness and impaired mentalisation can become a key feature of emerging adolescent psychosis (Myin-Germeys and van Os, 2007; Kettle *et al.*, 2008). With the cognitive development of formal operations the adolescent is able to distance themselves from their immediate experience and consider the mental and emotional state of themselves and others which allows for the emergence of more complex emotions and cognitions (Fonagy *et al.*, 2007). Social withdrawal and dissociation can be a response to the internal experience becoming too overwhelming, especially if mentalising capacity is limited or compromised; for example, in the context of an emergent psychosis, stressful situations are likely to distort the information and emotions associated with their internal experiences. The significant developmental impact of the experience of psychosis and poorer adaptation and emotional recovery is in part attributed to its destructive effects on adolescent development (Harrop and Trower, 2003).

In the context of psychosis the term 'mentalisation' subsumes conceptually other forms of cognitive capacity and awareness of cognitive states of mind, such as the theory of mind concept (Frith, 1992) and metacognition, defined as an awareness of one's thought processes (e.g. Wells, 1997; Fonagy *et al.*, 2002). With a focus on theory of mind capacity in individuals with schizophrenia and psychosis, Sprong and colleagues (2007) in a meta analysis of 831 participants in 29 studies established a clear effect for compromised theory of mind in psychosis samples. Key differences between mentalisation and theory of mind lie in the emphasis that is placed upon affect and interpersonal aspects of the overall capacity to attend to and understand thoughts, intentions and beliefs within self and others. Operationalisations of the theory of mind concept tend to be exclusively focused on cognitive and rational aspects, whereas mentalisation includes a strong emphasis on affect and relational components of behaviours and social interactions.

For the individual, impairments in mentalisation or their capacity for the awareness and understanding of mental states of self and others may be related to the development and experience of key features of psychosis. For example, difficulties in separating own thoughts and actions from external stimuli has been related to the development of delusions and hallucinations (Bentall *et al.*, 2007); deficits in the metacognitive evaluation of one's cognitive performance were related to poor understanding of the disorder (Lysaker *et al.*, 2005); and deficits in metacognitive evaluations have been linked to poor understanding of the illness and poor self reflective capacities (Koren *et al.*, 2004). Other more specific aspects of metacognition represent a unique barrier to recovery through impaired regulation of behaviour and internal states; for example, Lysaker and colleagues (2010) identified a clear association of impairments in self reflectivity making it difficult to differentiate personal goals, plans and intentions, with lower indicators of rehabilitation. The only study that directly linked attachment states of mind and mentalisation to psychosis in a first episode sample is that by MacBeth and colleagues (2011). In a small sample of 34 first episode psychosis clients within the first 12 months of treatment, the authors of this study establish a clear association between AAI based attachment states of mind and reflective function. In this sample 26.5 per cent of participants displayed a secure attachment style, in contrast to previous literature that asserted a predominance of insecure dismissive attachment in psychosis (van Ijzendoorn and Bakermans-Kranenburg, 2008, p. 84). Participants with insecure preoccupied attachment style showed significantly lower reflective function than participants with secure or insecure dismissive attachment. The authors further found that reflective function was linked to service engagement in that participants with insecure dismissive attachment showed lower service engagement than the other two groups.

This study did not find a direct association between reflective function and psychotic symptoms which may indicate that reflective function is not directly linked to a clear deficit in mentalisation reducible to a specific deficit or symptomatology in this first episode psychosis (Lysaker *et al.*, 2007), but rather to the difficulties in understanding their own thoughts and feelings and those of others and consequently their affective experience of psychosis and more importantly their social functioning and ability to seek support. In terms of psychotherapeutic interventions this may mean that attachment mental states and reflective function give us not only a meaningful understanding of the individual's ability to integrate their experience of psychosis and to adapt to the emotional and developmental impact of their experiences, but also their continued vulnerability to specific life events, lack of emotional recovery and future recurrence.

It is important to note that even though there is an overrepresentation of relative insecure and disorganised attachment classifications in populations of individuals suffering from psychosis (e.g. Dozier, 1990; Fonagy *et al.*, 1996), it is more likely that the underlying processes associated with these attachment classifications, such as reflective function and mentalising capacity as well as impaired affect regulation, are responsible for this, rather than there being a direct relationship between attachment classification and specific manifestations of psychopathology, such as psychosis. Attachment mental states and associated psychopathology and its outcomes are therefore likely to be mediated and moderated by a range of associated psychological processes, such as affect (dys)regulation, interpersonal sensitivities, attentional control, mentalisation and reflective function.

As outlined above, attachment theory and psychosis have been linked on a theoretical level in an attempt to enhance and develop further current conceptualisation of psychosis in terms of pathways of emotional dysfunction in psychosis, patterns of help seeking and engagement with services, and particular models of psychotic experiences. By contrast the impact of mentalisation and reflective function on the experience, adaptation and recovery from psychosis are largely unexplored. This area would benefit from further investigation and development in the literature.

One of the current difficulties in relating mentalisation to psychosis and its psychotherapeutic treatment is that the current literature reflects a very broad and multifaceted concept. In the context of mentalisation and affectivity in borderline personality disorder, Fonagy and Luyten (2009) develop a multidimensional structure of mentalisation, differentiating four dimensions: automatic/controlled, cognitive/affective, internal/external and self/other focused. There is no current research relating these postulated dimensions to functions of different aspects of mentalisation in psychosis, but a similar conceptual approach may aid a clearer and more coherent understanding of these aspects in individuals with psychosis, integrating developmental, neurophysiological and clinical observations with different components of vulnerability and observed deficits. This approach may further resolve the perceived dichotomy of trait-like mentalisation capacities in psychosis from situation-specific reactions, where we would expect differences in the quality of mentalisation depending on the quality of the relationship within which the aspect of interpersonal cognition is observed. The implication would be that mentalisation will show considerable fluctuations over time and across different interpersonal contexts, which will allow for considerable flexibility and modulation through psychotherapy.

Psychotherapeutic implications

One particular application of the concept of mentalisation could be in relation to the experience of psychosis itself. Going through a period of psychosis does not only consist of the experience of core symptoms and their underlying processes, but also the impact it makes on the social world of the individual. In this context it is the disruption of social relationship and the understanding of self in relation to others that majorly influence the individual's capacity to regulate unwanted and intolerable affect. Predominantly the observed combination of low mentalising and dismissive attachment patterns produces a focus on minimised expression of affect and increased self regulation, which is linked to the development and entrenchment of specific psychotic experiences and compromised emotional recovery. This leads to a more general disruption of interpersonal processes; for example, close confiding relationships are often experienced as overstimulating and overwhelming (e.g. Lysaker *et al.*, 2005).

In this context there may be the potential for specifically emphasised forms of psychotherapy in psychosis to allow for a compensatory interpersonal and attachment model and lead to the reconstruction of a personal narrative that may facilitate the processing and development of self and other understanding in the context of social and emotional recovery (e.g. Gumley and Schwannauer, 2006; Brent, 2009; Lysaker *et al.*, 2010). The psychotherapeutic framework for this may involve both a sensitisation and tolerance of affect that would allow increased mentalising capacity. In related areas of psychotherapeutic application, mentalisation based approaches that focused on affect dysregulation and patterns of interpersonal relating observed a clear shift in reflective function and mentalisation (e.g. Levy *et al.*, 2006). Brent (2009) further argues that the use of mentalisation based and psychodynamically informed therapy can successfully address individual deficits in the capacity to recognise and relate to emotional and mental states in self and others and the resulting incoherent sense of self, and thus address the effects of trauma related to early negative experiences and abuse with caregivers.

A clear focus on mentalisation and associated areas of cognitive, interpersonal and social functioning within psychotherapeutic treatment in psychosis allows us to combine and integrate the co-construction of a coherent narrative of significant attachment experiences, emotional reaction and adaptation in the context of past trauma and current life events and stressors, with a positive outlook to emotional and social recovery. Within this approach, recovery after psychosis allows for the expression of symptoms and individual adaptive coping strategies to be understood as a reflection of the individual's attempts to make sense and regulate the affective impact of past experience and transitions. Attachment theory and mentalisation provide both a framework for understanding and a link to possible mechanisms of change within psychotherapy.

Conclusion

It is argued here that attachment theory can provide a helpful foundational framework for modelling a rich understanding of cognitive and emotional regulation in the experience and expression of psychosis. Future work needs to be undertaken to fully elaborate possible dimensions of mentalisation in individuals with psychosis, and to apply this to clinical approaches in therapy, utilisation of services and recovery.

References

Alexander, P.C. (1992) Application of attachment theory to the study of sexual abuse, *Journal of Consulting and Clinical Psychology* 60: 185–195.

Allen, J.P., Insabella, G.M. and Porter, M.R. (2006) A social-interactional model of the development of depressive symptoms in adolescence, *Journal of Consulting and Clinical Psychology* 74(1): 55–65.

Bentall, R., Fernyhough, C., Morrison, T., Lewis, S. and Corcoran, R. (2007) Prospects for a cognitive developmental account of psychotic experiences, *British Journal of Clinical Psychology* 46: 155–173.

Bowlby, J. (1969/1980) *Attachment and Loss, Vol. 1: Attachment*, London: Hogarth Press.

Bowlby, J. (1973) *Attachment and Loss, Vol. 2: Separation, Anger and Anxiety*, London: Hogarth Press.

Bowlby, J. (1980) *Attachment and Loss, Vol. 3: Loss, Sadness and Depression*, London: Hogarth Press.

Bowlby, J. (1988) *A Secure Base: Clinical Applications of Attachment Theory*, London: Brunner-Routledge.

Brent, B. (2009) Mentalization-based psychodynamic psychotherapy for psychosis, *Journal of Clinical Psychology: In Session* 65: 803–814.

Bretherton, I. and Munholland, K.A. (1999) Internal working models in attachment relationships, in J. Cassidy and P. Shaver (eds) *Handbook of Attachment. Theory, Research and Applications*, New York: Guilford Press, 89–111.

Briere, J. (2002) Treating adult survivors of severe childhood abuse and neglect: further development of an integrative model, in J.E.B. Myers, L. Berliner, J. Briere, C.T. Hendrix, T. Reid and C. Jenny (eds) *The APSAC Handbook on Child Maltreatment*, 2nd edn, Newbury Park, CA: Sage.

Brown, G.W., Andrews, B., Harris, T.O., Adler, Z. and Bridge, L. (1986) Social support, self-esteem and depression, *Psychological Medicine* 16: 813–831.

Chadwick, P. and Birchwood, M. (1994) The omnipotence of voices. A cognitive approach to auditory hallucinations, *British Journal of Psychiatry* 164(2): 190–201.

Cole, P.M. and Putnam, F.W. (1992) Effect of incest on self and social functioning: a developmental psychopathology perspective, *Journal of Consulting and Clinical Psychology* 60: 174–184.

Couture, S., Lecomte, T. and Leclerc, C. (2007) Personality characteristics and attachment in first episode psychosis: impact on social functioning, *Journal of Nervous and Mental Disease* 195: 631–639.

Dozier, M. (1990) Attachment organization and the treatment use for adults with serious psychopathological disorders, *Development and Psychopathology* 2: 47–60.

Dozier, M. and Lee, S.W. (1995) Discrepancies between self- and other-report of psychiatric symptomatology: effects of dismissing attachment strategies, *Development and Psychopathology* 7: 217–226.

Dozier, M., Lomax, L., Tyrrell, C.L. and Lee, S.W. (2001) The challenge of treatment for clients with dismissing states of Mind, *Attachment and Human Development* 3: 62–76.

Drayton, M., Birchwood, M. and Trower, P. (1998) Early attachment experience and recovery from psychosis, *British Journal of Clinical Psychology* 37: 269–284.

Fernandez-Duque, D., Baird, J.A. and Posner, M.I. (2000) Executive attention and metacognitive regulation, *Consciousness and cognition* 9(2): 288–307.

Fonagy, P. (1998) Moments of change in psychoanalytic theory: discussion of a new theory of psychic change, *Infant Mental Health Journal* 19: 163–171.

Fonagy, P. and Luyten, P. (2009) A developmental, mentalization-based approach to the understanding and treatment of borderline personality disorder, *Development and Psychopathology* 21: 1355–1381.

Fonagy, P. and Target, M. (1997) Attachment and reflective function: their role in self-organization, *Development and Psychopathology* 9: 679–690.

Fonagy, P., Leigh, T., Steele, M., Steele, H., Kennedy, R., Mattoon, G. *et al.* (1996) The relation of attachment status, psychiatric classification, and response to psychotherapy, *Journal of Consulting and Clinical Psychology* 64: 22–31.

Fonagy, P., Gergely, G., Jurist, E.L. and Target, M. (2002) *Affect Regulation, Mentalization and the Development of the Self*, London: Karnac.

Fonagy, P., Gergely, G. and Target, M. (2007) The parent–infant dyad and the construction of the subjective self, *Journal of Child Psychology and Psychiatry* 48: 288–328.

Fraley, C.R. (2002) Attachment stability from infancy to adulthood: meta-analysis and dynamic modeling of developmental mechanisms, *Personality and Social Psychology Review* 6: 123–151.

Freud, S. (1933) New introductory lectures on psycho-analysis, in J. Strachey (ed.) *Standard Edition* Vol. 22, London: Hogarth Press, 1962.

Frith, C.D. (1992) *The Cognitive Neuropsychology of Schizophrenia*, Hillside, NJ: Lawrence Erlbaum Associates, Inc.

Gumley, A. and Schwannauer, M. (2006) *Staying Well After Psychosis: A Cognitive Interpersonal Approach to Recovery and Relapse Prevention*, Chichester: Wiley.

Harrop, C.E. and Trower, P. (2003) *Why Does Schizophrenia Develop at Late Adolescence?*, Chichester: Wiley.

Hofstra, M.B., van der Ende, J. and Verhulst, F.C. (2002) Child and adolescent problems predict DSM-IV disorders in adulthood: a 14-year follow-up of a Dutch epidemiological sample, *Journal of the American Academy of Child and Adolescent Psychiatry* 41: 182–189.

Holmes, J. (2001) *The Search for the Secure Base: Attachment Theory and Psychotherapy*, Hove, UK: Psychology Press.

Kettle, J.W.L., O'Brien-Simpson, L. and Allen, N.B. (2008) Impaired theory of mind in first episode schizophrenia: comparison with community, university and depressed controls, *Schizophrenia Research* 99: 96–102.

Kobak, R. and Cole, H. (1994) VIII Attachment and meta-monitoring: implications for adolescent autonomy and psychopathology, *Disorders and Dysfunctions of the Self* 5: 267.

Kochanska, G., Murray, K.T. and Harlan, E. (2000) Effortful control in early childhood: continuity and change, antecedents, and implications for social development, *Developmental Psychology* 36: 220–232.

Koren, D., Seidman, L.J., Poyurovsky, M., Goldsmith, M., Viksman, P., Zichel, S. and Klein, E. (2004) The neuropsychological basis of insight in first-episode schizophrenia: a pilot metacognitive study, *Schizophrenia Research* 70: 195–202.

Laible, D.J. and Thompson, R.A. (1998) Attachment and emotional understanding in preschool children, *Developmental Psychology* 34: 1038–1045.

Lecours, S. and Bouchard, M.-A. (1997) Dimensions of mentalisation: outlining levels of psychic transformation, *International Journal of Psychoanalysis* 78: 855–875.

Levy, K.N., Meehan, K.B., Kelly, K.M., Reynoso, J.S., Clarkin, J.F. and Kernberg, O.F. (2006) Change in attachment patterns and reflective function in a randomized control trial of transference-focused psychotherapy for borderline personality disorder, *Journal of Consulting and Clinical Psychology* 74: 1027–1040.

Lysaker, P.H., Carcione, A., Dimaggio, G., Johannesen, J.K., Nicolò, G., Procacci, M. and Semerari, A. (2005) Metacognition amidst narratives of self and illness in schizophrenia: associations with neurocognition, symptoms, insight and quality of life, *Acta Psychiatrica Scandinavica* 112: 64–71.

Lysaker, P.H., Dimaggio, G., Buck, K.D., Carcione, A. and Nicolò, G. (2007) Metacognition within narratives of schizophrenia: associations with multiple domains of neurocognition, *Schizophrenia Research* 93: 278–287.

Lysaker, P.H., Dimaggio, G., Carcione, A., Procacci, M., Buck, K.D., Davies, L.W. and Nicolò, G. (2010) Metacognition and schizophrenia: the capacity for self-reflectivity as a predictor for prospective assessments of work performance over six months, *Schizophrenia Research* 122: 124–130.

MacBeth, A., Gumley, A., Schwannauer, M. and Fisher, R. (2011) Attachment states of mind, mentalization, and their correlates in a first-episode psychosis sample, *Psychology and Psychotherapy: Theory, Research and Practice* 84(1): 1–112.

McGlashan, T.H. and Carpenter Jr, W.T. (1979) Affective symptoms and the diagnosis of schizophrenia, *Schizophrenia Bulletin* 5(4): 547–553.

Main, M. (1991) Metacognitive knowledge, metacognitive monitoring, and singular (coherent) vs. multiple (incoherent) models of attachment, in C.M. Parkes, J. Stevenson-Hinde and P. Marris (eds) *Attachment across the Life Cycle*, London: Routledge, 127–159.

Meins, E., Fernyhough, C., Russell, J. and Clark-Carter, D. (1998) Security of attachment as a predictor of symbolic and mentalising abilities: a longitudinal study, *Social Development* 7: 1–24.

Morgan, H.J. and Shaver, P.R. (1999) Attachment processes and commitment to romantic relationships, in J.M. Adams and W.H. Jones (eds) *Handbook of Interpersonal Commitment and Relationship Stability*, New York: Plenum, 109–124.

Myin-Germeys, I. and van Os, J. (2007) Stress-reactivity in psychosis: evidence for an affective pathway to psychosis, *Clinical Psychology Review* 27: 409–424.

Ponizovsky, A., Nechamkin, Y. and Rosca, P. (2007) Attachment patterns are associated with symptomatology and course of schizophrenia in male inpatients, *American Journal of Orthopsychiatry* 77: 324–331.

Rosenstein, D.S. and Horowitz, H.A. (1996) Adolescent attachment and psychopathology, *Journal of Consulting and Clinical Psychology* 64: 244–253.

Rothbart, M.K., Derryberry, D. and Posner, M.I. (1994) A psychobiological approach to the development of temperament, in J.E. Bates and T.D. Wachs (eds) *Temperament: Individual Differences at the Interface of Biology and Behavior*, Washington, DC: American Psychological Association, 83–116.

Rothbart, M.K., Derryberry, D. and Hershey, K. (2000) Stability of temperament in childhood: laboratory infant assessment to parent report at seven years, in V.J. Molfese and D.L. Molfese (eds) *Temperament and Personality Development across the Life Span*, Mahwah, NJ: Lawrence Erlbaum Associates, Inc., 85–119.

Rutter, M. (2000) Resilience reconsidered: conceptual considerations, empirical findings, and policy implications, in J.P. Shonkoff and S.J. Meisels (eds) *Handbook of Early Childhood Intervention*, 2nd edn, New York: Cambridge University Press, 651–682.

Sartre, J.-P. (1939) Esquisse d'une théorie des emotions. Trans. B. Fretchman (1948) *The Emotions: Outline of a Theory*, London: Philosophical Library.

Shaver, P.R. and Mikulincer, M. (2007) Adult attachment strategies and the regulation of emotion, in J.J. Grass (ed.) *Handbook of Emotion Regulation*, New York: Guilford Press, 446–465.

Slade, A., Belsky, J., Aber, J.L. and Phelps, J.L. (1999) Mothers' representations of their relationships with their toddlers: links to adult attachment and observed mothering, *Developmental Psychology* 35: 611–619.

Sprong, M., Schothorst, P., Vos, E., Hox, J. and van Engeland, H. (2007) Theory of mind in schizophrenia: meta-analysis, *British Journal of Psychiatry* 191: 5–13.

Tait, L., Birchwood, M. and Trower, P. (2003) Predicting engagement with services for psychosis: insight, symptoms and recovery style, *British Journal of Psychiatry* 182: 123–128.

Tait, L., Birchwood, M. and Trower, P. (2004) Adapting to the challenge of psychosis: personal resilience and the use of sealing-over (avoidant) coping strategies, *British Journal of Psychiatry* 185: 410–415.

Tyrrell, C. and Dozier, M. (1997) The role of attachment in therapeutic process and outcome for adults with serious psychiatric disorders. Paper presented at the biennial meeting of Society for Research in Child Development, Washington, DC.

van Ijzendoorn, M.H. and Bakermans-Kranenburg, M.J. (2008) The distribution of adult attachment representations in clinical groups: a meta-analytic search for patterns of attachment in 105 AAI studies, in H. Steele and M. Steele (eds) *Clinical Applications of the Adult Attachment Interview*, New York: Guilford Press, 69–98.

Waters, E., Merrick, S., Treboux, D., Crowell, J. and Albersheim, L. (2000) Attachment security in infancy and early adulthood: a twenty-year longitudinal study, *Child Development* 71: 684–689.

Weinfeld, N.S., Sroufe, L.A. and Egeland, B. (2000) Attachment from infancy to early adulthood in a high risk sample: continuity, discontinuity, and their correlates, *Child Development* 71: 695–702.

Wells, A. (1997) *Cognitive Therapy for Anxiety Disorders*, Chichester: Wiley.

Zimmerman, L. and Fassler, I. (2003) The dynamics of emotional availability in childcare: how infants involve and respond to their teen mothers and childcare teachers, *Infants and Young Children* 16(3): 258.

Chapter 7

Suffering the impact

Psychosis and the professional caregiver[1]

Robert D. Hinshelwood

> Schizophrenia is an expertise in producing disquiet in others.
> (Berke, 1979, p. 23)

In considering emotions in the condition called schizophrenia, it might be worth addressing the impact, especially the emotional impact on those who encounter people with the condition. The long-standing professional view of schizophrenia as a condition characterised by a flattening of affect is unfortunate, given the suffering that comprises the condition. More than this if the patient appears to have lost his emotional experiences, invariably his carers are reciprocally invaded by extreme 'disquiet'.

When Samuel Beckett went to the Tavistock Clinic in 1934 for psychotherapy with the novice therapist Wilfred Bion, he took an interest in mental illness and visited the Bethlem hospital. Beckett's verdict on one patient he encountered was: '[the patient] was like a hunk of meat. There was no-one there. He was absent' (Knowlson, 1996, p. 202).

We are rather shocked, I think. He shouldn't be so derogatory about a patient. I want in this chapter to think about reactions like this to psychiatric patients. If ordinary people are disturbed by the encounter with psychotic patients, what impact occurs with professionals? In fact, a reaction to psychosis is a regular occurrence whether the person is a professional carer or not, and serious organisational results can ensue from that. A comment somewhat similar to Beckett's was made a little before:

> I did not like those patients . . . They make me angry and I find myself irritated to experience them so distant from myself and from all that is

1 An early version of this paper was given at a conference in Santiago de Chile, on Institutional and Clinical Experiences of Psychosis, June 2007.

> human. This is an astonishing intolerance which brands me a poor psychiatrist.
>
> (Freud, 1928, quoted in Dupont, 1988, p. 251)

Freud of course was very aware of relational problems with these patients. But this is an interesting passage. On the one hand he regarded such a patient as subhuman, and on the other he conveyed that he should not think like that as a psychiatrist. Presumably, he should regard the patient as a fellow human being. Something therefore about the way in which Freud and people with schizophrenia related had created a conflict.

This chapter is therefore about the emotional impact of 'schizophrenia'. As the epigraph indicates, there is a provocative disquiet that has to be coped with. The way professional carers, the staff of a psychiatric service, struggle to cope with the distress of the extreme suffering of people with schizophrenia is complex and has effects on the organisation, and indeed reflexively back on those who are cared for. I shall indicate why perhaps diagnostic psychiatry associated particularly with Kraepelin's seminal work in the nineteenth century may have support from the emotional reactions of staff, as well as the evident benefits of diagnostic categorising. Such an emotional commitment can have as it were its own side effects. The claim is that the condition of schizophrenia is not merely a loss of the mind but an intense emotional experience that overwhelms the person, and by contact threatens the stability of carers.

The impact of persons with schizophrenia

It is a matter of common observation that patients with schizophrenia make an impact on those who meet them. The result is that people can often pull away from the patient. This is true of visitors, of families who in the end want their relative removed to a psychiatric service, and also the team of professional caregivers. This appears a tragic situation, for the loved ones who are deeply involved in the condition of the patient, as well as the patient himself or herself, who is stripped of his customary support from familiar people. But it is not only friends, relatives and staff who push the patient away and may reduce him or her to a non-personal status; the patient can depersonalise themselves. One of the core problems experienced by people with schizophrenia is that they suffer an intense anxiety about their own identity, existence even. Processes of identification can therefore be very abnormal and result in greater anxieties about their 'self'. Hence the result is an unintended collusion between the tendency to depersonalise patients and a core problem of the condition itself (Hinshelwood, 1999). At the same time, the common impulse is to give succour to those in distress, an impulse that has usually taken carers into their chosen business (Roberts, 1994).

The problem for psychiatric staff to stay in contact with the humanity of the psychotic patient was recognised by the Chestnut Lodge group.

Freda Fromm-Reichmann, developing the ideas of Harry Stack Sullivan, said:

> The schizophrenic patient and the therapist are people living in different worlds and on different levels of personal development with different means of expressing and of orienting themselves. We know little about the language of the unconscious of the schizophrenic, and our access to it is blocked by the very process of our own adjustment to a world the schizophrenic has relinquished. So we should not be surprised that errors and misunderstandings occur when we undertake to communicate and strive for a rapport with him.
>
> (Fromm-Reichmann, 1939, p. 416)

Fromm-Reichmann then counselled that the psychiatric caregiver has to conduct an extremely difficult act of entering this completely foreign world. We know it is possible to do that with training and support. However, it is an arduous task and, unfortunately, she states there is not much tolerance in the patient for mistakes.

Staff are subjected to a very difficult task of finding the meaning in the patient's experience, when the patient himself has little sense of himself or of it being his experience. Moreover, the origins of the staff experience are their own way of relating to the patient, which can lead staff unconsciously to keep an emotional distance. Thus, there appears to be a collaboration between the patient and all those around him to demolish his existence as a human being. It is no surprise that psychiatric teams find it easier to take a neutral scientific attitude to their patients (as I have shown, Hinshelwood, 1999) which leads to both the patient and the team being stuck in a set of mutual attitudes, resulting in chronicity.

It is important to understand that these processes described here are not intended consciously, and being unconscious are not observed. This creates a lot of difficulty – and indeed neglect of this level of interaction in a psychiatric service. It is all the more reason for studying them, and making constant attempts to find ways of doing something about them.

Psychiatric culture

Bob Barratt (1996), an Australian psychiatrist, made observations of the standard processes that occurred in a psychiatric team dealing with psychiatric patients. Like an anthropologist, he carefully described the psychiatric setting and concluded that there were four steps in the typical course of a patient through the psychiatric unit:

1 At first, the patient is perceived (and dealt with) as an object, one who does not live in the world of ordinary meanings.

2 Then, he is dismantled into a set of symptoms and pathologies that can be recorded objectively.
3 This is followed by a reconstruction as a 'worked-up' case, in which the patient's various 'objective' signs and symptoms are combined into a picture which is meaningful psychiatrically; he has a diagnosis, a set of treatment interventions and a prognosis about his future.
4 Only then can another piece of work start. Having been through the process as an object of scientific study and record, the patient needs to be reinvested with subjectivity as a person again. This fourth step is interestingly described by Barratt as involving the reactions of the professionals, that is, their subjectivity. Assuming that, the patient is sufficiently recognised as a set of parts.[2] The attempt to restore those parts to a whole can only be partly successful – and its partial nature needs much more recognition.

This final step is important. It requires the patient to be restored as an agent with volition – and his volition requires moral evaluation from us. In other words, his subjectivity is confirmed by our moral evaluation of his volition. We hold patients responsible for how they are and what they do. In other words there must be an engagement again with him in a world of meaningful intentions and actions. Thus, the patient is returned to being a person, and rescued from the category of a 'case'.

However, professionals normally avoid moral judgements about their patients, but in doing so they inevitably denude patients of a personhood. Their behaviour and symptoms are believed to be 'caused' by the illness, and thus they deny the patient his own volition and agency. The moral human being is accredited with a responsibility for his actions and his states of being. The 'schizophrenic' is absolved of this, and thus of his essential humanity, with which he, the patient, appears willing to collude. The task of the psychiatric team should be to restore his human and responsible nature. Central to the restoration of responsibility and human agency is the notion of a meaning and intention to those actions, rather than merely a cause – in the case of schizophrenia a pathological cause. The essential impact of schizophrenia is the apparent meaninglessness of the person's behaviour and utterances. They are so difficult to understand, and distant from all that is human. And that incomprehensibility is shared by the patient; without his proper sense of identity, his experiences and behaviour are incomprehensible too. Where we cannot find meaning we attribute madness and the loss of what is

2 It is of course interesting that this dismembering process, conducted in a conscious scientific way, parallels the unconscious institutional process. The patient comes apart psychically through projection with various 'bits' lodged in separate caregivers.

human.[3] This confrontation with the apparent meaninglessness is the especial problem for psychiatric teams. And that is what we the caregivers need particular support to withstand. We need to know, to make sense, to give ourselves meaningful explanations. And often that neediness gets in the way of a really open curiosity.

Organisational reactions

What then happens? Our reactions are to keep us away from these feelings – that is, an emotional distancing of some kind. Perhaps we especially flee from meaninglessness. Such pressures in common lead to the unconscious co-ordination of the members of an organisation, or its subgroups. All individual members of the working team suffer similar anxiety, therefore they tend to evade the experience in similar ways. I'll mention a number of ways in which the team members can collectively help themselves.

Ideology

One reaction to meaninglessness is a demand for certainty. It is a desperate need to *know*. In place of the incomprehensible an ideology is substituted.[4] Kraepelin was one of the first of those who developed an approach that now looks like an ideology. It was a pattern of thinking that was applied across the board. The correct ideological attitude was that you must look for signs and symptoms in a dispassionate and emotionally neutral way. This approach was the scientific ideal of the nineteenth century when Kraepelin was working (Kraepelin, 1919). It has served very well, in many ways. We should not complain about diagnostic psychiatry; however it is ideological in the sense that other people with a different point of view are devalued and excluded. There is a need to say 'This is the *right* way to practice psychiatry.' Not all staff will agree, and sometimes patients will not agree. For instance, staff with jobs that are related to a psychotherapeutic approach may criticise the emotional distance of scientific psychiatry, and can develop an ideology

3 There is a valid debate about what has happened to meaning in the mind of patients. It appears on the surface frequently to abandon him or her. The various possible positions are that: (a) meaning does not exist in his utterances and behaviour; (b) meaning does exist but is repressed or concealed in some way which needs to be discovered; or (c) meaning has been actively destroyed. Which of these conceptions is the valid one (or which is valid in any specific case) is not germane to the argument here, which rests on the confounding experience of meaninglessness which disquiets anyone meeting a person with schizophrenia.

4 In the practice of clinical psychoanalysis, Britton and Streiner (1994) have described the need to clutch at an idea, which thereby becomes over-valued, instead of waiting with evenly hovering attention, as Freud described that state of mind without certainty as yet, until a more synthetic idea emerges, the selected fact.

of their own – with the core of it being the same *need to know* the right answer to psychosis, but in that case, the *right* way is to give importance to relating to the patients, however difficult, and meaning must be found in their experiences. Both contesting points of view derive from a common need to know and a strategy to protect against the potential feeling of meaninglessness.

A great deal of benefit does come from knowing, but a great deal is closed off by the *need to* know.[5] If we cling to the 'right' idea, it leads to being closed to other points of view, and therefore fraught relations and potential friction with each other. Of course this is not everywhere in psychiatry but there is often a tendency for different groups of staff and different disciplines to have mutual antipathies to each other. It is legendary for multidisciplinary meetings to become multidisciplinary fragmentation. Seamless inter-agency working is often demanded, but where people have to be exhorted to work that way, it usually signals some ideological intrusion and friction. Ideology can therefore give everyone a sense of certainty and knowing. It is both helpful in the job, but can also distort judgements and work relations.

Stereotyped patients

Another organisational reaction is that the team will deny the feelings of helplessness and despair that come from incomprehension and locate those feelings in their patients – and only in the patients. The staff are then caught in a rigid perception of themselves and of their patients:

> Only roles of health or illness are on offer; staff to be only healthy, knowledgeable, kind, powerful and active, and patients to be only ill, suffering, ignorant, passive, obedient and grateful. In most hospitals staff are there because they seek to care for others less able than themselves, while the patients hope to find others *more* able than themselves. The helpful and the helpless meet and put pressures on each other to act not only in realistic, but also fantastic collusion . . . [The] helpful will unconsciously *require* others to be helpless while the helpless will *require* others to be helpful. Staff and patients are thus inevitably to some extent creatures of each other.
>
> (Main, 1975, p. 61)

5 We can also note that our patients give themselves a constructed kind of meaning which replaces the vast gaps they have in understanding themselves, others and the world in general. This reconstructive effort on the part of the patient gives rise to the hallucinations and delusions. This is the radical insight that Freud tried to communicate to psychiatry – the delusions and the hallucinations are not the illness, they are the attempts at self-recovery; the actual illness is the preceding loss of meaning in everything, which renders the world as if it is dead or destroyed in some catastrophe.

Scapegoating

Sometimes this process of stereotyping can be focused down on to one patient who is elected into a position to carry all the hopelessness. He is 'scapegoated'. Then, he usually gets worse clinically – and that confirms the way the staff have decided to see him – a hopeless case. Often the end result is that he is moved out of the unit – i.e. the 'helplessness' is moved out. Sometimes, however, a member of staff is scapegoated – he is seen as the problem that the staff have, and everything will be better when he leaves.

Depersonalisation

The subhuman depersonalisation of patients has been described above. Having identified patients as the location of madness and helplessness, there is then a move away from empathy into the experience of staff as effective and sane. Anxiety about madness is very corrosive to the staff's ability to continue with sympathy and understanding. The distance to which the staff retreat can then be institutionalised by a systematic process of turning the work into a set of routines – one could say meaningless routines.[6]

Splitting and fragmentation

Alternatively the staff team can collectively change their direction of interest. Instead of feeling hopeless about their patients, a new attitude grows up that the patients could be helped but there are not enough resources in the team. The problem is believed to be the authorities or managers who keep them so short of staff, of training, of money and so on. They feel solidarity amongst themselves, but they feel as if under siege by their employers who don't understand them, or who are stupid, or who may be deliberately malign. The team can feel happy together, and maybe even with their patients, so long as they have their own managers as an enemy they must fight.

Related to this is a process of division within the team itself. Because each person absorbs the feeling of being hopeless from the patients, they can then export that feeling into others in the team. It is not just a division between managers and clinicians, but some groups of colleague clinicians become the hopeless ones; and 'my' group is not hopeless. It suddenly becomes 'us' and 'them' amongst the staff who once worked together to support each other. This may lead to a lot of mutual denigration of each other. Often this is not openly expressed. So nobody can really get a proper picture of who is doing good work and who is not. Realistic perceptions and mutual support are lost. The team loses its coherence and becomes fragmented. In this process different

6 This is similar to the depersonalisation described in Menzies' (1959) study of the practices of a nursing service.

teams can get into mutual denigration of each other: the domiciliary team, the day hospital, the inpatient ward, etc. Then the service itself becomes fragmented. Such a division amongst the staff is augmented by the ideological division. Each pushes the other away, emotionally and ideologically as we touched on with Kraepelin's 'scientific' psychiatry and psychotherapists.

This account (incomplete no doubt) aims to emphasise the various strategies that staff need for coping with the impact of feelings arising in the work with patients suffering from schizophrenia.

Community psychiatry

The long history of crisis intervention and outreach work goes back (in modern times) to the 1950s (Jones, 1968; Scott, 1973), and was part of the social psychiatry movement in the post-war period. The increasing impetus for care in the community certainly abolished the large mental hospitals with their institutionalised social pathology described above. However without learning the lesson of their debility has risked a comparable proliferation of similar organisational pathologies in the community (Hinshelwood, 2010).

The dynamics of fragmentation in which different subgroups and units within the service have pulled away from each other due to unconscious inter-group projections has had an unfortunate and ill-understood impact on units serving the community. The move from institutional psychiatry to community psychiatry has added to this unconscious fragmenting process a structuring of the service which can give a physical form to the fragmentation. Many units, and even individuals, are actually geographically separated from each other. Where there are little or even no face-to-face contacts with each other the projective systems are freer to proliferate mutual lack of respect without the restraints of the reality of actual colleagueship.

These effects have not of course gone unnoticed and have mostly been countered by exhortation to better multidisciplinary and seamless working together. Research into the effects of these troubles is mixed (Atwell and Caldwell, 2002). Good team working does improve performance (Whyte and Brooker, 2001) and reduce burn-out (e.g. Hills *et al.*, 2000); but closer working can also provoke more conflict (Jones, 2006). Exhortation has not on the whole been accompanied by analysis of why some teams work better than others; the unconscious dynamic influences have been especially ignored.

The idea that people who are particularly stressed might have less good relations with colleagues is not in itself counter-intuitive, and could seem like commonsense. It is however difficult to understand that this is at an unconscious level and can become a collective organisational problem. It points specifically to a need to focus more directly on the kind of stress that is generally experienced in our work, and some thought about how to contain it better before it gets to the level of unconscious defensiveness in the individuals, and certainly before it becomes an institutionalised problem within the culture of the whole service.

Social defence system

When tension and stress impact on the staff as a general outcome of the work, disorders of the whole organisational system may result. Those distortions of the system have the function of protecting each member of the staff group from some of the stress of the work. This is known as a 'social defence system' described by Jaques (1990) who referred to 'how much institutions are used by their individual members to reinforce mechanisms of defence against anxiety' (Jaques, 1953/1990, p. 420). He also said:

> Individuals may put their internal conflicts into persons in the external world, unconsciously follow the course of the conflict by means of projective identification . . . and re-internalise the course and outcome of the externally perceived conflict by means of introjective identification.
> (Jaques, 1990, pp. 496–497)

Thus the internal conflicts become external relations; and back again. Take the instance when one group identifies another as the hopeless ones; this relieves the members of their sense of failure. This first group no longer feels hopeless. The group attitudes have taken over a function which supports the individuals' defence mechanisms. Collective defences grow up unwittingly and unconsciously, and this phenomenon was described vividly by Menzies (1959) in her classical account of a nursing service in a general hospital.[7] Similarly defences aimed at relieving the despair of the work with psychotic patients, for example, the group adoption of an ideology, protect the members psychologically against the stress of meaninglessness. The model of the social defence system gives us an idea of processes that can cause the observed depersonalisation, lifelessness and over-control of large mental health institutions – just those characteristics which led them to be closed down. It can also account for the strong adherence to a scientific attitude in psychiatry which relies on an objective approach that eschews personal or subjective influences, thus engendering suspicion of knowledge based on empathic relating, attempts to convert intersubjective impressions to quantitative scales, and maybe funded by pharmaceutical companies with an interest in treating the biological substrate of the mind rather than experience itself. Such a privileging of objectivity is understandable, but has its side effects, described above as an unhappy collusion that reinforces one of the most torturing of the experiences of patients.

7 See also Hinshelwood and Skogstad (2000) for several cases of mental healthcare units.

Secondary anxiety

This conceptual model relies on the psychoanalytic notion of unconscious anxiety and defence can be applied at the social level where the *collective* defensiveness relieves the *individual's* anxiety at work. However, the effect of social defensiveness may be double-edged. That is, it protects individuals against their initial anxieties, but it may also have the effect of enhancing other anxieties. For instance, as described when a group of staff adopts an ideology based on an exclusively pharmacological model and holds it tenaciously, it alienates other groups of staff who have different views, e.g. supporting the idea of a psychological relationship with the patient. Then each group benefits from an ideological certainty, but at the same time is undermined by mutual denigration between the groups. Communication problems arise and become endemic so that the two groups can no longer work together properly. This enhances the overall sense of failure in the system as the staff feel they no longer do a good job. The social defence system adds another problem to the initial stress of the work – instead of the stress of meaninglessness, a working against each other develops as well.

Such a secondary stress will enhance the original sense of failure and can affect the whole team, resulting in the various familiar effects of demoralisation such as high rates of sick leave, absenteeism and turnover of persons in the team. When all those things happen, the team feels unstable and unsupportive, the individuals feel less secure and morale falls even lower. A disastrous spiral, or vicious circle, takes place. Thus the effect of the collective defences can in the end contribute to additional excessive stress.

One of the prevailing problems in the psychiatric services is that different groups and teams operate unconsciously in different ways. They have different defensive strategies. For instance, the nurses, as exemplified in Menzies' (1959) study, tend to depersonalise patients so that they are not affected by their patients' suffering. At the same time, doctors have a different strategy. They may relate more, with their 'bedside manner', but have the opportunity to leave the patient and attend to another one, to the telephone or to some emergency elsewhere in the hospital. They can leave the ward to go to their outpatients, and so on. These strategies of moving away in a more physical sense have the same defensiveness as the nurses' emotional distance. Although the doctors do indeed have to move from one thing to another, there is an important unconscious effect of that – to keep the doctor distant from the stress of being with any patient for too long.

Management anxiety

I should like now to turn briefly to stresses which affect (and have to be coped with by) the managers of a service with such stressed clinical staff. In addition to the different kinds of collective defences in the various subgroups in the service, there are different kinds of anxiety for different groups. With these various phenomena occurring at the team level, the quality of the service must get worse. Changing staff, high levels of absence and temporary staff, scapegoating of patients and staff, and splits within and between teams must all have a very bad effect on the work done. Although this has been made the responsibility of the management of health services, they are not really in a position to deal with these unconscious processes. As a response to the manifest problems, there have been constant attempts to improve NHS management over the last 20 years, in all branches including the psychiatric services. In addition, in mental health there has been a move from large hospitals containing thousands of chronic patients to community care. The problems have not gone away, and if anything they have simply got worse.

In fact, unintentionally the management changes have given a different pattern to the anxieties but not contained them. The NHS was reorganised to resemble a market system, in order to create a sense of competition, through the stimulus that comes from anxiety about survival (Hinshelwood, 1994).[8] Unfortunately, adding a new anxiety – the business management anxiety of competition and survival – appears to have the opposite effect to that intended; in the last 15 years, with increases in the usual indicators – increased turnover of staff, increased absenteeism and sick leave, and a consequent drop in moral and constructive teamwork.

Management 'survival anxiety' supervenes on top of clinical anxiety. Managers exist in a marketplace in which the fittest survive – poorly performing enterprises die. This is a very explicit culture, but it has entered the health services where another very explicit culture exists – that those who are ailing should not die but should be brought back to health. Assumptions and attitudes in the two cultures are remarkably contrasting and this sets the two groups apart as the assumptions underlying their two ways of thinking conflict. There is a culture clash.

However, managers are also somewhat lost in a highly professionalised service, which they understand little of, and are often especially perplexed by the levels of stress and despair they find before adding their own. They are required to manage that distress without understanding it; indeed one might say that the stress of the meaninglessness is meaningless to managers.

Managerial defences

Business management anxiety about survival can also be dealt with by its own typical social defence system. That is, managers may as a group develop

8 Although it remained a public service the various hospitals and other parts of the service had to compete for work, and received budgets according to the amount of work they attracted. This ensured that there was a competition where there had been none before, and indeed a new anxiety where there had been none before. This anxiety led to pressures on the organisation to change in certain ways, rather as the clinical anxiety had.

collective forms of managing which are aimed at protecting them from their stresses, and, as in the clinical field, this risks introducing maladaptive practices. Managers who have no intimate involvement with the provision of healthcare suddenly have responsibility for all clinical services. They have responsibility without control, and they tend to deal with this stress in ways characteristic of bureaucracies. One of the attitudes to help managers deal with their insecurity is: If we know everything that goes on, then we are in charge of what goes on. Much activity is then spent on meetings and papers on any and all topics. But more significantly, as Weber once remarked, the language of bureaucracy is statistics. So invariably, managerial practice is established on the basis that they will know everything if they have the numbers for everything. Statistical analysis is not always a bad strategy. However, when it is used as a means of dealing with managerial anxiety to control everything, including meaninglessness, it malfunctions. Statistics are generated on the basis that the more statistics managers have, the more they know about the business they control. In fact, no manager of any organisation can know everything about his organisation. The impossible assumption is implicit and probably unconscious. Managers set off on an endless task of trying to capture a view of everything. They manage their anxiety, rather than manage the organisation.

Numbers and frequencies can never tell you everything. Indeed they add to the clinical defensiveness against relating to patients as persons. Nevertheless, pressing in this direction affects clinical practice as well. Clinicians are resentfully drawn into helping to generate quantities of statistics intruding upon the work of clinicians. However it is not just time consuming, it intrudes in a different sense. The stresses of clinicians and managers are different, and the defensive forms of protection they each use to quell the stress are different:

(a) For clinicians, the stress is failure and meaninglessness, and the collective defences are concerned with emotional distancing (from patients and each other) and with ideologies of one form or another, especially by administering drugs in order to keep control.
(b) For managers, the stress is to be responsible for every risk outside their own actions, and the collective protection is to cultivate the feeling of being responsible, being in control, by collecting numbers.

These two forms of dealing with stress are both held with ideological conviction. However, clinicians and managers suffer quite different concerns and anxieties which lead to quite different collective defences that clash with each other.

Conclusions

I have tried to show that there is a particular stress that impacts upon us working in mental health, which derives specifically from the condition we call schizophrenia. It is a kind of transference, to which we react in a personal way – a form of countertransference. The problem is how can the sophisticated human brain cope with meaninglessness. It is a problem for those who suffer, as well as the family carers, and the professional caregivers. For patients, they break down; for staff, there is a low job satisfaction; and for organisations there is a tendency to fragment into isolated groupings. My chapter gives a brief glimpse of how I think we might try to reflect on how we are affected by the caregiving to the severely disturbed. If we are not aware of what impacts on us, our conscious efforts will be untargeted and ineffective. We need to be aware of the Kraepelin phenomenon – making a knowledge science out of incomprehension.

The particular work which mental health workers do is inherently stressful, and we cannot change that. However, we can know more about the resulting malfunctioning of the organisation itself, and how it comes about. Lack of such knowledge has led, in Britain at least, to increased levels of anxiety unwittingly emerging in clinical services. The link between individual work stress and organisational malfunctioning explains how many well-meaning changes are ineffective and may make things worse. This hypothesis indicates that we should pay attention to this level of the organisation. It is difficult to expect clinicians and managers alike to recognise the unconscious levels at which these processes operate. However, certain things are well known. It is common knowledge that although intensity of anxiety may stimulate performance up to a point, beyond that point further anxiety diminishes performance. That knowledge is available, even though it may not be understood how the effects occur. In Britain, the NHS was persuaded to abolish the large mental hospital system, but we did not examine exactly how those institutions got into their bad state by mid-twentieth century. Consequently we risk not learning the lessons of why psychiatric institutions can adopt maladaptive elements in their cultures (Hinshelwood, 2001). In addition we continue to let staff work in (unconscious) conditions which if conscious would surely contravene health and safety regulations.

Acknowledgements

I must acknowledge the many helpful suggests and comments by the editors, which have made this chapter much more like what I wanted to say.

References

Atwell, A. and Caldwell, K. (2002) Do multidisciplinary integrated care pathways improve interprofessional collaboration?, *Scandinavian Journal of Caring Sciences* 16: 360–367.

Barratt, R. (1996) *The Psychiatric Team and the Social Definition of Schizophrenia*, Cambridge: Cambridge University Press.

Berke, J. (1979) *I Haven't Had to Go Mad Here*, London: Penguin.
Britton, R. and Streiner, J. (1994) Interpretation: selected fact or overvalued idea?, *International Journal of Psychoanalysis* 75: 1069–1078.
Freud, S. (1928) quoted in J. Dupont (1988) Ferenczi's 'madness', *Contemporary Psychoanalysis* 24: 250–261.
Fromm-Reichmann, F. (1939) Transference problems in schizophrenics, *Psychoanalytic Quarterly* 8: 412–426.
Hills, B., Norman, I. and Forster, L. (2000) A study of burnout and multidisciplinary team-working amongst professional music therapists, *British Journal of Music Therapy* 14: 32–40.
Hinshelwood, R.D. (1994) The relevance of psychotherapy, *Psychoanalytic Psychotherapy* 8: 283–294.
Hinshelwood, R.D. (1999) The difficult patient: the role of 'scientific' psychiatry in understanding patients with chronic schizophrenia or severe personality disorder, *British Journal of Psychiatry* 174: 187–190.
Hinshelwood, R.D. (2001) *Thinking about Institutions*, London: Jessica Kingsley Publishers.
Hinshelwood, R.D. (2010) Organisational schism: looking after a psychiatric service, *Psychoanalytic Psychotherapy*, 24: 202–212.
Hinshelwood, R.D. and Skogstad, W. (eds) (2000) *Observing Organisations*, London: Routledge.
Jaques, E. (1953/1990) On the dynamics of social structure: a contribution to the psycho-analytical study of social phenomena deriving from the views of Melanie Klein, in E. Trist and H. Murray (eds) *The Social Engagement of Social Science: A Tavistock Anthology. Vol. 1: The Socio-Psychological Perspective*, London: Free Association Books.
Jones, A. (2006) Multidisciplinary team working: collaboration and conflict, *International Journal of Mental Health Nursing* 15: 19–28.
Jones, M. (1968) *Beyond the Therapeutic Community. Social Learning and Social Psychiatry*, New Haven, CT: Yale University Press.
Knowlson, J. (1996) *Damned to Fame: The Life of Samuel Beckett*, London: Bloomsbury.
Kraepelin, E. (1919) *Dementia Praecox and Paraphrenia*, Edinburgh: Livingstone.
Main, T. (1975) Some psychodynamics of large groups, in L. Kreeger (ed.) *The Large Group*, London: Constable, 57–86.
Menzies, I. (1959) A case study in the functioning of social systems as a defence against anxiety, *Human Relations* 13: 95–121.
Roberts, V. (1994) The self-appointed impossible task, in A. Obholzer and V.Z. Roberts (eds) *The Unconscious at Work: Individual and Organizational Stress in the Human Services*, London: Routledge.
Scott, R.D. (1973) A 24-hour family oriented psychiatric and *crisis* service, *Journal of Family Therapy* 3: 177–186.
Whyte, L. and Brooker, C. (2001) Working with a multidisciplinary team in secure psychiatric environments, *Journal of Psychosocial Nursing and Mental Health Services* 39: 26–34.

Chapter 8

Discrimination about psychosis

Stigma, emotions and changing emotional attitudes about psychosis to improve outcomes

Michelle Campbell, Rory Byrne and Anthony P. Morrison

Introduction

This chapter will focus on discrimination about psychosis and outline the importance of stigmatised representations of psychosis and their implications for public health and clinical services. Discrimination is a major concern for service users. It has a variety of negative consequences including the prevention of help seeking, increasing the duration of untreated psychosis (DUP), decreasing self-esteem and increasing social anxiety. The chapter will describe how community-based interventions focused on the reduction of discrimination can facilitate change in public attitudes, promoting early detection and intervention for individuals experiencing psychosis and maximising the likelihood of recovery. It will also describe individual and group interventions to address negative consequences of discrimination.

Stigma versus discrimination

The literature in this area largely focuses on stigma about psychosis. However, there are a growing number of authors making a point of referring to the process of 'discrimination'. It is argued that talking about stigma individualises social problems of discrimination and can inadvertently lead to the victim of such discrimination being blamed (Sayce, 1998; Bracken and Thomas, 2000; Perkins, 2001; Thornicroft *et al.*, 2007). For example, we don't talk about the stigma of being a female, we talk about sexism. Some authors use the term discrimination to refer specifically to behavioural responses related to stigmatising attitudes (Corrigan *et al.*, 2003). However, the term discrimination is used here to refer to a social process by which people think, feel and behave in a way which discredits those people who receive a label of psychosis.

Stigmatised representations

If we are to understand the existence of discrimination about psychosis it is important to look into its origins. Historically, Britain's mental health system involved people with mental health problems being 'treated' in asylums. Asylums were closed institutions, where people were isolated, locked away and removed from society. Arboleda-Florez (2005) suggests that the stigmatised messages which such an approach gave to the general public were:

- People who experience mental health problems like psychosis are fundamentally different to the 'ordinary' person and as such they must be treated in 'special' and 'separate' institutions.
- People who experience serious mental health problems are dangerous. Consequently they must reside in locked institutions to protect the public.

These negative messages about psychosis and mental ill health were compounded by the fact that deinstitutionalisation occurred without adequate support. People had spent many years of their lives in asylums and as a result were not prepared for life in the community and some people found it difficult to reintegrate. This situation is thought to have exacerbated the discriminatory attitudes which were already in existence.

Researchers have made attempts to disentangle the different factors that constitute prejudice about mental health problems like psychosis. For example, Rusch *et al.* (2005) highlight some of the core assumptions of stigmatising attitudes:

- *Fear and exclusion*: people with mental health problems like psychosis are feared and therefore should be kept out of communities.
- *Authoritarianism*: people diagnosed with psychosis are irresponsible so life decisions should be made by other people.
- *Benevolence*: people with serious mental health problems like psychosis are childlike and need to be cared for.

It has been suggested that discriminatory attitudes tend to worsen if the attribute instils fear and an element of danger (Arboleda-Florez, 2005), which is extremely relevant with regard to the depictions of psychosis. However, the facts about psychosis indicate that most people who receive this label are not dangerous (Steadman *et al.*, 1998). The increase in risk to others for those diagnosed with schizophrenia is tiny and such diagnoses do not predict dangerousness (BPS/DCP, 2000). Better predictors of violence are being male, being young, alcohol or drug abuse, social exclusion and having a past history of violence (Monahan and Steadman, 1994). Interestingly, these characteristics are not discriminated against by western society as a whole. Moreover, people who have psychotic experiences are at risk themselves as they are more likely than other people to be victims of violence. Despite these facts, mental health policy remains biased with regard to recommended approaches to risk assessment (Hewitt, 2008).

Discriminatory beliefs are maintained by numerous variables including the fact that up-to-date research regarding the nature, course and outcome of psychosis is not well publicised. For example, little news about recovery from psychosis has made its way into the mass media; rather, the general tone of articles has been found to be predominantly negative (Huang and Priebe, 2003). Consequently, the general public remain misinformed. Moreover, the mass media have been found to exacerbate discrimination about psychosis. Leudar and Thomas (2000) carried out a study of the content of stories relating to voice hearing in British national newspapers between the years 1993 and 1996. They qualitatively analysed 14 cases where individuals were reported to have committed a terrible deed as a result of hearing voices. They concluded that the tie between hearing voices, mental health problems and violence was a major recurrent theme.

More recently, Foster (2006) examined British national and local media regarding the proposed Mental Health Bill (2002). Interestingly, most articles presented the Mental Health Bill as unnecessarily repressive and were sympathetic towards mental health service clients (except the tabloids). However, when the implicit representations within the articles were considered, evidence of links between mental ill health and violence were found. Service users were also portrayed as being passive and pitiful. Foster (2006) concludes that the continued use of such images may arise from the fact that serious mental health problems have long been constructed as being other, or abnormal, and this is deeply engrained in British society.

There are various levels of discrimination that operate in society (Rusch *et al.*, 2005):

- *Public stigma*: this refers to the everyday life negative attitudes and discriminations that people with serious mental health problems encounter. Public stigma occurs within interpersonal interactions and in stereotyping images in the media.
- *Structural discrimination*: this is when private and public institutions intentionally or unintentionally restrict the opportunities of people with psychosis and other mental health problems.
- *Self stigma*: this is when the individual diagnosed with a serious mental health problem internalises the stigmatising attitudes and beliefs they have been exposed to, often causing them to feel shame, guilt and experience low self-esteem. Research has shown that self stigma and empowerment are on opposite poles on a continuum (Corrigan, 2002), which strongly suggests that discrimination is a form of social control.

Discrimination about mental health problems is a powerful force that we need to understand in order to change.

The extent of discrimination about serious mental health problems

Research from several countries indicates that a significant proportion of the general population hold discriminatory attitudes towards people with serious mental health problems (Crisp *et al.*, 2000), especially psychosis. The public have been found to most commonly regard individuals with psychosis as dangerous and unpredictable (Walker and Read, 2002) and these attitudes increase the desire for social distance.

A recent telephone survey carried out in Germany highlights the general public's views and knowledge about schizophrenia (Gaebel *et al.*, 2002). A large (n=7246) representative random sample was recruited and found the following:

- 76.5 per cent believed that people with schizophrenia often needed drugs to control their symptoms.
- A staggering 81.1 per cent believed most people would pass over a job application of a former patient.
- Nearly 100 per cent would reject a patient with schizophrenia if they offered to look after their child.
- On a more positive note, 80 per cent of the people interviewed believed that more should be done to increase acceptance of people with schizophrenia.

Helper or hindrance?

Discrimination and mental health professionals

People with psychosis and other mental health problems seek help from mental health professionals. Paradoxically, however, the research suggests that such professionals are often the source of discriminatory attitudes (Farina *et al.*, 1976). Lauber *et al.* (2004a) recruited a Swiss sample of psychiatrists (n=90) and individuals from the general population (n=786). It was found that these two groups did not differ in the extent to which they desired social distance from people with mental health problems, which suggests that the psychiatrists themselves held discriminatory attitudes about their own clients.

Families of individuals with psychiatric diagnoses have also identified the medical profession as a source of discrimination. Work carried out by Angermeyer *et al.* (2003) used focus groups with relatives of people diagnosed with schizophrenia. They found that relatives encounter structural discrimination and psychiatry was identified as an important source of negative attitudes. These relatives called for changes in training, mental health care, education and support for relatives. Gaebel *et al.* (2002) point out that negative attitudes and rejecting behaviour are the main obstacles to successful treatment; thus mental health professionals may be a barrier to their own clients' recovery.

Negative consequences of discrimination

There are countless reasons why discrimination about psychosis needs to be eliminated. Some of the main damaging consequences are highlighted below:

A barrier to recovery

It is well documented that discriminatory attitudes are a major barrier to recovery, especially in relation to psychosis (NICE, 2009). In fact, some service users describe discrimination as more long lasting and disabling than psychosis itself. Recovery often involves overcoming discrimination, but exposure to prejudice or keeping one's psychiatric history a secret are major stressors which can increase the likelihood of relapse (Birchwood *et al.*, 2000a).

Increased duration of untreated psychosis (DUP)

Fear of discrimination can mean that people may not accept or seek help from professionals until a very late stage (Bertolote and McGorry, 2005). In addition, if they are met with discriminatory attitudes when they do seek help this is likely to reduce the likelihood that they will seek help in the future, thus further compounding the vicious cycle of discrimination and ill health. A longer duration of untreated psychosis (DUP) is associated with worse symptoms and functioning and less chance of remission in people with first episode psychosis (Drake *et al.*, 2000). Thus, the negative consequences of such discrimination on people's lives are far reaching.

Reduced self-esteem

A recent study found that self-esteem explained 55 per cent of variance in subjective distress in 105 people with first episode psychosis (Vracotas *et al.*, 2007), so it is of clear importance to service users. Perceived stigma correlates with reduced self-esteem and life satisfaction (Gumley and MacBeth, 2006); thus, in order to improve people's quality of life, discrimination about psychosis needs to be tackled. When individuals who have experienced psychosis view this to be shameful and humiliating (i.e. they hold self-stigmatising attitudes) they are highly likely to experience post-psychotic depression (Birchwood *et al.*, 2000b). People do not develop their beliefs in a social vacuum and social stigma and discrimination are major contributors to self stigma and, therefore, poorer outcomes for people with psychosis.

Increased social anxiety

Many people who have been diagnosed with psychosis will at some point have experienced social anxiety. Such anxiety can be closely linked to the discriminatory attitudes and emotions that the public hold about the label 'psychosis'. For example, diagnosed individuals may avoid telling people about their diagnosis for fear of being criticised, rejected, attacked or humiliated. This can obviously have a detrimental impact upon people's close relationships as well as their confidence to relate to members of the public. When applying for jobs people who have received a diagnosis of psychosis may be understandably reluctant to admit to this in case their application is rejected as a result. People often feel they have to keep their diagnosis a secret but living with such a secret can be very stressful and distressing in itself. A recent study has shown that first episode patients who also have social anxiety experienced greater shame attached to their psychotic diagnosis and felt that the diagnosis placed them apart from others (Birchwood *et al.*, 2007).

Social exclusion

After an acute episode people with psychosis often find it very hard to return to work or study and have few opportunities to form new relationships (NICE, 2009). In the research literature the concept of desire for social distance is examined. Social distance refers to the level of 'willingness to engage in relationships of varying intimacy with a person' (Lauber *et al.*, 2004b, p. 265). Discriminatory attitudes and negative emotions about serious mental health problems predict an increase in one's desire for social distance. Thus, prejudice, discrimination, social exclusion and recovery are closely linked. Research certainly supports this link; for example, a recent international study of 729 patients meeting criteria for a diagnosis of schizophrenia (Thornicroft *et al.*, 2009) found that negative discrimination was experienced by 47 per cent in making or keeping friends, by 43 per cent from family members, by 29 per cent in finding a job, by 29 per cent in keeping a job, and by 27 per cent in intimate or sexual relationships.

Deprivation

The level of deprivation that people with psychosis endure is another formidable reason for tackling discrimination about psychosis effectively. This group represents a disproportionate amount of those who are homeless and poor. Consequently, they are more likely to be victimised, which includes exposure to sexual and/or physical assault (Read *et al.*, 2005). Such traumatic events serve to further increase an individual's vulnerability, stress and, therefore, the likelihood of a psychotic relapse.

Health inequalities

The wider consequences of discrimination about psychosis are that people who receive such a label do not receive the quality of physical health care to which other people have access (DRC, 2006). In addition, prejudice and discrimination have been major barriers to mental health reforms as restrictive methods of treatment are used even when advances in treatment have been made. Often the most effective treatments are not offered or provided due to a lack of resources and it is due to discrimination that money is not invested into mental health services or mental health research (Thornicroft, 2006).

Consequences for families

It is not only the individual diagnosed with psychosis who experiences discrimination. Their family may also experience similar negative attitudes and reactions when it is disclosed that a family member has psychosis. Neighbours may be reluctant to talk to them; friends of the family may decline their support and people (including mental health professionals) may criticise or blame the family for their relative's mental health problems. This has implications for such relationships as it places enormous stress on the family unit. Families and carers may not know where to turn to get support and help about their negative experiences and may feel they can only suffer in silence. Given that it is largely people with mental health problems and their families that suffer the burden of prejudice, in recent years advocacy groups have made beating discrimination a central priority (Stuart, 2005).

Changing stigma and discrimination

Public health interventions

One in four people will experience mental health problems at some time in their lives. However, discrimination about mental health problems detrimentally impacts upon people's ability to seek support for psychological problems when they arise. Information about mental health is essential if we are to promote good mental health in the public. Mental health promotion is an activity that aims to bring information about mental health to communities. In line with this, tackling stigma and discrimination has been made a priority for the NHS as acknowledged in mental health policy documents and guidance for the UK. In these documents mental health promotion has been put on the agenda in a variety of ways. For example, in the recent update of the NICE guidelines for schizophrenia it is highlighted that stigma must be tackled in order to enhance recovery for people with psychosis (NICE, 2009). This is supported by the mental health policy implementation guide (DH, 2001), which identifies the reduction of stigma as one of the objectives of early intervention teams for psychosis. Raising awareness of psychotic illness for professionals and lay people and active involvement in community-based programmes are central recommendations.

The fact that NHS policy and guidance reflect the importance of mental health promotion in combating discrimination about mental ill health is encouraging because this could lead to large-scale change. However, the mental health promotion campaign 'Time to Change' is ahead with regard to mobilising a large-scale national campaign. This campaign is run by charitable organisations and aims to tackle all three levels of stigma and discrimination (public, structural and self): by educating the public about mental health problems; by working with the law; by training professionals who work with people with mental health problems; and by working to support people with experience of mental ill health to challenge stigma and discrimination. This campaign is unusual because of its scope and resources, which reflects the positive steps forward that have been made with regard to tackling discrimination about psychosis and other mental health problems. They have recently been advertising their campaign on television and they have a dedicated website (www.time-to-change.org.uk/).

Community-based interventions

On a global scale the World Psychiatric Association (WPA) initiated a programme against stigma and discrimination because of schizophrenia in 1996. A *World Psychiatry* report (Stuart *et al.*, 2005) was published which presented research into stigma about schizophrenia from across the globe. They have a campaign website called 'Open the Doors' that has information about schizophrenia and campaign resources which are available in many different languages. The WPA is helping to encourage the reduction of discrimination worldwide.

There are a variety of anti-discrimination approaches that have been carried out in order to challenge negative views about psychosis. Historically these have mainly adopted a biogenetic view of psychosis. Biogenetic mental health promotion campaigns are based on the medical approach to 'mental illness'. Jorm (2000) is a well-known advocate of campaigns from this perspective. He talks about the importance of increasing the public's *health literacy*. He has outlined six important components of this:

1. The ability to recognise specific disorders or different types of psychological distress.
2. Knowledge and beliefs about different risk factors and causes.
3. Knowledge and beliefs about self-help interventions.
4. Knowledge and beliefs about professional help available.
5. Attitudes which facilitate recognition and appropriate help seeking.
6. Knowledge about how to seek mental health information.

However, there are many authors who have espoused grave concerns with the central message of biogenetic mental health promotion campaigns and the evidence base supports these concerns. Pure biogenetic campaigns are considered ineffective by many because populations have shown no improvement in their negative attitudes about mental health problems over time (Green *et al.*, 1987; Huxley, 1993). However, more concerning is that research in this area suggests that as biogenetic causal beliefs increase so do negative attitudes (Read and Law, 1999) and responses (Angermeyer and Matschinger, 2003).

Consequently, more effective alternatives have been sought. Psychosocial approaches aiming to reduce discrimination about psychosis have been explored. The findings from these studies are encouraging. There is strong evidence to suggest that viewing psychiatric symptoms as understandable reactions to life events can reduce negative attitudes, fear, distance and discrimination (Read *et al.*, 2005). A psychosocial anti-discrimination workshop targeting teenagers that has been found to be effective is reported by Pinfold *et al.* (2003). They carried out this workshop with 472 year ten secondary school pupils where two 1-hour educational interventions were delivered. Questionnaires measuring negative attitudes and knowledge about mental health problems were administered. Data was gathered before the intervention, immediately after the intervention and at six months follow-up. It was found that the workshop had a small but positive effect on the students' views of mental health problems and the 'them and us' phenomenon. However, the study was limited by the fact that no control data was gathered. Those students that learnt most from the workshops were female or knew someone with a mental health problem.

In a more recent study the same research group reported the impact of two school-based anti-stigma programmes (one in the UK, five schools, and one in Canada, two schools) involving a brief educational intervention (Pinfold *et al.*, 2005). The programmes aimed to do the following:

- provide basic information about mental health problems;
- tackle stigma and discrimination;
- deliver clear normalising messages that are relevant to young people.

Group exercises, discussions and short talks were employed. In the UK the programmes placed an emphasis on schizophrenia whereas in Canada the emphasis was on mental health. Questionnaires were administered that examined factual recall, self-reported attitude change, changes in feelings toward the stigmatised group and social distance. Improvements were found in factual recall, negative attitudes and the desire for social distance. The findings of this research indicated that discrimination can be favourably influenced by short awareness-raising campaigns, but if real progress is to be made mental health awareness should have a place in the school curriculum.

Similar conclusions were drawn from a large and robust study carried out in Germany (Schulze *et al.*, 2003). This was a weeklong anti-discrimination workshop which involved ninety 14 to 18 year olds and a control group (n=60). Contact with someone with a diagnosis of schizophrenia was central to the campaign. A questionnaire measuring attitudes and behavioural intentions towards people with serious mental health problems was administered before and after the intervention and at one month follow-up. It was found that the workshop led to a reduction in negative stereotypes about people with mental health problems and this effect remained at the one month follow-up. The authors concluded their report by suggesting that discrimination regarding schizophrenia is susceptible to change and anti-discrimination approaches at a school level could be a promising way forward to prevent negative stereotypes from being reinforced. However, like Pinfold *et al.* (2003) they believe that in the long term continued exposure to such anti-discrimination information is crucial and should be included as a regular slot on the school curriculum.

Therefore, psychosocial anti-discrimination campaigns have produced some positive results with regard to the reduction of stigma and discrimination about psychosis. However, Link and Phelan (2001) point out that if anti-discrimination efforts are to be effective they must be multifaceted and multilevel. At present psychosocial campaigns have been operating at a single level (i.e. one target group with a time-limited programme). Thus, it seems that these approaches are heading in the right direction, but in order to tackle the roots of discrimination interventions will need to be directed at the various levels of society where prejudice operates. This will require changes to the national curriculum, to mental health services, to employers' approaches to recruitment, to the law, to the training of mental health professionals and to the approach to changing negative attitudes of the public. Psychosocial campaigns are part of a wider movement which will be necessary to combat fully discrimination about psychosis and other serious mental health problems.

The emphasis on providing psychosocial explanations for mental health problems such as psychosis is also more consistent with the views held by service users themselves. For example, a study found that far more individuals with a diagnosis of schizophrenia endorsed social, supernatural and psychological explanations for their experiences than biological ones (McCabe and Priebe, 2004). Another recent study (Dudley *et al.*, 2009) found that people with psychosis attributed their experiences to a combination of factors that were predominantly psychosocial as opposed to biological (drug usage, traumatic experiences in adulthood, personal sensitivity and developmental vulnerabilities).

Health service interventions

The responsibility for delivering mental health promotion and reducing discrimination about psychosis has officially been laid at the door of early interventions services (DH, 2001). However, child and adolescent mental health services (CAMHS) also have a responsibility for delivering mental health promotion to young people (DH and DfES, 2007). Thus, it will be important for mental health professionals working in these services to find a way to deliver effective mental health promotion and anti-discrimination messages to the public. Target audiences for such anti-discrimination messages include schools, mental health professionals, workplaces, prisons and at risk groups. It is likely that these services will need to be supported in their endeavours by researchers in the area as well as by professionals working in voluntary sector services who have developed expertise in delivering mental health promotion to communities.

It is unclear what resources are available to mental health services in delivering mental health promotion. Therefore, the role of the mental health professionals may include applying for funding and resources, liaising with communities in the design and delivery of such interventions and communicating with communities and members of parliament (MPs) to lobby the government to drive forward changes. It may mean that services need to pool existing resources and share information, knowledge and skills.

Promoting early detection and intervention

There is evidence that people with psychosis do not access services due to fear of stigma and discrimination (Bertolote and McGorry, 2005; Thornicroft, 2007). This is certainly maintained by the unhelpful views and attitudes of mental health professionals (Gaebel *et al.*, 2002; Lauber *et al.*, 2004a, 2004b) and the media (Clement and Foster, 2008). Reducing this fear and discrimination through promotion of more positive images of psychosis, provision of normalising information and changing attitudes of professionals and the media would bring about more positive engagement with services and facilitate rapid access and appropriate help seeking (Bertolote and McGorry, 2005).

Individual interventions

Stigma and discrimination about psychosis is a pervasive problem. It is clear that treatments for psychosis must incorporate strategies which help clients to alleviate the negative consequences of the discrimination that they face. Cognitive behaviour therapy (CBT) has been identified as a recommended treatment for psychosis by the National Institute of Clinical Excellence (NICE). Ideally, any individual therapy for psychosis would also take into account the impact and consequences of stigma and discrimination. For example, within a contract of CBT for psychosis treatment interventions focusing on alleviating social anxiety and low self-esteem would usefully be incorporated in order to reduce self stigma.

Established treatments for social anxiety (e.g. Wells, 1994) can be incorporated into CBT for psychosis if social anxiety is on the person's problem list. Presenting a formulation of social anxiety which complements a formulation of a person's psychotic experiences will be important. These would form the rationale for suggesting that the individual be exposed to anxiety-provoking situations (including being videotaped in such situations) whilst dropping their safety behaviours and directing their attention externally. Socialising a client with experience of psychosis to this model may be more gradual given that the threat which they may perceive in social situations could be more severe. It would also be important to acknowledge and validate a client's experience of discrimination and to take some time to explore people's coping strategies for dealing with discrimination. However, the treatment approaches for social anxiety would nevertheless remain the same. The aim of these approaches would be to identify the processes that are leading a person to overestimate social threat but also to acknowledge that discrimination does exist and that clients have skills and abilities to deal with these situations effectively.

Similarly, when someone who experiences psychosis puts self-confidence or self-esteem on their problem list traditional treatment approaches to increase a person's self-esteem could be incorporated into their treatment package. For example, the CBT approaches for improving self-esteem outlined by Fennell (2009) could be adopted. It would be useful to acknowledge the impact that discrimination about psychosis has had upon a person's self-esteem via a self-stigmatising process. Normalising such self stigma in the face of discrimination (e.g. that experienced by women as a result of sexism and by older people as a result of ageism) could be highlighted along with the inaccuracy of the discriminatory beliefs held by society. Another approach to improving self-esteem is based on the idea of recognising that negative self-concept and unhelpful beliefs about self-worth is similar to self-prejudice and utilises discussion of prejudice and discrimination in order to help a person adopt a more accurate and positive belief (Padesky, 1993).

Group interventions

Group interventions are regularly offered by mental health services for people who experience psychosis. Often such groups take a CBT approach to recovery by focusing on enhancing effective coping strategies for psychotic experiences. Addressing discrimination and self-prejudice by allowing a space where discrimination can be explored would be a useful addition to group therapy. Sharing experiences of discrimination could be an especially powerful intervention as it would help people to become aware that they are not alone with their experiences, thus challenging beliefs that they are 'different' or 'abnormal'. Also, by hearing about others' negative experiences people may be able to appreciate the inaccuracy and injustice of such discrimination.

Enabling clients to access normalising information about psychosis would support this endeavour, as would an examination of the biased nature of prejudice and discrimination.

User involvement and reduction of discrimination

User involvement in mental health research and practice and reduction of discrimination

The increased involvement of service users in mental health research and practice is long overdue. It is now widely recommended (DH, 2005, 2006; BPS, NIMHE and CSIP, 2009) that service users routinely adopt such roles in mental health services. Meaningful inclusion of those with lived experience of psychosis as valued partners in the research process and in the provision of clinical services can offer significant improvements in the quality and effectiveness of professional interventions. For example, increased collaboration between professionals and service users can help to enhance professionals' understanding of them as equals and peers, and in this context, discriminatory beliefs held by professionals themselves can be challenged directly and disproved.

Importantly, user-collaborators' own self-stigmatising beliefs may be reduced with the improvements in self-esteem, self-worth and empowerment that can come with active involvement in challenging discrimination and in the improvement of mental health services. The inclusion of service user consultants in mental health services can also serve to illustrate to other service users the professional and social value of the life experiences that they themselves have had (challenging negative self-stigmatising beliefs). Indeed, direct personal contact with user researchers and consultants, and access to their own and others' stories of recovery 'can be inspiring and a great source of hope, particularly following an episode of psychosis' (Pitt *et al.*, 2007).

User-led interventions and reduction of discrimination in general population

An important way for user-researchers/consultants to reduce discrimination is through positive interpersonal contact ('contact interventions') with individuals and groups among the general population (e.g. Corrigan and Watson, 2007). It is notable that such contacts may be most effective when they occur in work or organisational settings (Pettigrew and Tropp, 2000). These circumstances provide service users with a forum to challenge discriminatory attitudes and emotions, and they provide others with the opportunity to realise that people explicitly labelled as having a mental health problem are just like them. An essential aspect of users' contribution involves presenting a testimonial of their experiences. Such personal stories are likely to increase understanding, compassion and empathy, while reducing discriminatory beliefs, feelings and behaviours. However, it must be acknowledged that being open about one's experiences in the face of potential discrimination can still be a very difficult task. It is also important to remember that mental health professionals who have used services themselves, and who are willing to disclose this, could contribute similarly to reductions of stigmatising beliefs among their colleagues, their clients and among the general public.

Formal involvement of users at executive levels of research conduct and service provision should aim to achieve a significant improvement in the imbalance of power that still defines relationships between mental health policymakers, professionals and users, and should directly challenge the generation and continuation of institutional/structural stigmatisation. Ideally, service users will adopt a lead role in the development and delivery of mental health interventions in the future. This should accelerate progress in the fight to eradicate discrimination about psychosis, and should contribute significantly to the kind of social liberation of mental health service users envisioned by, for example, Bentall (2003), Romme and Escher (1993) and Sayce (2000).

Conclusions

Discrimination about psychosis is a social problem which results in people who receive such a label being discredited and denigrated. Stigmatised representations strongly influence this process of discrimination. In Britain these representations have their origins in the country's mental health system and are maintained today by inaccurate and misleading portrayals of psychosis in the mass media. However, discrimination about psychosis is evident across the globe and worldwide interventions to tackle discrimination about psychosis (the WPA) have been mobilised.

There are myriad negative consequences of discrimination about psychosis, including increased DUP, significant deprivation and health inequalities which provide a powerful rationale for such discrimination to be eradicated. Changing stigma and discrimination about psychosis will require interventions to be targeted at all levels of society, including public health interventions (e.g. mental health promotion), community-based interventions (e.g. anti-discrimination campaigns) and health service interventions (including the promotion of early detection and intervention, and tailoring individual and group interventions to take the reality of discrimination about psychosis into account).

At the heart of all anti-discrimination interventions should be user involvement. User-collaborators will adopt a variety of roles including consultant, researcher and designer of interventions. User-collaborators' most valuable contributions may involve taking the lead in the design and delivery of mental health promotion and anti-discrimination campaigns. Not only is this recommended to improve the effectiveness of anti-discrimination campaigns, but it is also suggested as a direct challenge to the stigmatised representation of service users as passive and pitiful recipients of health care. Rather, users would be more accurately portrayed as activists campaigning for more compassion and a better general understanding of psychosis and other mental health problems.

References

Angermeyer, M.C. and Matschinger, H. (2003) The stigma of mental illness: effects of labelling on public attitudes towards people with mental disorder, *Acta Psychiatrica Scandinavica* 108: 304–309.

Angermeyer, M.C., Schulze, B. and Dietrich, S. (2003) Courtesy stigma: a focus group study of relatives of schizophrenia patients, *Social Psychiatry and Psychiatric Epidemiology* 38: 593–602.

Arboleda-Florez, J. (2005) Stigma and discrimination: an overview, *World Psychiatry* 4(Supplement 1): 8–10.

Bentall, R. (2003) *Madness Explained: Psychosis and Human Nature*, London: Allen Lane.

Bertolote, J. and McGorry, P. (2005) Early intervention and recovery for young people with early psychosis: consensus statement, *British Journal of Psychiatry* 187(48): 116–119.

Birchwood, M., Spencer, E. and McGovern, D. (2000a) Schizophrenia: early warning signs, *Advances in Psychiatric Treatment* 6: 93–101.

Birchwood, M., Iqbal, Z., Chadwick, P. and Trower, P. (2000b) Cognitive approach to depression and suicidal thinking in psychosis: 1. Ontogeny of post-psychotic depression, *British Journal of Psychiatry* 177: 516–521.

Birchwood, M., Trower, P., Brunet, K., Gilbert, P., Iqbal, Z. and Jackson, C. (2007) Social anxiety and the shame of psychosis: a study in first episode psychosis, *Behaviour Research and Therapy* 45: 1025–1037.

BPS/DCP (2000) *Recent Advances in Understanding Mental Illness and Psychotic Experiences*, Leicester: British Psychological Society.

BPS, NIMHE and CSIP (2009) *New Ways of Working for Applied Psychologists. Executive Summary: Good Practice Guide on the Contribution of Applied Psychologists to Improving Access for Psychological Therapies*, Leicester: British Psychological Society.

Bracken, P. and Thomas, P. (2000) Stigma or discrimination?, *Openmind* 105: 20.

Clement, S. and Foster, N. (2008) Newspaper reporting on schizophrenia: a content analysis of five national newspapers at two time points, *Schizophrenia Research* 98: 178–183.

Corrigan, P.W. (2002) Empowerment and serious mental illness: treatment partnerships and community opportunities, *Psychiatric Quarterly* 73: 217–228.

Corrigan, P.W. and Watson, A.C. (2007) The stigma of psychiatric disorders and gender, ethnicity, and education of the perceiver, *Community Mental Health Journal* 43(5): 439–458.

Corrigan, P.W., Markowitz, F.E., Watson, A.C., Rowan, D. and Kubiak, M.A. (2003) An attribution model of public discrimination towards persons with mental illness, *Journal of Health and Social Behaviour* 44: 162–179.

Crisp, A.H., Gelder, M.G., Rix, S., Meltzer, H.I. and Rowlands, O.J. (2000) Stigmatisation of people with mental illnesses, *British Journal of Psychiatry* 177: 4–7.

DH (2001) *The Mental Health Policy Implementation Guide*. Retrieved 16/4/2009 from www.dh.gov.uk/en/Publicationsandstatistics/Publications/PublicationsPolicyAndGuidance/DH_4009350.

DH (2005) *Creating a Patient-led NHS: Delivering the NHS Improvement Plan*. Retrieved 16/4/2009 from www.dh.gov.uk/en/Publicationsandstatistics/Publications/PublicationsPolicyAndGuidance/DH_4106506.

DH (2006) *Health Reform in England: Update and Commissioning Framework*. Retrieved 16/4/2009 from www.dh.gov.uk/en/Publicationsandstatistics/Publications/PublicationsPolicyAndGuidance/DH_4137226.

DH and DfES (2007) *National Service Framework for Children, Young People and Maternity Services: The Mental Health and Psychological Well-being of Children and Young People*. Retrieved 16/4/2009 from www.dh.gov.uk/en/Publicationsandstatistics/Publications/PublicationsPolicyAndGuidance/Browsable/DH_4094607.

DRC (2006) *Part 2 of the DRC's Formal Investigation Report: Report of the DRC Formal Inquiry Panel to the DRC's Formal Investigation into the Inequalities in Physical Health Experienced by People with Mental Health Problems and People with Learning Disabilities*, Manchester: Disability Rights Commission.

Drake, R., Hayley, C.J., Akhtar, S. and Lewis, S. (2000) Causes and consequences of duration of untreated psychosis in schizophrenia, *British Journal of Psychiatry* 177: 511–515.

Dudley, R., Siitarinen, J., James, I. and Dodgson, G. (2009) What do people with psychosis think caused their psychosis? A Q methodology study, *Behavioural and Cognitive Psychotherapy* 37: 11–24.

Farina, A., Hagelauer, H.D. and Holzberg, J.D. (1976) Influence of psychiatric history on physicians' response to a new patient, *Journal of Consulting and Clinical Psychology* 44: 499.

Fennell, M. (2009) *Overcoming Low Self-Esteem: A Self-Help Guide Using Cognitive Behavioural Techniques*, London: Robinson.

Foster, J.L.H. (2006) Media presentation of the Mental Health Bill and representations of mental health problems, *Journal of Community and Applied Social Psychology* 16: 285–300.

Gaebel, W., Baumann, A., Witte, A.M. and Zaeske, H. (2002) Public attitudes towards people with mental illness in six German cities: results of a public survey under special consideration of schizophrenia, *European Archives of Clinical Neuroscience* 252: 278–287.

Green, D.E., McCormick, I.A., Walkey, F.H. and Taylor, A.J.W. (1987) Community attitudes to mental illness in New Zealand twenty-two years on, *Social Science and Medicine* 24(5): 417–422.

Gumley, A.I. and MacBeth, A. (2006) A trauma based model of relapse in psychosis, in W. Larkin and A.P. Morrison (eds) *Trauma and Psychosis: New Directions for Theory and Therapy*, London: Routledge.

Hewitt, J.L. (2008) Dangerousness and mental health policy, *Journal of Psychiatric and Mental Health Nursing* 15: 186–194.

Huang, B. and Priebe, S. (2003) Media coverage of mental health care in the UK, USA and Australia, *Psychiatric Bulletin* 27: 331–333.

Huxley, P. (1993) Location and stigma: a survey of community attitudes to mental illness – Part 1. Enlightenment and stigma, *Journal of Mental Health* 2: 73–80.

Jorm, A.F. (2000) Mental health literacy, *British Journal of Psychiatry* 177: 396–401.

Lauber, C., Anthony, M., Ajdacic-Gross, V. and Rossler, W. (2004a) What about psychiatrists' attitudes to mentally ill people?, *European Psychiatry* 19: 423–427.

Lauber, C., Nordt, C., Falcato, L. and Rossler, W. (2004b) Factors influencing social distance toward people with mental illness, *Community Mental Health Journal* 40(3): 265–274.

Leudar, I. and Thomas, P. (2000) *Voices of Reason, Voices of Insanity: Studies of Verbal Hallucinations*, London: Routledge.

Link, B.G. and Phelan, J.C. (2001) Conceptualising stigma, *Annual Review of Sociology* 27: 363–385.

McCabe, R. and Priebe, S. (2004) Explanatory models of illness in schizophrenia: a comparison of four ethnic groups, *British Journal of Psychiatry* 185: 25–30.

Monahan, J. and Steadman, H.J. (1994) Towards a rejuvenation of risk assessment research, in J. Monahan and H.J. Steadman (eds) *Violence and Mental Disorder: Developments in Risk Assessment*, Chicago, IL: University of Chicago Press.

NICE (2009) *Schizophrenia: Core Interventions in the Treatment and Management of Schizophrenia in Adults in Primary Care and Secondary Care. Update.* Retrieved 16/4/2009 from http://www.nice.org.uk/Guidance/CG82.

Padesky, C.A. (1993) Schema as self-prejudice, *International Cognitive Therapy Newsletter* 5/6: 16–17.

Perkins, R. (2001) Stigma or discrimination?, *Openmind* 112: 6.

Pettigrew, T.F. and Tropp, L.R. (2000) Does intergroup contact reduce prejudice: recent meta-analytic findings, in S. Oskamp (ed.) *Reducing Prejudice and Discrimination*, Mahwah, NJ: Lawrence Erlbaum Associates, Inc.

Pinfold, V., Toulmin, H., Thornicroft, G., Huxley, P., Farmer, P. and Graham, T. (2003) Reducing psychiatric stigma and discrimination: evaluation of educational interventions in UK secondary schools, *British Journal of Psychiatry* 182: 342–346.

Pinfold, V., Stuart, H., Thornicroft, G. and Arboleda-Florez, J. (2005) Working with young people: the impact of mental health awareness programmes in schools in the UK and Canada, *World Psychiatry* 4(Supplement 1): 50–54.

Pitt, L., Kilbride, M., Nothard, S., Welford, M. and Morrison, A.P. (2007) Researching recovery from psychosis: a user-led project, *Psychiatric Bulletin* 31: 55–60.

Read, J. and Law, A. (1999) The relationship of causal belief and contact with users of mental health services to attitudes to the 'mentally ill', *International Journal of Social Psychiatry* 45(3): 216–229.

Read, J., van Os, J., Morrison, A.P. and Ross, C.A. (2005) Childhood trauma, psychosis and schizophrenia: a literature review with theoretical and clinical implications, *Acta Psychiatrica Scandinavica* 112(5): 319–345.

Romme, M. and Escher, S. (1993) *Accepting Voices*, London: Mind.

Rusch, N., Angermeyer, M.C. and Corrigan, P.W. (2005) Mental illness stigma: concepts, consequences, and initiatives to reduce stigma, *European Psychiatry* 20: 529–539.

Sayce, L. (1998) Stigma, discrimination and social exclusion: what's in a word?, *Journal of Mental Health* 7: 331–343.

Sayce, L. (2000) *From Psychiatric Patient to Citizen: Overcoming Discrimination and Social Exclusion*, London: Macmillan.

Schulze, B., Richter-Werling, M., Matschinger, H. and Angermeyer, M.C. (2003) Crazy? So what! Effects of a school project on students' attitudes towards people with schizophrenia, *Acta Psychiatrica Scandinavica* 107: 142–150.

Steadman, H.J., Mulvey, E.P., Monahan, J., Robbins, P.C., Appelbaum, P.S., Grisso, T., *et al.* (1998) Violence by people discharged from acute psychiatric inpatient facilities and by others in the same neighbourhoods, *Archives of General Psychiatry* 55(5): 393–401.

Stuart, H. (2005) Why stigma matters and why it should be beaten, *World Psychiatry* 4(Supplement 1): 6–7.

Stuart, H., Arboleda-Florez, J. and Sartorious, N. (2005) Stigma and mental disorders: international perspectives, *World Psychiatry* 4(1): 1–62.

Thornicroft, G. (2006) *Shunned: Discrimination Against People with Mental Illness*, Oxford: Oxford University Press.

Thornicroft, G. (2007) Most people with mental illness are not treated, *Lancet* 370: 807–808.

Thornicroft, G., Rose, D., Kassam, A. and Sartorius, N. (2007) Stigma: ignorance, prejudice or discrimination?, *British Journal of Psychiatry* 190: 192–193.

Thornicroft, G., Brohan, E., Rose, D., Sartorius, N. and Leese, M. (2009) Global pattern of experienced and anticipated discrimination against people with schizophrenia: a cross-sectional survey, *Lancet* 373: 408–415.

Vracotas, N., Schmitz, N., Joober, R. and Malla, A.K. (2007) Subjective distress in first-episode psychosis: role of symptoms and self-esteem, *Early Intervention in Psychiatry* 1: 251–258.

Walker, I. and Read, J. (2002) The differential effectiveness of psychosocial and biogenetic causal explanations in reducing negative attitudes toward 'mental illness', *Psychiatry* 65(4): 313–325.

Wells, A. (1994) *Cognitive Therapy of Anxiety Disorders: A Practice Manual and Conceptual Guide*, Chichester: Wiley.

Chapter 9

Towards a systemic understanding of family emotional atmosphere and outcome after psychosis

Frank R. Burbach

There is compelling evidence for the importance of family emotional atmosphere in determining the course of psychosis, but considerable debate about the theoretical underpinnings of research in this area, and their clinical implications.

The most influential body of literature derives from the research using the expressed emotion (EE) rating scales. This measure of emotional atmosphere has been used in a large number of research studies, including randomised controlled trials of family interventions, and has contributed to the widespread recognition of the need to involve relatives in mental health services and to offer formal family interventions. Unfortunately, the focus of the research effort on relapse has led to a widespread, oversimplified perception of expressed emotion as a unidirectional, binary concept.

Despite a number of useful reviews, casual browsing of the current EE literature can quickly lead to confusion, due to the range of research studies exploring different facets of EE and their relationship to other concepts. EE is increasingly recognised as reflecting interactions between the person with psychosis and their relative/caregiver, but relatively little use has been made of systemic theory to guide research in this area. However, two recent research foci – coping styles and appraisal processes – have bought EE research and systemic theory within touching distance. This chapter will focus on the more recent research, which could help to develop a systemic, and specifically cognitive-interactional, formulation of family emotional atmosphere and outcome after psychosis.

Expressed emotion – the original studies

The expressed emotion (EE) rating scales were developed in the course of three research projects in the 1950s and 1960s by George Brown and colleagues (1972) investigating family relationships associated with relapse.

The first study appeared to show that patients with schizophrenia were more likely to relapse if they returned to live with parents or wives, whereas those with other disorders appeared to do better on their return to live with the family. The second study found that ratings based on the relatives' comments effectively predicted deterioration in the patient's clinical state in the follow-up period, while ratings based on the patient did not. They also found that low face-to-face contact could be protective for those returning to 'highly emotionally-involved' homes. In the third study, a structured interview schedule, the Camberwell Family Interview (CFI), was used with parents while patients were still hospitalised, and was repeated nine months after discharge when 35 out of 101 people had relapsed. The audiotape of this interview was rated on five subscales (criticism, hostility, emotional overinvolvement (EOI), warmth and positive comments), taking into account both the content and tone of the comments.

In order to simplify the analysis, the three scales most clearly related to relapse (criticism, hostility, EOI) were combined into a single index of EE and relatives assigned to either a High-EE or Low-EE group. This combined index of EE gave a better prediction of relapse than any individual component: 58 per cent of patients returning to High-EE relatives relapsed, compared with 16 per cent discharged to Low-EE homes.

Warmth was also related to relapse, but had complex interrelationships with the other scales. Those rated low in warmth also tended to be highly critical, whereas those high in warmth tended to be associated with over-involvement. However, if relatives showed considerable warmth without criticism or overinvolvement, patients did very well (9 per cent relapse rate).

The findings of an independent, small-scale replication study (Vaughn and Leff, 1976) were remarkably consistent with the original study (Brown *et al.*, 1972), which allowed the results to be combined to explore the interaction between medication, the family environment, contact with relatives and relapse rates. While these findings suggested that either low face-to-face contact or regular maintenance on medication gives a measure of protection in a High-EE environment, the role of medication in Low-EE environments was unclear. However, the aggregate analysis of data from 25 studies by Bebbington and Kuipers (1994) indicated that medication reduces the relapse rate for those living with High-EE or Low-EE relatives (see Table 9.1). An additional analysis confirmed that high contact with a High-EE relative increases the risk of relapse but indicated that high contact with Low-EE families may be protective.

Current status of EE

The predictive validity of the expressed emotion index in a range of settings has been confirmed by numerous studies, with few negative results. Following their meta-analysis of 26 studies, Butzlaff and Hooley (1998) concluded that EE was now established as a robust predictor of schizophrenic relapse (High-EE relapse rate=65 per cent; Low-EE=35 per cent) and suggested that further replication studies were no longer required. Research has also

Table 9.1 Four characteristic response styles (Vaughn and Leff, 1981)

Low-EE relatives	*High-EE relatives*
1 Respect the patient's desire for social distance.	1 Are highly intrusive, 'making repeated attempts to establish contact or to offer unsolicited (and frequently critical) advice' (p. 43).
2 Are not overly anxious and able to exert a calming influence when family members are distressed.	2 Respond with anger and/or acute distress (which relatives recognised tended to upset the patient further).
3 Take the view that the patient is suffering from a legitimate illness.	3 Doubt that the patient is genuinely ill and blame them/hold them responsible for their difficulties.
4 Are tolerant of disturbed behaviour and long-term social impairment.	4 Are intolerant of symptom behaviours and low performance.

confirmed that EE is significantly associated with relapse in depression (with particular sensitivity to criticism by partners) and in a range of other mental health problems, including bipolar disorder, anorexia, post-traumatic stress disorder and childhood psychological disorders. Research is required in all of these areas to corroborate these findings (see Wearden *et al.*, 2000 for a review of EE research with both psychiatric and medical conditions).

Throughout the past four decades, EE has thus proved a popular research tool due to its predictive validity. However, researchers have also struggled to define its meaning and construct validity.

Construct validity

A key question has been the construct validity of the EE ratings. There was an assumption that the attitudes expressed by relatives reflected their behaviour towards the person with schizophrenia, but this was not confirmed until a Californian research team (Valone *et al.*, 1983) found that parents who expressed attitudes rated as High-EE were significantly more critical in face-to-face interactions with their disturbed, but non-psychotic adolescent children.

This research team has also conducted the first study supporting the construct validity of EE with people diagnosed with schizophrenia (Miklowitz *et al.*, 1984). EE was rated at the time of hospitalisation and followed with two family discussions approximately two weeks after discharge. These were rated on dimensions of affective style: critical statements (benign or harsh) and neutral-intrusive statements (implying that the parent has a special insight into their child's attitudes, ideas or emotions). This study confirmed that High-EE parents (n=34) made more negative affective statements than Low-EE parents (n=28) in the interaction task. When parents rated as highly critical were compared with those rated as highly emotionally over-involved (EOI), the former tended to make more critical comments (CC) during interactions, whereas the latter used more intrusive, invasive statements.

Using a more detailed family-interaction coding system Hahlweg *et al.* (1989) found that High-EE critical relatives were characterised by a negative interactional style – more negative non-verbal affect, criticism and negative solution proposals – than either Low-EE or High-EOI relatives when discussing an emotionally sensitive family problem with the patient. The latter groups also made more overtly positive and supportive comments than did the High-EE critical relatives.

So what is EE measuring?

Although the construct validity studies reviewed above confirm that the attitudes expressed by relatives do reflect their behaviour towards the person with schizophrenia, it still remains a challenge to describe what EE is measuring.

In a further analysis of their data, Vaughn and Leff (1981) have identified four characteristic attitudes and behaviours that tend to distinguish relatives who are highly critical or over-involved from those who are not (see Figure 9.1). Their content analysis indicated that High-EE relatives were significantly more likely to take an unsympathetic view of the illness, exert 'considerable pressure on the patient to behave as a normal individual might be expected to act' (p. 44), and drew attention to the centrality of illness appraisals.

A critique of EE

An originator of the field, Julian Leff (1989), has acknowledged that it was 'unfortunate that the general term Expressed Emotion was applied to (the) index' (p. 135) as it has led to assumptions that any emotional expression by a relative is harmful to the person with psychosis. Leff reviewed the psychophysiological evidence that Low-EE relatives may be 'providing active emotional support which enables the patients to habituate to an arousing situation' (p. 135). If the 'warmth' scale had not been excluded from the EE index, or other positive scales such as 'compassion' or 'tolerance' had been included, then the research effort may have had an equal emphasis on resilience or recovery. Unfortunately, the index focused research on the negative impact of relatives' attitudes to the person with psychosis.

This linear causal perspective on EE has predominated, despite Brown *et al.* (1972) recognising that EE reflects 'a quality of relationship with a particular person (the patient), not a general tendency to react to everyone in the same way' (p. 246). Unfortunately, relatively few studies have involved a two-way examination of this process within the particular relationships.

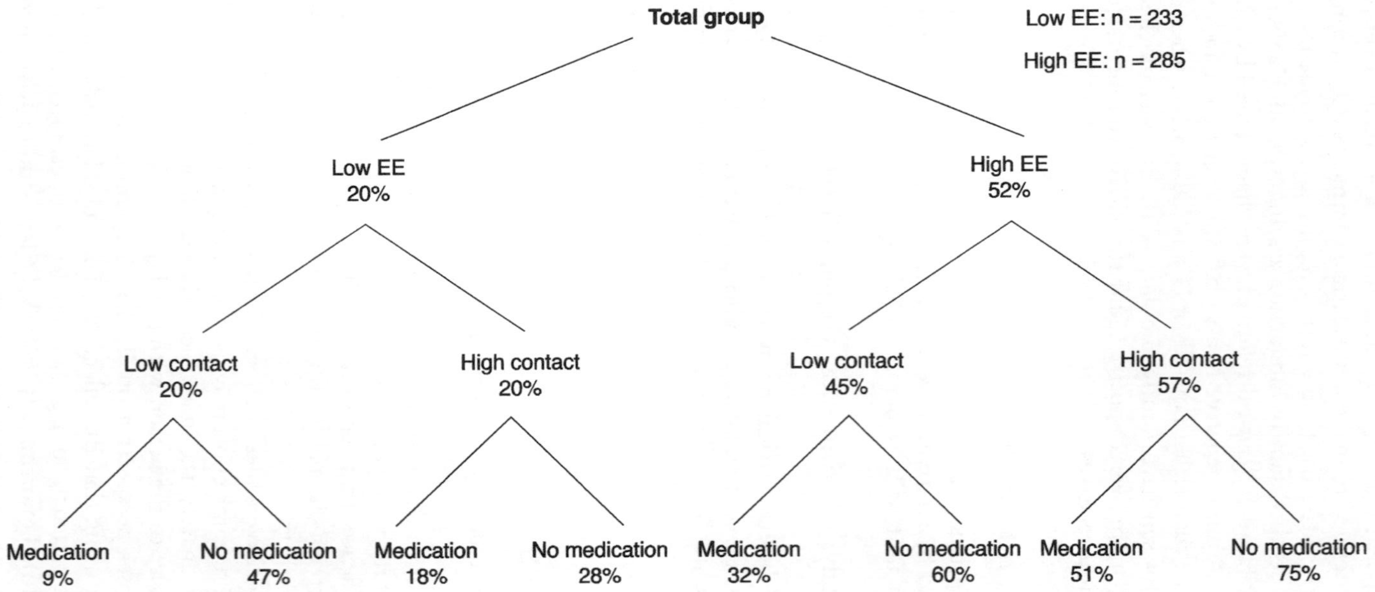

Figure 9.1 Percentage relapse according to EE, contact and medication status from Bebbington and Kuipers' (1994) aggregate analysis.

Furthermore, it has been a fairly recent development to view EE as a normal coping strategy and developmental process, rather than a pathological one. It is also unfortunate that the patient's construal of his or her parents remains under-researched, despite literature reviews recognising that the way 'High-EE is perceived by the patient, and how the stress is translated into florid symptoms' is a gap in our understanding (Kuipers and Bebbington, 1988, p. 905).

Studies involving direct observation of family interactions

The Californian researchers have studied the reciprocal influencing processes between parents and children with recent onset schizophrenia. Miklowitz *et al.* (1989) found that families rated as High-EE (critical) used many more harshly critical statements in direct interactions than those rated as critical initially, and later as Low-EE or emotionally over-involved. They also found that the patient's coping style was not related to their clinical attributes, but rather to the relatives' interactional affective style and their pattern of EE attitudes. Interactions involving consistently Low-EE relatives featured tolerant, low-key exchanges, with a low rate of criticism; neutral behaviour by relatives; and autonomous statements by patients. In contrast, consistently High-EE attitudes were associated with reciprocal levels of criticism by both parties.

Subsequent studies found that, when discussing emotionally loaded family problems, it made no difference whether the patient or parents instigated a negative sequence. High-EE families were characterised by patterns of 'attack–counterattack' (criticism followed by returned criticism) and 'attack–justify' (e.g. parent criticises, patient makes excuses). In other studies, the Californian group has shown that such patterns are apparent in verbal content and non-verbal behaviour and therefore conclude that these are transactional patterns that are 'reciprocal and systemic in nature, rather than linear and unidirectional, as was the original EE concept' (Strachan *et al.*, 1989, p. 180). In Rosenfarb *et al.*'s (1995) study High-EE relatives were more likely to respond critically to the first unusual thought verbalised by the patient; and this, in turn, evoked further unusual thoughts.

This work has resulted in the widespread acknowledgement that EE is best understood as an index of a transactional process. Tarrier (1991) concluded that these results 'argue against a trait model of EE, and support a conceptualisation of EE as representing coping and response styles that develop over time and interact with patients' behaviour' (p. 321). Hooley (1985) similarly concluded that 'EE is a complex measure reflecting the interaction between a patient and a relative at a particular point in time' (p. 137).

Studies of relatives' coping behaviours and attributional styles

Two particularly fruitful research avenues shed further light on aspects of the family atmosphere measured by the EE index – coping and attributions.

Greenley (1986) reanalysed Brown's original data set and found that families who expressed fear and anxiety about the patient were more likely to express high levels of criticism and overinvolvement, and that this behaviour changed depending on whether the family attributed the patient's behaviour to a 'real' illness or not. EE may thus be described as a coping behaviour and a form of social control. Hooley (1985) reached a similar conclusion from an attributions perspective: 'High-EE relatives may . . . be individuals who attempt to cope by trying to exert control over what may actually be uncontrollable behaviour in the patient' (p. 134).

Birchwood and Cochrane's (1990) study of the coping behaviours of family members found that 'coercion' was more commonly adopted when dealing with a relative with low social functioning. Another small study (Raune *et al.*, 2004) investigating carer appraisal in first episode psychosis found that even at this early stage 43 per cent of relatives had high levels of EE linked to increased levels of subjective burden, avoidant coping (disengagement and substance use) and perceived poor interpersonal functioning in patients. As a result, High-EE criticism or EOI have come to be conceptualised as forms of maladaptive coping. Furthermore, it is now clear that, despite any objective differences in symptom severity, High-EE and Low-EE relatives appear to differ in their beliefs about the individual with psychosis and the problem behaviours associated with their illness.

In their comprehensive review of the field, Barrowclough and Hooley (2003) reported that all studies to date confirmed that criticism and hostility in relatives reflected their underlying beliefs that the person could do more to control their symptoms and problems, and that their failure to do so was due to some specific quality (e.g. a habit or trait) that was unique to him or her.

It is interesting to note that, from an attributional perspective, high EOI relatives are very similar to relatives rated as Low-EE. There is a tendency for high EOI relatives to make even fewer blaming attributions than Low-EE relatives, and to make significantly more attributions implicating illness as the sole cause for the patient's problems.

Importantly, a few studies have also found that the more family members viewed ill relatives as having control over their symptoms and behaviour, the less likely they are to express warmth. Further research into the reflexive capacity of relatives and attributive processes related to sympathy and compassion may be theoretically and clinically important. Two other findings in this literature are interesting: (1) Hostile relatives identify *fewer* causal attributions (Brewin *et al.*, 1991), i.e. they simply blame the patient, which appears to indicate the importance of helping families to develop multifaceted causal explanations. (2) In High-EE dyads there was a greater discrepancy between the illness models of schizophrenia held by patients and relatives, with the relatives having a more negative model of illness than the patients (Lobban *et al.*, 2006). The authors note that this implies the need for a systemic approach, focusing on both the patients' and relatives' beliefs, and the discrepancies between them.

Patients' perceptions of their parents

Although largely ignored in the EE literature, there is some evidence of the effect of the perception of parents on the course of illness. Warner and Atkinson (1988), using the Parental Bonding Instrument (PBI), demonstrated that the manner in which patients remember their parents' care and protection in the first 16 years of life was associated with varying severity of illness. Those who perceived their parents positively and were in frequent contact with them experienced a better outcome. The opposite was true for those who perceived their parents negatively. Scott *et al.* (1993) used the Family Interpersonal Perception Test (FIPT) to simultaneously assess how family members see themselves and each other, and how they think family members see them. Parents' and patients' views of each other were more negative in those with worse outcome, but of particular significance was how patients expected their parents to see them. They concluded that this revealed 'patterns of interaction in which the patients' role in outcome is at least as important as that of the parents' (p. 62).

An interactional view of family emotional atmosphere

Any understanding of the family emotional climate and outcome after psychosis has to take into account the interactional processes partially measured by the unidirectional EE index. In addition, appraisals, affect and behaviour need to be considered. Unfortunately, many clinicians are still reliant on the original research manuals and are not aware of recent developments in the field. However, some therapists have overcome problems inherent in the earlier linear psycho-educational approaches by integrating systemic family therapy and psycho-educational family management (Burbach and Stanbridge, 1998, 2006; Meddings *et al.*, 2010), and have made particular use of circular questioning – therapeutic questions which reveal relationships between members of a family. Many contemporary systemic therapists also adopt constructivist or social constructionist approaches, exploring how people use language in a way that shapes and defines appraisals. There is a particular interest in the way in which family members both construe one another, and behave in a way which is coherent with that construction, and how the actions of each validate or invalidate the other's construction of their relationship.

These elegant approaches are therapeutically useful and compatible with the emerging literature on appraisals, interactions and family emotional atmosphere.

Although their classic cognitive-behavioural family interventions text (Barrowclough and Tarrier, 1997) has not been updated, Barrowclough and Lobban (2009) presented a format for the formulation of problem behaviours in the context of family interactions, reflecting the more recent research on appraisals and interactions. They describe their approach as a 'basic family CBT model' of 'linked vicious circles' with behaviours of one person triggering thoughts/beliefs, feelings and behaviours of another. Their joint formulation diagram mirrors the earlier work of Harry Procter (1985, 1987) who integrated George Kelly's personal construct therapy and systemic therapy. His bow-tie diagram and interview format link 'the individual processes of meaning making to the delicate social ecology of intimate personal relationships that sustain them' and is 'particularly useful as a means of clarifying complex interactive sequences in conflicted couples and families, and in suggesting a road map for intervention' (Neimeyer, 2009, p. 41). A simplification of this diagram is used in the 'cognitive-interactive approach' (Burbach, 2000) developed in the Family Interventions Service in Somerset. This 'cognitive-interactional' diagram can be used to illustrate the patterns of interaction commonly described in the EE literature (see Figure 9.2).

A complementary pattern of interaction is likely to become increasingly entrenched over time. The more frustrated, critical or intrusive the parent becomes, the more the young person feels overwhelmed and hopeless, and consequently does less and withdraws. Sustained or increasing inactivity and withdrawal strengthen the parents' belief that their child is lazy and results in increased attempts to control their behaviour through criticism or intrusiveness. In behavioural terms, these processes can be described as intermittent reinforcement of the parents' behaviour (e.g. the young person sometimes complies with demands) and negative reinforcement of the young adult's behaviour (e.g. withdrawal reduces exposure to parental criticism). In systemic terms, the family members could be described as being caught up in a pursuit–withdrawal cycle.

Further detailed research will be required to clarify the common interactional patterns underlying family emotional atmosphere and their relationship to outcome after psychosis, but the Californian group has clearly described how High-EE (critical) relatives tend to become locked into chains of negative interactions with their offspring with schizophrenia. Critical relatives display more negative verbal and non-verbal behaviour, and less positive verbal and non-verbal behaviour. The patients in these interactions are themselves more critical of their parents, use more justifications for their behaviour, express more disagreements and display more negative non-verbal behaviour. In contrast, Low-EE relatives were able to break negative chains of interaction sooner and to adopt a more neutral, non-critical,

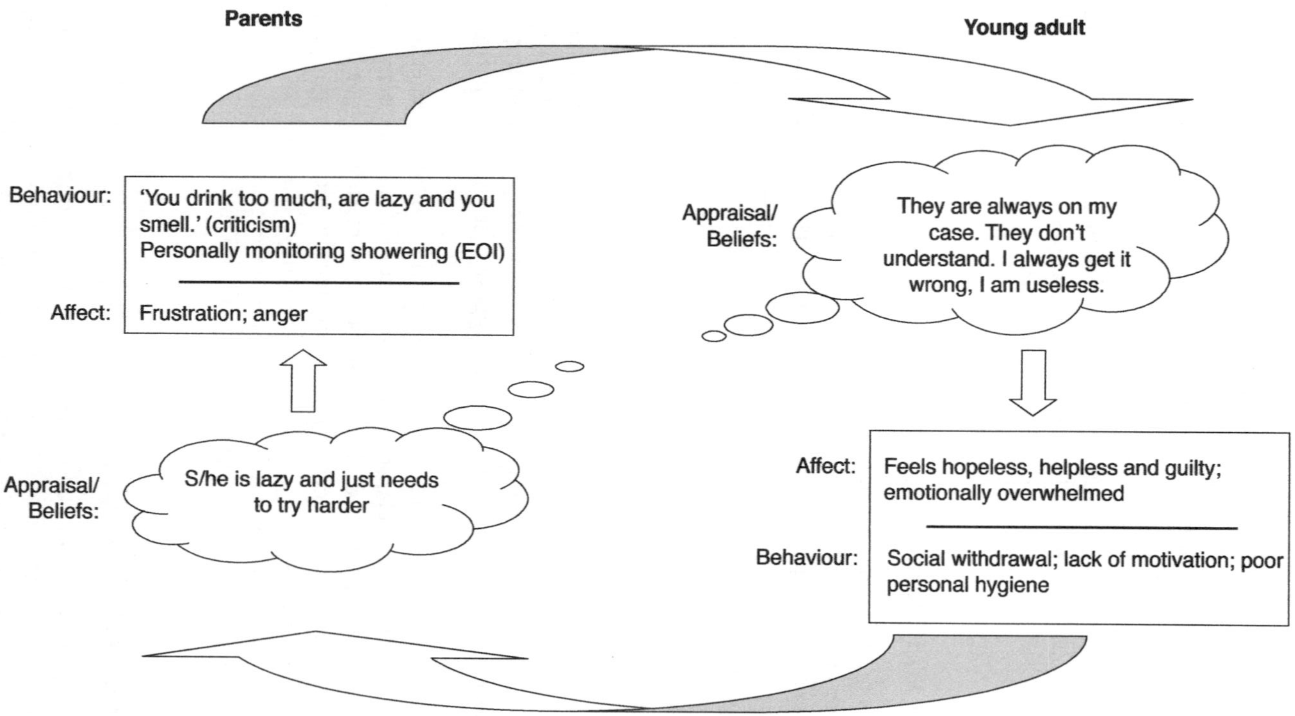

Figure 9.2 A cognitive-interactional diagram of a complementary transactional pattern.

facilitative stance. This was associated with more frequent use of autonomous statements by the young person with schizophrenia and enabled more effective problem solving by the family.

Miklowitz *et al.* (1989) found that High-EE-critical families became locked either into symmetrical critical interactions or complementary interactions. Figure 9.2 illustrates the complementary pattern, in which the young person with schizophrenia is self-denigrating and appears to have internalised the criticism. A symmetrical pattern of mutual criticism is illustrated in Figure 9.3. The previous examples are of simple dyadic relationships. Young people with psychosis commonly receive different messages because various family members perceive them differently. A common example is illustrated in Figure 9.4.

Causality and blame

One of the main difficulties with the EE research literature has been the definitive categorisation of families as either High-EE or Low-EE. As a result, minor changes in ratings may result in the recategorisation of the family. In addition, the correlation of High-EE with relapse is commonly misunderstood by professionals as implying causation. The fact that EE ratings are based on the relatives' views of the patient, and that many professionals hold unsophisticated linear understanding of causation, has resulted in many families being labelled as 'problem families' and being blamed for ongoing mental health problems in the patient (Hatfield *et al.*, 1987). Such unidirectional models of understanding have predominated, despite Brown *et al.* (1972) stating that they 'cannot specify the direction of cause and effect, but the fact that a decrease in expressed emotion at follow-up accompanied an improvement in the patients' behaviour strongly suggests that there is a two-way relationship' (p. 255).

Although the initial research effort was devoted to proving the empirical link between High-EE and relapse (point 1 in Figure 9.5), subsequent studies have demonstrated that relatives' EE levels may, in part, develop as a result of prolonged contact with a poorly functioning family member (point 2 in Figure 9.5). For example, in a cross-sectional study, Hooley and Richters (1995) found that relatives' critical comments were clearly related to the duration of the patient's illness, appearing to peak and stabilise just over three years into the illness.

Developmental view

More recently, EE has come to be seen as reflecting a normal developmental process of adjustment to the onset and development of a devastating illness. Consequently, EE measures the constantly changing, interactive, mutually reciprocal family relationships (point 3 in Figure 9.5). Studies examining the

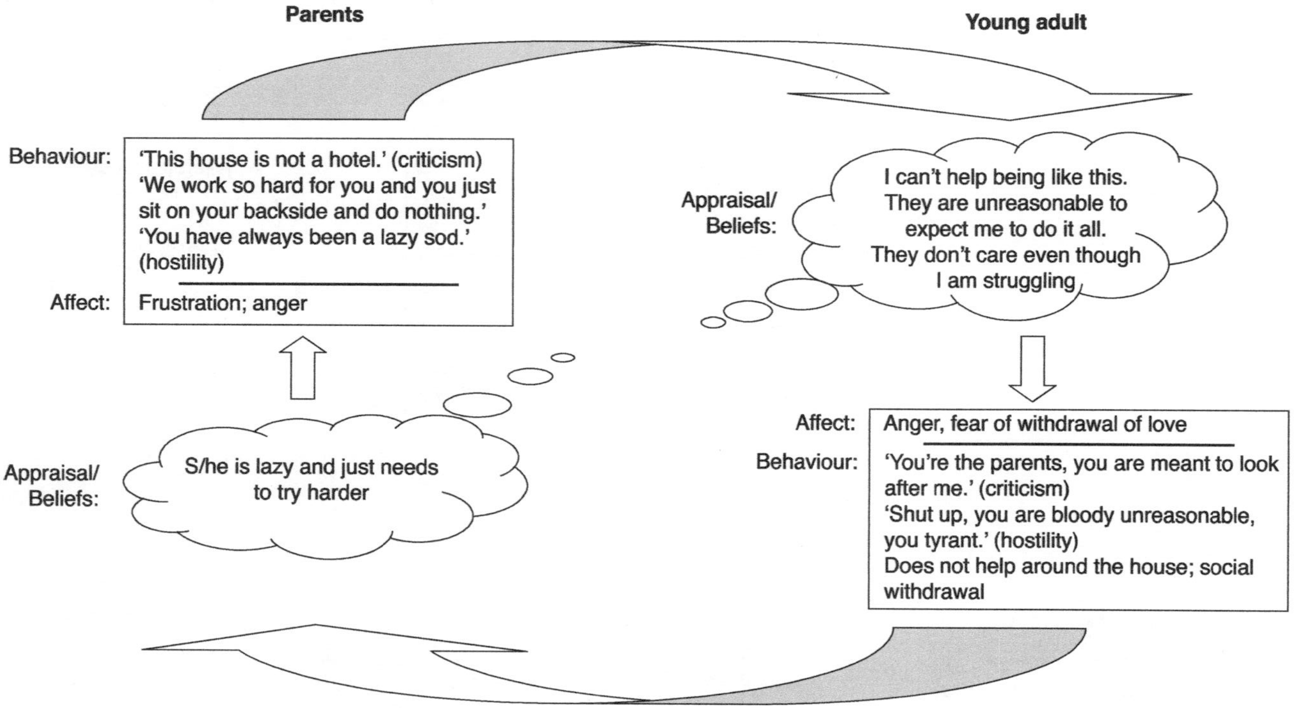

Figure 9.3 A cognitive-interactional diagram of symmetrical counter-criticism.

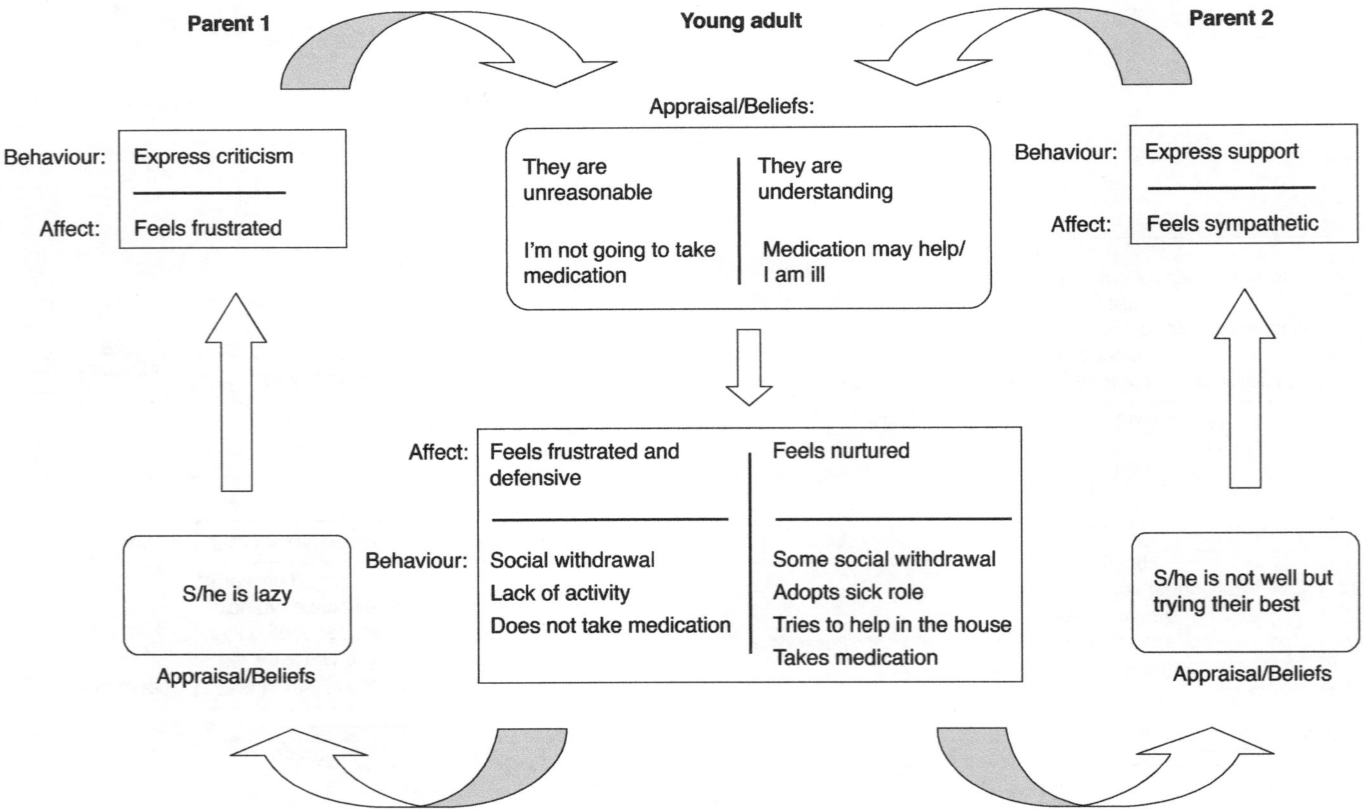

Figure 9.4 A cognitive-interactional diagram illustrating mixed messages and resultant confusion.

family emotional climate during the development of the first episode psychosis are beginning to shed some light on this developmental process. A study involving relatives of 30 people admitted for a first episode psychosis (Stirling *et al.*, 1993) found that while 13 out of 16 High-EE households (81 per cent) contained at least one key relative with high emotional over-involvement at admission, only 4 out of 11 (36 per cent) High-EE households were rated High-EOI at 18-month follow-up (mostly due to critical comments).

Another small-scale first episode psychosis study (Patterson *et al.*, 2005; see also Chapter 10, Patterson, this volume) also found considerable variation in EE status over time, with 28 per cent of relatives obtaining a different EE rating at nine-month follow-up. Loss appeared to be a major feature in EOI relationships for both relatives and patients, and was linked to subjective 'burden' of carers. At nine-month follow-up, loss had decreased in those changing from High-EOI to High-CC or Low-EE and the authors noted that 'the results are consistent with Bowlby's attachment theory, where EOI and coercive criticism may be understood as adaptive reactions to perceived loss' (p. 59). These developmental patterns can be represented as 4(i) and 4(ii) in Figure 9.5. (The coping and attributions literature is also summarised in Figure 9.5.)

A recent study by McFarlane and Cook (2007) compared the components of EE in parents of young people experiencing attenuated psychotic symptoms and judged to be at high risk of psychosis (n=16) with two groups in which patients had a well-established disorder. The parents of the prodromal or high-risk group were found to be 'warmer, less rejecting, less protective, and less fused with their child compared with parents of people with established cases of schizophrenia' (p. 194). The study also found significant positive correlations between duration of the prodromal phase and rejection and protectiveness, as well as a decrease in warmth. This suggests that expressed emotion, specifically EOI, develops out of parents' initial concerns about the young person's deterioration in functioning. They hypothesised that 'rejection and criticism emerge, on average, after chronicity develops and perhaps as family members begin to both lose hope and find themselves increasingly frustrated and unable to help the afflicted member of the family', and suggested that 'a better term might well be *expressed exasperation*' (p. 195).

Although contemporary theories about EE are no longer simple unidirectional ones, they still place an emphasis on the symptoms/problem behaviours of the child (e.g. Kavanagh, 1992). A truly systemic understanding would accept that such interactional cycles might begin so subtly that it is impossible to determine the person initiating the interaction. In some cases, this process would begin following the development of symptoms/problem behaviours in the young person, and in others the parental High-EE may result in such patterns developing from the earliest interactions with the newborn infant.

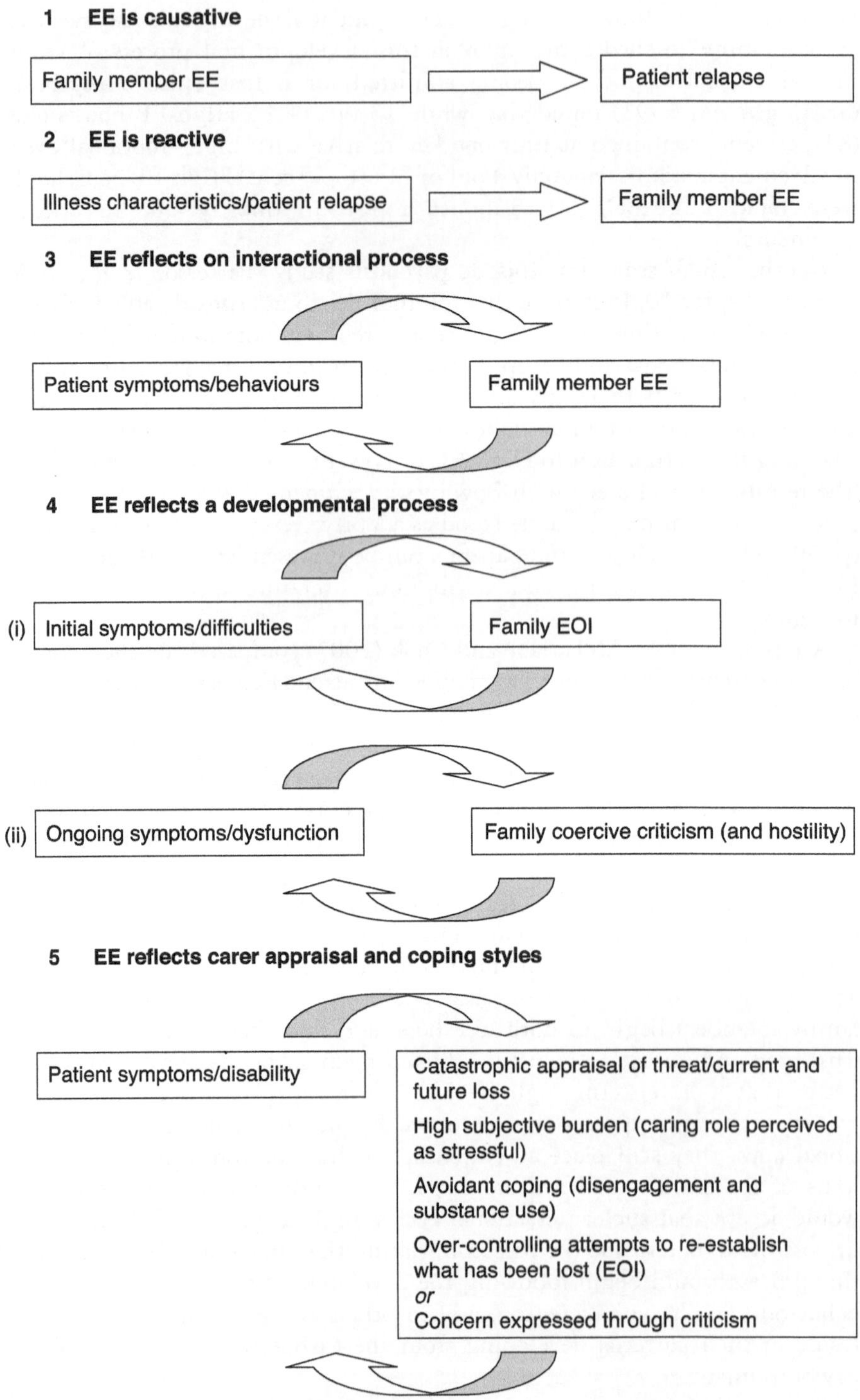

Figure 9.5 Models of expressed emotion (EE).

There may be many different developmental processes involved in High-EE and the onset or relapse of psychosis in those who have a predisposition to such symptoms. This does not imply that parental attitudes and behaviours, as reflected in the EE measure, are uniquely and ubiquitously associated with the onset of psychosis. It simply reflects the need to develop more comprehensive models regarding stress and vulnerability in psychosis. The Finnish adoption study (Tienari *et al.*, 2004) has demonstrated that common family dynamics are implicated in triggering the onset of psychosis in genetically predisposed individuals. They found that genetically at-risk adoptees – reared in families which had higher levels of criticism/conflict; constricted/flat affect; poor intergenerational boundaries; a chaotic family structure or unusual communication – were more likely to develop schizophrenia spectrum disorders, whereas there was no increase in such disorders among genetically predisposed adoptees raised in healthier families.

Conclusion

In 1992, Birchwood and Shepherd commented that 'the *precise* changes to the family interior that are the goal of family interventions are undifferentiated and scatter-shot in nature. This is not a criticism but an inevitable consequence of an empirical construct such as EE' (p. 311), and called for theoretical innovation. Fortunately, there has been considerable progress in exploring the nature of the family emotional atmosphere and its relationship with outcome in psychosis since that paper.

The original hypothesis of Brown *et al.* (1972) was 'that a high degree of expressed emotion is an index of characteristics in relatives which are likely to cause a florid relapse of symptoms, independently of other factors such as length of history, type of symptomatology or severity of previous behavioural disturbance' (p. 242). The initial research studies summarised in this chapter largely confirmed this hypothesis. However, subsequent studies have shown that EE is not the stable index it was once conceived to be, but is influenced by a range of variables. Interactional studies, in particular, clearly indicate that a more subtle developmental perspective is required to understand the processes creating High-EE and poor outcome as a variety of responses from relatives and the patient can contribute to the development of helpful or harmful interactional cycles.

Kuipers and Bebbington (1988) hypothesised three basic family EE patterns: (1) High-EE families that have difficulty with any stress, and remain High-EE at reassessment; (2) families with effective coping strategies, who deal with all problems with little expression of negative emotion, and remain Low-EE; (3) those who are usually Low-EE, except at times of extreme stress, such as an exacerbation of symptoms or rehospitalisation, when they become High-EE. Most families probably fall into the third category, with the trauma related to the onset of psychosis and its treatment severely affecting the ability of the family to function effectively in multiple ways. These families can be described in systemic terms as 'trauma-organised systems'. Families differ in their ability to meet the new demands imposed by the illness; with the result that in some cases their reactions protect against further episodes, and in others they contribute to the risk of relapse. Family members are often extremely concerned and stressed by the psychosis, and act with the best of intentions (e.g. trying to maintain established patterns of interaction), but inadvertently reinforce dysfunctional behaviour. One can hypothesise about the various interactional patterns that evolve over time in the other groups of families identified by Kuipers and Bebbington (1988).

The initially Low-EE group may perhaps better be described in terms of four possible developmental trajectories: some relatives adjust well to the new situation and continue to do so, remaining Low-EE; but many of those who are initially Low-EE become frustrated and critical (High-EE) over time. Other Low-EE families may be unhelpfully detached and cool, with such severely lowered expectations that they inadvertently reinforce a 'sick (overly dependent) role'. These families may become more detached with time (remaining Low-EE), but others may become critical over time (High-EE).

It is argued that the High-EE group can also be better understood in terms of circular causality rather than unidirectional (linear) causality. Although many writers in the field have understandably focused on the family emotional climate associated with relapse, rather than on similar factors associated with the onset of psychosis, it is possible to place this small research literature in the same theoretical framework. There are clearly a minority of families where the parents, perhaps due to their own attachment difficulties or mental health problems, are unable to cope with stressful life-cycle transitions such as having a child. As the Finnish adoption study has demonstrated, children raised in families that function in a range of suboptimal ways might be at higher risk of psychosis. Systemically oriented family interventions may involve the exploration of the onset and subsequent development of psychosis in terms of reciprocal interactions. This would include validating parental perceptions that 'something was not right', and their attempts to positively influence their child's behaviour. In addition it would include the recognition that children who have increased vulnerability to psychosis due to a range of psychosocial stressors and their genetic inheritance may well be adversely affected by inappropriate parental overinvolvement, poor communication, criticism, etc.

Acknowledgements

I would like to acknowledge the contribution of colleagues and families in Somerset who have been instrumental in developing these ideas over the years. Many thanks also to Sarah Angus for her cheerful typing of successive drafts, Sandy Burbach for support and expert editorial assistance, and Wendy Cull and Denise Hodgkin for their help in tracking down the many papers reviewed in this chapter.

References

Barrowclough, C. and Hooley, J.M. (2003) Attributions and expressed emotion: a review, *Clinical Psychology Review* 23: 849–880.

Barrowclough, C. and Lobban, F. (2009) Family intervention in psychosis: using an illness cognition framework. Workshop presented at the BABCP Conference, Exeter, July.

Barrowclough, C. and Tarrier, N. (1997) *Families of Schizophrenic Patients: Cognitive Behavioural Intervention*, London: Chapman and Hall.

Bebbington, P. and Kuipers, L. (1994) The predictive utility of expressed emotion in schizophrenia: an aggregate analysis, *Psychological Medicine* 24: 707–718.

Birchwood, M. and Cochrane, R. (1990) Families coping with schizophrenia: coping styles, their origins and correlates, *Psychological Medicine* 2: 857–865.

Birchwood, M. and Shepherd, G. (1992) Controversies and growing points in cognitive-behavioural interventions for people with schizophrenia, *Behavioural Psychotherapy* 20: 305–342.

Brewin, C.R., MacCarthy, B., Duda, K. and Vaughn, C.E. (1991) Attributions and expressed emotion in the relatives of patients with schizophrenia, *Journal of Abnormal Psychology* 100: 546–554.

Brown, G.W., Birley, J.L.T. and Wing, J.K. (1972) Influence of family life on the course of schizophrenic disorders: a replication, *British Journal of Psychiatry* 121: 241–258.

Burbach, F.R. (2000) Combining psychoeducational family work and systemic approaches. Paper presented at Working with Families: Making it a Reality Conference, Stratford-upon-Avon, March.

Burbach, F.R. and Stanbridge, R.I. (1998) A family intervention in psychosis service integrating the systemic and family management approaches, *Journal of Family Therapy* 20: 311–325.

Burbach, F.R. and Stanbridge, R.I. (2006) Somerset's family intervention in psychosis service: an update, *Journal of Family Therapy* 28: 39–57.

Butzlaff, R.L. and Hooley, J.M. (1998) Expressed emotion and psychiatric relapse: a meta-analysis, *Archives of General Psychiatry* 55: 547–552.

Greenley, J.R. (1986) Social control and expressed emotion, *Journal of Nervous and Mental Disease* 174: 24–30.

Hahlweg, K., Goldstein, M.J., Nuechterlein, K.H., Doane, J.A., Miklowitz, D.J. and Snyder, K.S. (1989) Expressed emotion and patient–relative interactions in families of recent onset schizophrenia, *Journal of Consulting and Clinical Psychology* 57: 11–18.

Hatfield, A.B., Spaniol, L. and Zipple, A.M. (1987) Expressed emotion: a family perspective, *Schizophrenia Bulletin* 13: 221–226.

Hooley, J.M. (1985) Expressed emotion: a review of the critical literature, *Clinical Psychology Review* 5: 119–339.

Hooley, J.M. and Richters, J.E. (1995) Expressed emotion: a developmental perspective, in D. Cicchetti and S.L. Toth (eds) *Emotion, Cognition and Representation*, New York: University of Rochester Press, 133–166.

Kavanagh, D. (1992) Recent developments in expressed emotion and schizophrenia, *British Journal of Psychiatry* 160: 601–620.

Kuipers, L. and Bebbington, P. (1988) Expressed emotion research in schizophrenia: theoretical and clinical implications, *Psychological Medicine* 18: 893–909.

Leff, J. (1989) Controversial issues and growing points in research in relatives' expressed emotion, *International Journal of Social Psychiatry* 35: 133–145.

Lobban, F., Barrowclough, C. and Jones, S. (2006) Does expressed emotion need to be understood within a more systemic framework? An examination of discrepancies of appraisals between patients diagnosed with schizophrenia and their relatives, *Social Psychiatry Psychiatric Epidemiology* 41: 50–55.

McFarlane, W.R. and Cook, W.L. (2007) Family expressed emotion prior to onset of psychosis, *Family Process* 46: 185–197.

Meddings, S., Gordon, I. and Owen, D. (2010) Family and systemic work, in C. Cupitt (ed.) *Reaching Out – The Psychology of Assertive Outreach*, Abingdon: Routledge.

Miklowitz, D.J., Goldstein, M.J., Falloon, I.R.H. and Doane, J.A. (1984) Interactional correlates of expressed emotion in the families of schizophrenics, *British Journal of Psychiatry* 144: 482–487.

Miklowitz, D.J., Goldstein, M.J., Doane, J.A., Nuechterlein, K.H., Strachan, A.M., Snyder, K.S. and Magana-Amato, A. (1989) Is expressed emotion an index of a transactional process? I. Parents' affective style, *Family Process* 28: 153–167.

Neimeyer, R.A. (2009) *Constructivist Psychotherapy: Distinctive Features*, Hove, UK: Routledge.

Patterson, P., Birchwood, M. and Cochrane, R. (2005) Expressed emotion as an adaptation to loss: perspective study in first-episode psychosis, *British Journal of Psychiatry* 187: 59–64.

Procter, H.G. (1985) A construct approach to family therapy and systems intervention, in E. Button (ed.) *Personal Construct Theory and Mental Health*, Beckenham: Croom Helm.

Procter, H.G. (1987) Change in the family construct system, in R.A. Neimeyer and G.J. Neimeyer (eds) *Personal Construct Therapy Casebook*, New York: Springer.

Raune, D., Kuipers, E. and Bebbington, P.E. (2004) Expressed emotion at first episode psychosis: investigating a carer appraisal model, *British Journal of Psychiatry* 184: 321–326.

Rosenfarb, I.S., Goldstein, M.J., Mintz, J. and Nuechterlein, H. (1995) Expressed emotion and subclinical psychopathology observable within the transactions between schizophrenic patients and their family members, *Journal of Abnormal Psychology* 104(2): 259–267.

Scott, R.D., Fagin, L. and Winter, D. (1993) The importance of the role of the patient in the outcome of schizophrenia, *British Journal of Psychiatry* 163: 62–68.

Stirling, J., Tantam, D., Thomas, P., Newby, D., Montague, L., Ring, N. and Rowe, S. (1993) Expressed emotion and schizophrenia: the ontogeny of EE during an 18-month follow-up, *Psychological Medicine* 23: 771–778.

Strachan, A.M., Feingold, D., Goldstein, M.J., Miklowitz, D.J. and Nuechterlein, K.H. (1989) Is expressed emotion an index of a transactional process? II. Patient's coping style, *Family Process* 28: 169–181.

Tarrier, N. (1991) Family factors in psychiatry, *Current Opinion in Psychiatry* 4: 320–323.

Tienari, P., Wynne, L.C., Sorri, A., Lahti, I., Laksy, K., Moring, J., Naarala, M., Nieminen, P. and Wahlberg, K. (2004) Genotype-environment interaction in schizophrenia-spectrum disorder, long-term follow-up study of Finnish adoptees, *British Journal of Psychiatry* 184: 216–222.

Valone, K., Norton, J.P., Goldstein, M.G. and Doane, J.A. (1983) Parental expressed emotion and affective style in an adolescent sample at risk for schizophrenia spectrum disorders, *Journal of Abnormal Psychology* 92: 339–407.

Vaughn, C.E. and Leff, J.P. (1976) The measurement of expressed emotion in the families of psychiatric patients, *British Journal of Social and Clinical Psychology* 15: 157–165.

Vaughn, C.E. and Leff, J.P. (1981) Patterns of emotional response in relatives of schizophrenic patients, *Schizophrenia Bulletin* 7: 43–44.

Warner, R. and Atkinson, M. (1988) The relationship between schizophrenic patients' perceptions of their parents and the course of their illness, *British Journal of Psychiatry* 153: 344–353.

Wearden, A.J., Tarrier, A., Barrowclough, C., Zastowny, T.R. and Rahill, A.A. (2000) A review of expressed emotion research in health care, *Clinical Psychology Review* 20: 633–666.

Chapter 10

Attachment, loss and expressed emotion

Developmental processes in psychosis

Paul Patterson

As our understanding of the aetiology of common mental disorders improves, a greater emphasis on the period of life when many of these illnesses first become evident – the period of adolescence and youth – must also occur. Young people often still living in the family home and in reciprocal affective relationships with parents and carers are the group most vulnerable to onset of a major mental illness such as psychosis. This chapter explores some of the developmental and transactional processes that may be related to the emergence and maintenance of mental illness in a family member, and suggests a model of early attachment experiences as playing a major role in the aetiology, response and recovery processes involved.

The attachment experience

What does it mean to be 'attached' to something or someone? It is often not apparent until we are separated from the object of our attachment. Imagine a young family member going missing or becoming ill. How do you react? Commonly, an initial sense of panic or heightened anxiety is apparent, as you begin searching for the missing person, refusing to believe that they have disappeared, or seek support and help for the ailing child if they are becoming more unwell. As this period is extended, concern may well become interspersed with moments of angry retribution aimed at yourself, others, and even the attached person (especially if they are missing), as anxiety levels remain high and the sense of frustration increases. If the person refuses to be found or does not appear to be recovering – depending on how closely 'attached' you are – it may be difficult to think of anything else, as you search yet again through the same possible locations, refusing to accept that they may actually be lost, or maintaining a vigil while imploring the world to help them recover. If there is no resolution, feelings of anger, helplessness and guilt may increase, interspersed with a refusal to accept the new situation and ever-increasing wish to have the world back to how it was before the changes. For closely attached relationships, the searching or the vigilant monitoring is unlikely to decrease, and accepting a longer term change in relationship status almost impossible, as you retain the hope or possibility that the individual will 'reappear' or the illness subside. The affective dynamics involved in such situations are amongst the most powerful and imperative in the human canon – and moving to a stage of resolution in cases of more permanent 'loss' can be amongst the most difficult challenges for individuals. In these situations, the necessity for a person to reorganise memories, expectations and intentions to reflect the changed status of the object of attachment and cope with 'loss' is the more or less extended experience of cognitive disruption and reorganising we call 'mourning', that carries the possibility of resolution and of 'moving on'. There are of course many cases where such resolution cannot occur, and it can come as no surprise that with the unpredictable course of many mental illnesses such as psychosis, the dynamics are likely to be salient and recurring within familial and carer/patient interactions reflecting cycles of crisis, relapse and recovery.

These processes of attachment, separation and loss and the emotional correlates of these behaviours is the subject of an influential trilogy of works by John Bowlby (1969, 1973, 1980), who directed a considerable proportion of his professional life to investigating the origins, consequences and import of attachment as a behavioural system encompassing many of the most important facets of care, protection, personal and social relationships into a developmental model of human behaviour. (For a fuller introduction to attachment theory see Chapter 6, Schwannauer, this volume.)

Expressed emotion

Mental illnesses such as psychosis often first appear during adolescence or early adulthood (Kessler *et al.*, 2007), at a time when the unwell individual is highly likely to be living at home with closely 'attached' family members. It has also been well established that familial expressed emotion (EE, Vaughn and Leff, 1976) involves affective transactions that have a direct bearing on the recovery of individuals experiencing psychosis and other disorders, yet a coherent theoretical understanding of what drives EE remains elusive. In this context, examining the correspondence between such key models of affective discourse as EE and attachment theory may help to refine our theoretical understanding and clinical intervention strategies for these immensely disruptive disorders.

Expressed emotion (EE) is a measure of the 'emotional temperature' in a family household and for many years has been regarded as a robust predictor of outcome in studies of familial influence on psychiatric disorders. Its importance is reflected in the vast body of research carried out over the past five decades and the original association linking high EE in family carers with increased risk of relapse in patients with schizophrenia (Vaughn and Leff, 1976) amongst other disorders has been regularly confirmed (Vaughn and Leff, 1976; Hooley *et al.*, 1986; Miklowitz *et al.*, 1988). In Chapter 9 of this volume Frank Burbach has skilfully demonstrated the relevance of EE to systemic family work with psychosis as well as providing an overview of many key historical and theoretical developments. EE is generally measured by employing recorded semi-structured interviews such as the 'gold standard' Camberwell Family Interview (CFI, Vaughn and Leff, 1976) or shorter interviews, with ratings for EE subscales based on carers' comments, attributions and verbal tone regarding the patient. More recent work has shown that by focusing on key components of EE, particularly those that are traditionally associated with poorer patient outcomes, such as critical comments (CC), emotional over involvement (EOI) and hostility (H), a better understanding of the concept may be reached.

Comparing EE and attachment

Research has demonstrated that the expression of high EE comments by a family member may be state related rather than a fixed trait (e.g. Schreiber *et al.*, 1995; McFarlane and Cook, 2007); reactive to symptoms in the patient as part of a transactional process (Stirling *et al.*, 1993; King and Dixon, 1996; Patterson *et al.*, 2005); and an early response to deterioration in the patient (McFarlane and Cook, 2007). Physiological studies have confirmed that transactional responses between carer and patient are associated with increased arousal and stress reactions, correlated over time with changes in EE status of relative (Sturgeon *et al.*, 1984; Tarrier, 1991). Carer attributions have also been related to differences in EE subscales (e.g. Barrowclough and Hooley, 2003). The parallels with current attachment research are striking (e.g. Berry *et al.*, 2008).

EE is believed to have a 'toxic' effect on patients through increased stress when in the company of 'high EE' carers, but a more 'therapeutic' impact in relation to 'low EE' carers (e.g. Tarrier, 1989). Two findings from attachment research may help us to clarify this situation. First, secure adults are found to be more likely than insecure adults both to seek support from their partners when distressed and to provide support to their distressed partners, in line with Bowlby's descriptions of attachment behaviour as involving caregiving and care eliciting (e.g. Simpson *et al.*, 1992). The anxiety-reducing impact of appropriate attachment behaviours would serve to reduce stress for unwell patients in the company of securely attached adults. Conversely, insecurely attached individuals when making attributions relating to their partner's behaviour during and following arguments have the result of escalating rather than alleviating their sense of insecurity (Simpson *et al.*, 1996). This would suggest a greater likelihood of increased 'stress' in situations where insecurely attached carers respond to illness in a family member. If sustained high EE is found to be associated with insecurely attached carers, this would give support to the supposition.

Attachment theory also suggests that some heightened emotional transactions are an appropriate response to any situation of risk or illness between attached members. This would imply that an initial response of high EE to a recently unwell family member may be normative, and it is only where this initial 'normal' response does not reduce in intensity over time – a situation of ongoing 'high EE' – could the dynamics be regarded as anomalous. The distinction between appropriate or abnormal attachment behaviours was first examined by Bowlby in situations of bereavement where healthy mourning was found to involve a range of increased affective responses, as described at the beginning of this chapter. These attachment, separation and loss processes encapsulate all the major affective dynamics encountered in situations of illness and protection – the same core affective elements in EE transactions. Bowlby found that healthy mourning could be long lasting and often involved aspects that could be regarded as pathological, including anger directed at self and others and disbelief that loss has occurred. Disorders such as psychosis involve very powerful dynamics of loss experienced by carers and family members, and a similar set of 'attachment' behaviours might be expected. If this is the case, we might predict that some of the 'normal' processes experienced early in a psychosis by family members may involve high levels of EE as reflecting the triggering of normative attachment responses. We know that EE close to onset of illness is often different to EE at follow-up periods and that it changes in intensity with course of illness (e.g. McFarlane and Cook, 2007). If we could suggest that changes to EE in response to illness in a family member are reflecting attachment behaviours, this could help in targeting interventions to address EE levels in some families.

Parental bonding, EE and psychosis

As previously noted, attachment behaviours including separation anxiety evoke similar patterns of responses to bereavement, which can involve disbelief, angry berating, refusal to recognise that the loss or changes may be permanent and an instinctive need to attempt to recreate the original pre-illness situation. It is perhaps then normative for heightened emotions within families to occur most strongly around the onset of illness in a family member and follow the 'grieving' cycle of responses – Bowlby's 'detachment' – should the situation not resolve. The early stages of coping with psychosis would seem likely to invoke attachment behaviours, and EE responses at this stage may indeed be a reflection of this adaptation (Birchwood and Cochrane, 1990; Patterson *et al.*, 2000). This is suggested in a small study employing measures of expressed emotion (Camberwell Family Interview, CFI), loss (Texas Revised Instrument for Grief, TRIG) and patient and family members perceived attachment (Parental Bonding Instrument, PBI, Parker, 1989) for a first-episode psychosis sample (Patterson *et al.*, 2005).

Table 10.1 Comparison of carers perceived loss scores (TRIG) by expressed emotion in three studies of psychosis

	Patterson et al. *(2000)*	*Atkinson (1994)*	*Miller* et al. *(1990)*
N	39	25	33
X	53.8 (9.4)	53.8 (4.1)	51.0

Table 10.2 Carers' perceived loss scores at baseline (TRIG) associated with High and Low EE carers

	High EE	*Low EE*	t	p
CC	42 (13.1)	56 (9.2)	3.54	<.001
EOI	60 (8.9)	48 (11.0)	3.57	<.001

The parental bonding instrument (PBI, Parker, 1986, 1989) was employed to measure perceived levels of care and overprotection, that is, perceived 'attachment styles' of parents. Two subscales – 'care' measuring warmth, empathy and emotional support, and 'protection' measuring overprotection, control and intrusiveness – are scored for the relationship with each parent.

Tables 10.1 and 10.2 display the consistently high levels of perceived loss displayed by relatives across studies employing carers of those with psychosis/severe mental illness. The 'loss' scores are of similar intensity to that reported by bereaved individuals, suggesting similarly high attachment responses are likely to be occurring in these carer–patient dyads.

When 'attachment' as measured by the PBI is examined, patients' perceived care and protection by their parents show consistently lower levels of perceived care and higher levels of overprotection than the population norms derived from Parker's (1983) study. Employing the four 'quadrants' of the PBI it can be seen that patients perceive their early parenting in mainly negative terms, with high levels of 'neglect' and 'affectionless control' and little 'optimal' parenting reported (Figures 10.1 and 10.2). The results echo Parker's (1989) findings that individuals diagnosed with schizophrenia experienced both their parents as being significantly less caring and fathers as more overprotective than controls. Parker also found that those who perceived their parents to have displayed predominantly 'low-care/high-overprotection' (affectionless control) parenting behaviours during their childhood had an earlier age of onset and were more likely to relapse after discharge, although this was not possible to compare in the current study as numbers of participants who perceived 'secure' parental bonding were too low for comparison. Attachment theory suggests that illness in a close family member should normally elicit

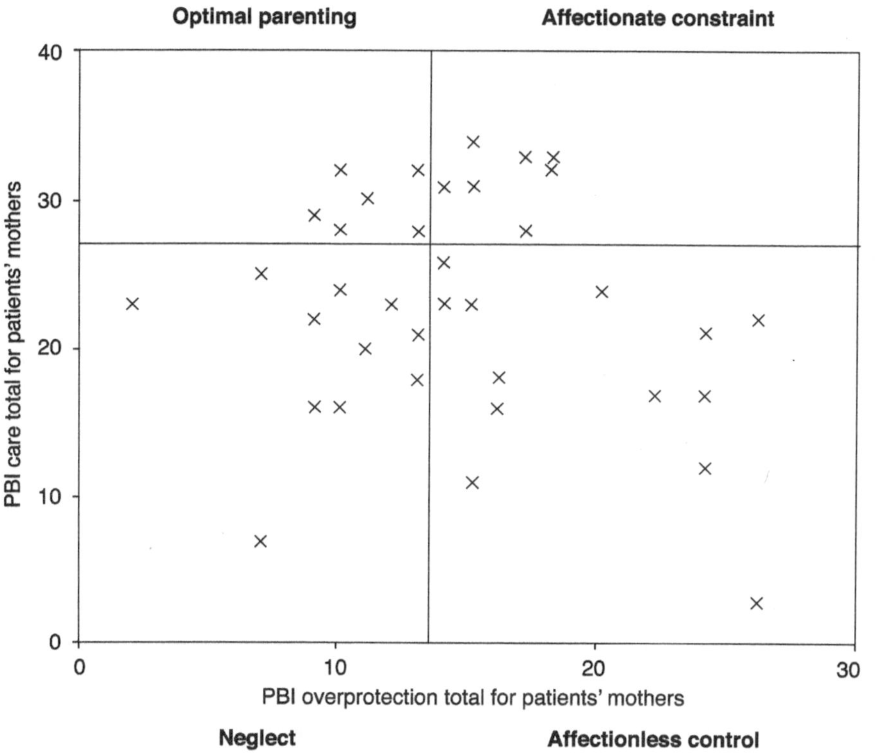

Figure 10.1 PBI scores by quadrant for patients' mothers n=37 (based on normative data from Parker, 1983).

caregiving, including some level of 'coercive' criticism and warmth from those securely attached, but the high rates of perceived insecure attachment are more likely to elicit frustrated attachment responses, with ongoing heightened criticism, hostility and EOI behaviours associated with an ongoing increase in household stress. This is likely to be associated with EE rates and when measures of carer burden were compared at nine-month follow-up those who were high in EE (n=22) had higher reported burden due to negative behaviours, ongoing illness symptoms and 'loss' then those with low EE (n=17). The potential negative impact of these perceived parenting styles on embryonic 'internal working models' is also salient here. The study demonstrates the very high level of 'insecure' or non-optimal parenting reported by patients.

Here, carers expressed EOI in attachment terms is likely to represent 'separation anxiety' with a refusal to accept changes and a searching for what has been lost. It is at this stage that carers and patients who employ anxious insecure attachment working models are likely to elicit a greater degree of clinging and 'needy' distress signals. Interestingly, Boye *et al.* (2002) found

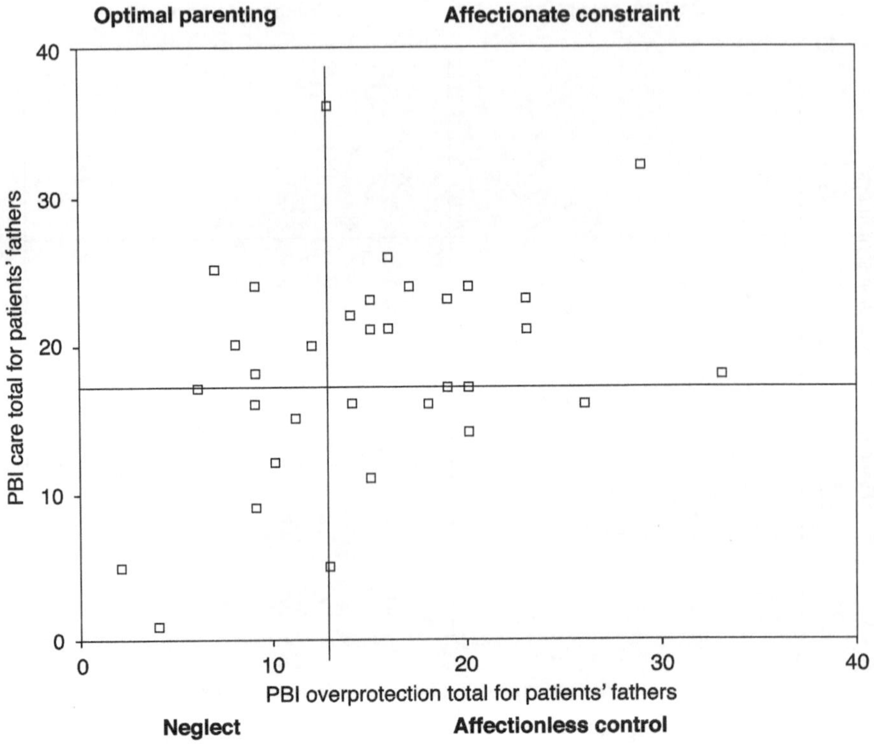

Figure 10.2 PBI scores by quadrant for patients' fathers n=33 (based on normative data from Parker, 1983).

EOI associated with anger suppression and guilt, but equally carers who employ avoidant attachment styles are likely to dismiss the illness as more under the control of the patient and demonstrate critical or hostile responses to symptoms, whilst conversely, 'insecure-avoidant' patients are more likely to underplay their symptoms and elicit EOI from carers (Dozier and Kobak, 1992). High EE carers perceived loss was associated more from those high in EOI whilst for those low in EE loss was associated more with critical responses displaying distinct profiles for 'loss' across EE categories.

Difficulties in responding appropriately to attachment 'distress' may be evident in the findings that high levels of CC in carers were associated with lower carer 'grief' scores, and conversely lower CC was associated with higher levels of 'grief'. This makes sense in relation to those insecurely attached who continue to try to critically coerce the individual with psychosis back to health but are unable to accept that the psychosis is not under the patient's control – and reduce or adapt this response to enter into a stage of detachment/ loss and 'mourning'.

Emotional overinvolvement and attachment behaviours

In studies of EE and professional staff caring for those with mental illness, high levels of EOI tend to be absent (e.g. Oliver and Kuipers, 1996), suggesting that this response is mainly a function of close familial interactions, and therefore more likely to involve attachment processes. High percentages of patients experiencing the onset of psychosis have been found to harbour and employ insecure internal working models, particularly avoidant attachment (Dozier, 1990; Dozier *et al.*, 1991, 1999) and high percentages of carers of these patients are likely to display an 'overinvolved' emotional response to psychosis (Dozier *et al.*, 1991). Patients' attachment behaviour can also influence EOI in carers. Dozier and colleagues (1991) also found an association between the repressive strategy of symptom expression (linked to avoidant attachment behaviour) – where patients maintain an air of invulnerability and fail to acknowledge the impact of symptoms – to increased overinvolvement in family carers. Overinvolved family members have been associated with longer premorbid history of symptoms in patients (Miklowitz *et al.*, 1983) and Dozier and colleagues' findings support a conclusion that emotional overinvolvement in certain carers may be a chronic response elicited by the perceived vulnerability of avoidant/repressive patients alongside increased length of illness or insidious onset of psychosis.

Dozier *et al.* (1991) argue that in the case of attachment 'preoccupied' patients, overinvolvement in relatives develops in response to overt expressions of distress; and in the case of dismissing patients, it may develop as relatives perceive the individual's underlying neediness or attempt to compensate for his or her lack of reliance on other sources of support. EOI on the part of relatives is hypothesised to perpetuate the use of both preoccupied and dismissing attachment strategies by patients, through confirming beliefs about vulnerability in the former case and through promoting withdrawal to avoid emotional intensity in the latter case (Dozier *et al.*, 1991). Heightened EOI as a response to the onset of psychosis can then be recognised as normative 'attachment behaviour' expected to elicit increased familial care-giving and care-receiving responses to an initial 'threat' of separation by illness. This is likely to be interspersed by directives of 'angry coercion' with CC attempting to pull the patient out of illness and 'back into line'. As the length of illness extends, securely attached individuals are more likely to recognise that these initial care-giving 'attachment' responses are ineffective and a more restrained approach is appropriate. Those that maintain heightened EOI over time are likely to be in dyads where one or both of the carer/patient displays an insecure attachment presentation, leading to an inability to successfully resolve the level of attachment response.

Critical comments and attachment behaviours

Carers with insecure working models/attachment styles tend to view providing care as burdensome. Additionally, they are likely to emphasise their own needs over the desires of others, and perceive support seeking by others as unnecessary or manipulative (George and Solomon, 1999). Mikulincer and Orbach (1995) have argued that dysfunctional anger emerges in the context of anxious-ambivalent attachment as a result of the expectation that others are unavailable and insensitive to their needs. Attachment research has also shown that secure individuals more often adopt functional anger strategies, insecure more often dysfunctional (Kobak *et al.*, 1991, 1993), particularly in stressful situations (Mikulincer *et al.*, 2003). Secure individuals have been found to respond to anger-inducing situations with a more rational analysis than insecurely attached individuals, whilst avoidantly attached individuals displayed high levels of hostility and were less aware of their own physiological signs of anger (Mikulincer, 1998). This 'cut-off' presentation of avoidantly attached individuals may play a role in the maintenance of tension and escalation. Mikulincer writes: 'Dissociated anger may result from avoidant persons' attempts to distance themselves from problematic situations, to suppress any painful affect of thought, and to present themselves in a positive way . . . These attempts may leave avoidant persons unaware of subjective and physiological signs of anger arousal, full of paranoid suspicions and hostile feelings, and unable to bridge discrepancies and to reduce tension.' A proposed model of how carers' and patients' internal working models (IWMs) driving attachment behaviour styles may influence EE is given in Figure 10.3. In this model, illness in a family member (e.g. psychosis) leads to activation of attachment behaviour with increased EE from relatives as an initial presentation, particularly where symptoms are acute. If symptoms do not resolve over time, maintained high EE responses are more common where one or both individuals have insecure IWM. Increased criticism/hostility is more likely if one or more individuals display insecure avoidant attachment style. In this model, dissociated IWM (not included) is likely to be associated with unresolved/ongoing symptoms and more chronic loss/depression in carers and additionally chronic high EE in relatives with insecure IWMs.

Integrating attachment theory and expressed emotion

Berry *et al.* (2008) reviewed the relevance of attachment theory in regard to psychosis giving a strong rationale for further exploration, while crossover research on attachment and EE may help to further strengthen the theoretical and aetiological understanding of each (e.g. Dozier *et al.*, 1991; Paley *et al.*, 1999; Liotti and Gumley, 2008). The importance of emotional dysfunction in vulnerability to psychosis has been increasingly recognised

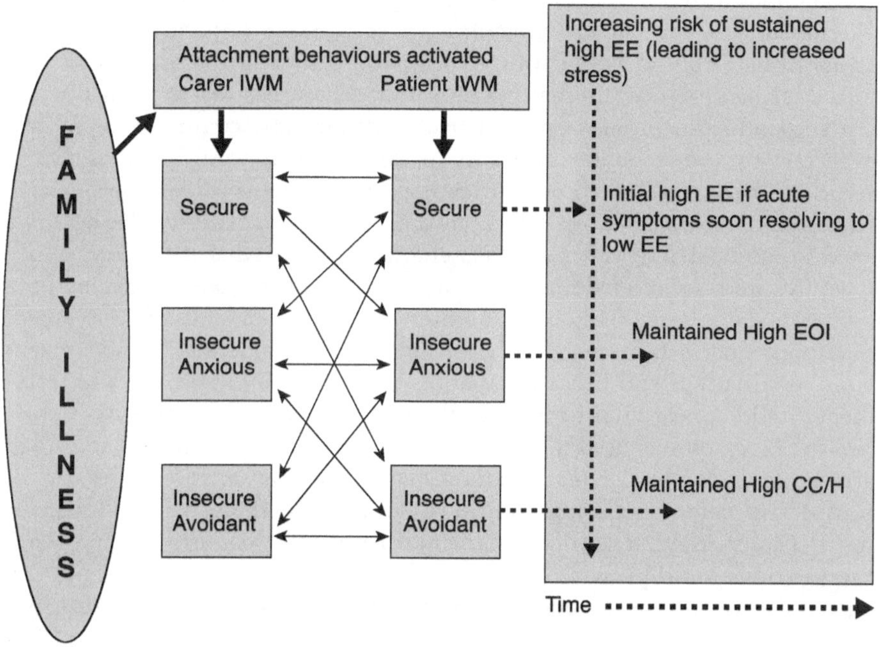

Figure 10.3 Proposed model for attachment behaviours' influence on expressed emotion.

(e.g. Birchwood, 2003; Freeman and Garety, 2003) including the role in development of positive symptoms (Garety *et al.*, 2001). Mentalisation research also suggests new understandings of attachment theory's role in cognitive development (Liotti and Gumley, 2008), whilst the work of Dozier and colleagues (1991) makes convincing arguments for prioritising attachment research in relation to psychosis. These approaches would help to answer the call for newer and creative approaches to family research involving EE (Bebbington and Kuipers, 1994; Butzlaff and Hooley, 1998), and may give fresh impetus to research focused on translating theory and rationale into clinical applications, since a common framework to enabling a better understanding of what drives EE has to date remained elusive.

Summary

The quality of early attachment behaviours and their legacy would appear to be vital for mental health and resilience throughout the lifespan (Bohlin *et al.*, 2000), and as our understanding of transactional processes between individuals and affective environment grow, opportunities to predict, identify and target insecure attachment processes with appropriate interventions should become increasingly available. Disturbances to the security of attachment in childhood and consequent difficulties with anxiety regulation may play an inordinate role in vulnerability to mental disorders for adolescents and into adulthood. Since internal working models are posited to persist across life and influence interactions, personal relationships, cognitive appraisals, expectations and responses to events in the world, it would make sense to prioritise this area for clinical investigation and to consider preventative strategies for emotional resilience at the earliest opportunity. Perhaps we need to accept that at times the constellation of parental accessibility, family pressures and social-environmental stress combine to cause tensions at a very vulnerable stage in a child's maturational development. EE may reflect developmental attachment processes and early vulnerability in certain familial situations and behavioural and systemic family approaches to treatment would appear vital to include alongside individual treatments. Public health strategies may need to consider introducing a greater understanding of attachment processes to early educational parenting interventions for all prospective parents, offering additional support for those who may benefit most. Closer integration of attachment theory with cognitive behavioural formulations could prove a firm basis for future preventative approaches and encourage supportive and effective interventions at the earliest opportunity.

References

Barrowclough, C. and Hooley, J.M. (2003) Attributions and expressed emotion: a review, *Clinical Psychology Review* 23: 849–880.

Bebbington, P. and Kuipers, L. (1994) The predictive utility of expressed emotion in schizophrenia: an aggregate analysis, *Psychological Medicine* 24: 707–718.

Berry, K., Barrowclough, C. and Wearden, A. (2008) Attachment theory: a framework for understanding symptoms and interpersonal relationships in psychosis, *Behaviour Research and Therapy* 46: 1275–1282.

Birchwood, M. (2003) Pathways to emotional dysfunction in first-episode psychosis, *British Journal of Psychiatry* 182: 373–375.

Birchwood, M. and Cochrane, R. (1990) Families coping with schizophrenia: coping styles, their origins and correlates, *Psychological Medicine* 20: 857–865.

Bohlin, G., Hagekull, B. and Rydell, A. (2000) Attachment and social functioning: a longitudinal study from infancy to middle childhood, *Social Development* 9(1): 24–39.

Bowlby, J. (1969) *Attachment and Loss, Vol. 1: Separation*, London: Hogarth Press.

Bowlby, J. (1973) *Attachment and Loss, Vol. 2: Separation*, London: Penguin.

Bowlby, J. (1980) *Attachment and Loss, Vol. 3: Loss*, New York: Basic Books.

Boye, B., Bentsen, H. and Malt, U.F. (2002) Does guilt proneness predict acute and long term distress in relatives of patients with schizophrenia?, *Acta Psychiatrica Scandinavica* 106: 351–357.

Butzlaff, R.L. and Hooley, J.M. (1998) Expressed emotion and psychiatric relapse: a meta-analysis, *Archives of General Psychiatry* 55: 547–552.

Dozier, M. (1990) Attachment organization and the treatment use for adults with serious psychopathological disorders, *Development and Psychopathology* 2(1): 47–60.

Dozier, M. and Kobak, R.R. (1992) Psychophysiology in attachment interviews: converging evidence for deactivating strategies, *Child Development* 63: 1473–1480.

Dozier, M., Stevenson, A.L., Lee, W. and Velligan, D.I. (1991) Attachment organization and familial overinvolvement for adults with serious psychopathological disorders, *Development and Psychopathology* 3: 475–489.

Dozier, M., Stovall, K.C. and Albus, K.E. (1999) Attachment and psychopathology in adulthood, in J. Cassidy and P.R. Shaver (eds) *Handbook of Attachment*, New York: Guilford Press, 497–519.

Freeman, D. and Garety, P. (2003) Connecting neurosis and psychosis: the direct influence of emotion on delusions and hallucinations, *Behaviour Research and Therapy* 41(8): 923–947.

Garety, P.A., Kuipers, E., Fowler, D., Freeman, D. and Bebbington, P.E. (2001) A cognitive model of the positive symptoms of psychosis, *Psychological Medicine* 31: 189–195.

George, C. and Solomon, J. (1999) Representational models of relationships: links between caregiving and attachment, *Infant Mental Health Journal* 17: 198–216.

Hooley, J.M., Orley, J. and Teasdale, J.D. (1986) Levels of expressed emotion and relapse in depressed patients, *British Journal of Psychiatry* 148: 642–647.

Kessler, R.C., Angermeyer, M., Anthony, J.C., de Graaf, R., Demyttenaere, K., *et al.* (2007) Lifetime prevalence and age-of-onset distribution of mental disorders in the World Health Organization's World Mental Health Survey Initiative, *World Psychiatry* 6: 168–176.

King, S. and Dixon, M.J. (1996) The influence of expressed emotion, family dynamics, and symptom type on the social adjustment of schizophrenic young adults, *Archives of General Psychiatry* 53: 1098–1104.

Kobak, R., Sudler, N. and Gamble, W. (1991) Attachment and depressive symptoms during adolescence: A developmental pathways analysis, *Development and Psychopathology* 3: 461–474.

Kobak, R.R., Cole, H.E., Ferenz-Gillies, R., *et al.* (1993) Attachment and emotion regulation during mother–teen problem solving: a control theory analysis, *Child Development* 64: 231–245.

Liotti, G. and Gumley, A.L. (2009) An attachment perspective on schizophrenia: Disorganized attachment, dissociative processes, and compromised mentalisation, in A. Moskowitz, M. Dorahy and I. Schaefer (Eds) *Dissocation and Psychosis: Converging Perspectives on a Complex Relationship*, John Wiley & Sons.

McFarlane, W.R. and Cook, W.L. (2007) Family expressed emotion prior to onset of psychosis, *Family Process* 46: 185–197.

Miklowitz, D.J., Goldstein, M.J. and Falloon, I.R.H. (1983) Premorbid and symptomatic characteristics of schizophrenics from families with high and low levels of expressed emotion, *Journal of Abnormal Psychology* 92: 359–367.

Miklowitz, D.J., Goldstein, M.J., Nuechterlein, K.H., Snyder, K.S. and Mintz, J. (1988) Family factors and the course of bipolar affective disorder, *Archives of General Psychiatry* 45: 225–231.

Mikulincer, M. (1998) Adult attachment style and affect regulation: strategic variations in self-appraisals, *Journal of Personality and Social Psychology* 75: 420–435.

Mikulincer, M. and Orbach, I. (1995) Attachment styles and repressive defensiveness: the accessibility and architecture of affective memories, *Journal of Personality and Social Psychology* 68: 917–925.

Mikulincer, M., Shaver, P.R. and Pereg, D. (2003) Attachment theory and affect regulation: the dynamics, development, and cognitive consequences of attachment-related strategies, *Motivation and Emotion* 27: 77–102.

Oliver, N. and Kuipers, E. (1996) Stress and its relationship to expressed emotion in community mental health workers, *International Journal of Social Psychiatry* 42: 150–159.

Paley, B., Cox, M.J., Burchinal, M.R. and Payne, C.C. (1999) Attachment and marital functioning: comparison of spouses with continuous-secure, earned-secure, dismissing and preoccupied attachment stances, *Journal of Family Psychology* 13: 580–597.

Parker, G. (1983) Parental 'affectionless control' as an antecedent to adult depression. A risk factor delineated, *Archives of General Psychiatry* 40: 956–960.

Parker, G. (1986) Validating an experiential measure of parental style: the use of a twin sample, *Acta Psychiatrica Scandinavica* 73: 22–27.

Parker, G. (1989) The parental bonding instrument: psychometric properties reviewed, *Psychiatric Developments* 7: 317–335.

Patterson, P., Birchwood, M. and Cochrane, R. (2000) Preventing the entrenchment of high expressed emotion in first episode psychosis: early developmental attachment pathways, *Australia and New Zealand Journal of Psychiatry* 34: 191–197.

Patterson, P., Birchwood, M. and Cochrane, R. (2005) Expressed emotion as an adaptation to loss: prospective study in first-episode psychosis, *British Journal of Psychiatry* 48: 59–64.

Schreiber, J.L., Breier, A. and Pickar, D. (1995) Expressed emotion: trait or state?, *British Journal of Psychiatry* 166: 647–649.

Simpson, J.A., Rholes, S.W. and Nelligan, J.S. (1992) Support seeking and support giving within couples in an anxiety-provoking situation, *Journal of Personality and Social Psychology* 62: 434–446.

Simpson, J.A., Rholes, S.W. and Phillips, D. (1996) Conflict in close relationships: an attachment perspective, *Journal of Personality and Social Psychology* 71: 899–914.

Stirling, J., Tantam, D., Thomas, P., *et al.* (1993) Expressed emotion and schizophrenia: the ontogeny of EE during an 18-month follow-up, *Psychological Medicine* 23: 771–778.

Sturgeon, D., Turpin, G., Kuipers, L., *et al.* (1984) Psychophysiological responses of schizophrenic patients to high and low expressed emotion relatives: a follow-up study, *British Journal of Psychiatry* 145: 62–69.

Tarrier, N. (1989) Electrodermal activity, expressed emotion and outcome in schizophrenia, *British Journal of Psychiatry* Supplement: 51–56.

Tarrier, N. (1991) Changes in the electrodermal activity of schizophrenic patients associated with changes in the expressed emotion status of their relatives, *Psychopathology* 24: 203–208.

Vaughn, C. and Leff, J. (1976) The measurement of expressed emotion in the families of psychiatric patients, *British Journal of Social and Clinical Psychology* 15: 157–165.

Chapter 11

Affect, emotion and the psychotic mind

Michael Robbins

Introduction

Schizophrenia, the most serious of the psychoses, has long been a lightning rod for mythology and misconception. Some of the misconception relates to affect and emotion. Although persons diagnosed with schizophrenia usually manifest in addition to cognitive and relational peculiarities some combination of emotional flatness and social inappropriateness along with occasional affect storms, general psychiatry that focuses on labeling and classifying illness according to signs and symptoms has tended to call it a thought disorder in contrast to the so-called affective disorders.

Mental life is inherently social and interpersonal, and individual identity takes shape through affective-emotional expressions and responses within this context. The terms *affect* and *emotion* are not synonymous, however. Affect may be looked upon as the primordial somatopsychic expressive core of mind whereas emotion refers to the thoughtful awareness and mental representation of feeling states. Charles Darwin made important contributions to the study of affect. In 1872 he published a book in which he inferred the existence of innate affect from observation of infant facial expression, gesture and vocalization. Awareness of specific emotions such as love, anger, shame, embarrassment, guilt, sadness and envy, in contrast, is proportional to maturation of mind and development of the capacity to think. The basic proposition of this chapter is that the failure to translate somatopsychic affective experience into emotional awareness and the deficiency in self-regulation that follows from it is a central characteristic of psychosis, especially schizophrenia.

The problem processing affect and identifying and bearing emotion has been explored in persons with psychosomatic problems and was named alexithymia by Sifneos (1975), meaning no words for emotions. This failure is part of a larger problem, socially inappropriate or maladaptive manifestations of a primordial form of mental activity that is normal in such contexts as infancy, dreaming and some forms of spirituality and creativity. This is what I call primordial mental activity (PMA). The belief that schizophrenia is a thought disorder is equally misleading, as the problem in psychosis is not that thought is disordered, but that the predominant mental activity is not thought at all, but primordial mental activity.

Background: Freud, Klein and Bion

Freud, Klein, Bion and others including Matte-Blanco, Mahler, Werner and Piaget whose work there is not space to discuss (Robbins, 2008, 2011) made pioneering efforts to explore this aspect of mind beginning with Freud's concept of the primary process (1900). He believed the primary process underlies dreaming as well as the mind of infancy and of psychosis. The primary creates a state of hallucinatory wish fulfillment. Klein subsequently formulated the paranoid-schizoid position and the mental activity called phantasy (1935, 1937, 1946) which, after being tweaked for decades by others, especially Bion (1957, 1959), has become the default psychoanalytic model of psychosis. Why then is another model of psychotic mind needed?

Although Klein did not seem to know about Freud's model of primary process, and employed a radically different conceptual language, both describe a concrete somatically experienced mind that is sensory-perceptual, auditory-visual and psychomotor; that is undifferentiated in the sense of not observing ordinary distinctions between self and other or world; that is immediate, discontinuous and stimulus-bound; and that lacks a thoughtful, reflective self and symbolic capability. Their models share confusions and misconceptions as well (Robbins, 2008, 2011). Because their primary data were mentally ill children and adults they share the bias that primordial mind is immature and psychotic, hence "normal" infants are psychotic. Infancy is conceived of as a kind of autoimmune disease of defense against one's feelings and an intolerable reality. The psychotic process involves creating a more palatable sense of satisfaction or good-ness. Freud explicitly uses the term hallucination, and Klein uses such terms as paranoid, schizoid and manic, as well as defenses of splitting and projective identification. With the advent of infant research (Stern, 1985) we now know that the normal infant is eager to adapt to reality in the best way it can.

Both their theories are also unclear about the distinction between primordial mind and thought. They describe it as somatic and perceptual rather than as thoughtful and emotional, as concrete, as perceiving the world in momentary unintegrated fragments, and as creating a convincing belief or "reality" that does not differentiate internal elements with external perception and experience. In "The Interpretation of Dreams" Freud states: "The primary process endeavors to bring about a discharge of excitation in order that . . . it may establish a 'perceptual identity.' The secondary process, however, has abandoned this intention and taken on another in its place – the establishment of a 'thought identity'" (1900, p. 602). He describes language in primary process dreaming as concrete rather than representational and symbolic (1900,

p. 295). The subjective experience of the dreamer is not one of thought but "a complete hallucinatory cathexis of the perceptual systems" (1900, p. 548). Yet there are every bit as many references in Freud's writings to the primary process as a thought-related symbolic activity, and his technical recommendations for dream interpretation are based on the assumption that dreams are a symbolically meaningful variant of thought. For example: "The dream-thoughts and the dream-content are presented to us like two versions of the same subject-matter in two different languages . . . The dream-content, on the other hand, is expressed as it were in a pictographic script, the characters of which have to be transposed individually into the language of the dream-thoughts" (1900, p. 277). Understanding dreams "presents no greater difficulties to their translators than do the ancient hieroglyphic scripts to those who seek to read them," because "the keys are generally known and laid down by firmly established linguistic usage" (1900, pp. 341–342).

Klein is similarly confusing in her formulation of the paranoid-schizoid position and phantasy. Phantasy is described as a process different from and antecedent to conceptual thought (depressive position); one in which aspects of self and other are undifferentiated, the psyche is unintegrated, and experience is concrete (Klein, 1930; Segal, 1957). Nonetheless the conceptual language with which she describes it is what the thoughtful analyst imagines (fantasizes) to be the subjective mental state of the infant, suggesting that infants are capable of thinking or imagining in terms involving self, other, impulses, feeling states, complex motives, body parts and functions, and executing defense mechanisms of splitting and projective identification against unwanted intrapsychic content in order to put it inside another person. While some Kleinian analysts (Meltzer, 1976) interpret *phantasies* by receiving projected impressions impressionistically and translating them by analogy, many clinical vignettes involve symbolic interpretations based upon the assumption that their analysands can comprehend symbolic thought or *fantasy*.

Bion's ideas about mind (1962, 1967) begin with dreaming, but unlike Freud who considered it a nocturnal psychosis and some Kleinians who consider dreams a product of phantasy, qualitatively different from thought, Bion believes dreaming is related to thought. The state of reverie that Bion was referring to in his now clichéd "without memory or desire," is for him a reflection of the continuous process of dreaming both waking and sleeping. It is the alpha function that creates an alpha screen or differential gradient between conscious thought and unconscious content. Dreams transform the raw chaotic sensory-perceptual-affective data he calls beta elements into elements that can be represented, symbolized and arranged in narrative sequence. In the normal course of development mother acts as container of infant projections, performs alpha function of reverie, metabolizes the experience, and returns to the infant the beta elements along with some of her capacity for performing alpha process. When containment, dreaming and the alpha function are disturbed then beta elements cannot be alpha-betized into thought so that there is no unconscious. Unmetabolized fragments of mind are then evacuated onto a delusional beta screen by projective identification.

I agree with Bion that the process underlying dreaming is a normal modality of learning, not one of defense against intolerable affect and reality. Moreover, I believe it underlies other normal phenomena of adult life. However, I believe the learning that takes place is not related to thought, but to what the attachment theorists call implicit or procedural processes. On the other hand, I concur with Freud and Klein that the dreaming function is concrete and actualizing, undifferentiated and unintegrated, quite unlike thought. Bion describes psychosis as the consequence of failure of the dreaming/learning function that creates thought and the thoughtful (repressive) barrier between conscious and unconscious, and usurpation of mind by a pathological mental process involving splitting and evacuation of concrete sensory-perceptual-affective beta elements. I believe, along with Freud and Klein, that psychosis is the product of the process that underlies dreaming. However, in contrast to Freud and Klein I believe that it is a normal process that has been co-opted by mind for purposes that are socially maladaptive.

Table 11.1 lists the salient features of primordial mental activity that underlies dreaming, infancy and psychosis, as well as numerous other phenomena including parent–infant bonding, creativity and modal mental activity in spiritual (non-western) cultures.

Attachment and the affective core of primordial mind

Bowlby (1969) proposed what is known as attachment theory and detailed film recordings of mother–infant interactions by the Robertsons (1971) demonstrate synchronized choreography of gesture, facial expression and vocalization. (For an introduction to attachment and psychosis see Chapter 6, Schwannauer, this volume.) Experimental findings are beginning to document the basis of this choreography in simultaneous activity of similar brain areas of mother and infant. Trevarthen (1980) describes mother–infant coordinated visual eye-to-eye messages, tactile and body gestures, and auditory prosodic vocalizations serving as a channel of communicative signals that induce instant emotional effects. Manning *et al.* (1997) note that most women hold their infants on the left side of their bodies and Schore (2003, 2005) believes that this position allows the mother's left eye and ear to contact the infant's left eye and ear and that these are processed by the respective right or non-verbal hemispheres of each. Lorberbaum *et al.* (2002) found that the infant's cry activates the mother's right brain and her vocal responses tend to be encoded in the infant's right hemisphere.

Table 11.1 Primordial mental activity in relation to thought

	PMA	*Thought*
What motivates mind?	*Somatic sensation and affect*	*Identified emotion and adaptation*
How meaning is experienced and expressed.	Psychosomatic: sensation, perception, motor, belief, "it is".	Reflective, recursive, referential. "I think that …"
Nature of personal narrative.	Chaining or linking of perception by idiosyncratic sensation and affect.	Integrates emotion and adaptation hence is logical, causal, recursive, aware of passage of time.
The center of experience and expression.	De-centered, existential, collectively referenced in cosmos.	Self-referenced, intrapsychic, reflective.
Is the world perceived in relative or absolute terms?	Absolutism. Immediacy or actuality of experience. Belief. Holistic syncretic perception.	Differentiation in a self–other referenced world in which time passes. Also within mind that compares, contrasts, can be subjective or objective.
The nature of expression, communication and learning.	Concrete, literal, forceful, peremptory.	Meaning exchanged in form of ideas and symbols.
Language.	Full vocabulary, grammar and syntax. Words used concretely as things.	Entire range of linguistic complexity; words carry meaning.
Development.	Utilizes learned material but process itself does not develop.	Developmental transformation in systemic complexity.

Another strand of neuroscience research related to primal attachment has to do with so-called "mirror neurons" located on the outer surface of frontal and parietal lobes (Gallese *et al.*, 1996; Tomasello, 1999; Molnar-Szaracs *et al.*, 2005; Pally, 2007) and speculation about their developmental significance. Dimberg *et al.* (2000) report that electromyographic studies of facial responses of subjects to facial expressions of others show that "both positive and negative emotional reactions can be unconsciously evoked, and that important aspects of emotional face to face communication can occur at an unconscious level" (p. 86). The mirror neuron system does not appear to differentiate subject from object. The subject responds behaviorally to perceived cues from another as though they were coming from the self, as expressed in the saying "monkey see, monkey do." This function of the mirror neuron system would appear to describe the mutual forceful inductive process that is part of primordial mental activity and distinguishes it from thoughtful communication of meaning, and suggests it is not an innate defense against attachment, but rather a part of the primordial learning and attachment process.

Relational theorists have formulated concepts such as unconscious implicit or procedural knowledge or memory (Squire, 1986; Clyman, 1991; Grigsby and Hartlaub, 1994; Stern *et al.*, 1998). Emde states:

> There is a major amount of nonconscious mental activity that is neither preconscious (i.e., readily accessible to consciousness using recent or working memory) nor defensively excluded (i.e., involving repressed memories or isolated affects) . . . a variety of organized automatically functioning procedures and rules for guiding behavior in particular contexts.
>
> (1983, p. 415)

Other terms for this aspect of mental life include unformulated experience (Stern, 1989); subsymbolic process (Bucci, 2000); primary affective memory or primary affective unconscious (Panksepp, 1998); implicit relational knowing (Stern *et al.*, 1998); and the unthought known (Bollas, 1987). As Lyons-Ruth puts it, "implicit processing may be particularly relevant to the quick and automatic handling of nonverbal affective cues, which are recognized and represented early in infancy in complex 'proto-dialogues' [Trevarthen, 1980] and so have their origins prior to the availability of symbolic communication" (Lyons-Ruth, 1999, pp. 586–587).

Mary Ainsworth (Ainsworth *et al.*, 1978) derived a "strange situation" experiment and classified infant behavior into four affect-based attachment categories: secure, anxious/avoidant, anxious/resistant and disorganized/disoriented. Lyons-Ruth (2003) and the Boston Change Process Study Group (Stern *et al.*, 1998) have formulated a model of disorganized attachment that involves external or interpersonal rather than intrapsychic conflict. If caregivers behave in ways that are rejecting and attacking, and distort the meaning of infant initiatives by responding to them with dissonant or inappropriate affects, the consequence in the infant is anticipatory procedural learning or reflexive dysphoric affective responses that may be adaptive in that context but ultimately maladaptive and self-destructive in a more normal social context.

Attachment theory and the concept of implicit or procedural learning and knowledge are very important contributions to understanding basic affective-relational patterns, both ordinary and disordered. However, it does not provide a sufficient characterization of primordial mind. There is an active mental process that exists from birth that assimilates (learns) and enacts the affective-relational pattern of response to caregivers that has been called implicit or procedural knowledge. It is not simply a matter of pathological reflex responsiveness to other human beings. This primordial mental activity builds upon the attachment configuration or implicit knowledge that has been assimilated at the beginning of life.

Primordial mental activity, affect and psychosis

Psychosis is the maladaptive expression of primordial mental activity (PMA) unregulated by thought. PMA is the somatic-psychic expression of mind, in contrast to thought, which is reflective and representational. Unprocessed somatic sensation, perception and affect is experienced and enacted. The affective experiences are amorphous states like somatic emptiness (a hole inside to be filled), global sour unhappy mood, protracted states of depression and despair, destructive tantrum-like enactments suggestive of rage, the spectrum of anxiety, panic and dread, and psychosomatic states including migraine headaches, skin disorders, gastrointestinal and genitourinary problems. Personal narrative chaining is driven by affect rather than by logic and rational causality.

Although no one who observes a person in the throes of acute schizophrenia doubts that distress is being experienced, the nature of the emotional suffering is not known to and borne thoughtfully by the person in the way that an empathic observer might imagine. Many successfully treated persons have told me that kind of suffering is much more painful than was the psychotic state.

In psychosis external (consensual) reality is undifferentiated from intrapsychic (subjective) reality. Self experience is not differentiated from object perception. There is experience without an integrated differentiated self to think about it. What is experienced and enacted is an affect-driven happening, a sensory-perceptual event rather than something to think about. One way for the observer to comprehend the psychotic process is to contrast the *experience* of dreaming that we all have at night with the recasting of the dream in language on awakening in order to think about it. Even after awakening we sometimes have to struggle to determine that the experience – that came from our minds alone – was not a real event.

To the observer a schizophrenic person manifests delusions and hallucinations and a sense of omnipotence. The subject, however, experiences his or her mind as equivalent to the world that we call reality, hence possessing omnipotent power to alter the world as though by magic. As the affects are mostly disturbing so the cosmos is a malignant one. Because the painful emotions arising from awareness of one's real place in the world are not identified and thoughtfully experienced, the result is a kind of narcosis or anesthesia within a malignantly conceived universe.

PMA in psychosis is a modality both of expression and of deep learning. It is literal rather than figurative; concrete and enactive. It exerts force and pressure to actualize beliefs. Such concrete expression and enactment of belief exerts pressure on the other person to lose boundaries and to enter into the subject's delusional belief system. Klein called this phenomenon projective identification; our difference is that she considered it a defense. The psychotic person similarly feels pressured and forced by the other and the environment.

This literal quality of mind along with undifferentiation of self from other leads the person to feel assaulted or persecuted by externally misperceived aspects of his or her own mind and contributes to phenomena known as paranoia and ideas of reference.

In the psychotic state mind is not integrated and sequenced by thoughtful rules of logic, causality, time and space. There is no sense of passage of time; the moment is everything and there is no remembered past or anticipated future. The person is psychologically neither here nor there. Narrative sequence is affect-driven. Without integration and differentiation there is no experience of contrast, contradiction conflict, reflection or ambivalence and it is not possible to consider alternatives and make decisions. While people diagnosed with schizophrenia often obsess, giving the impression they are in conflict within themselves, such paralytic obsessions are also experienced somatically and expressed motorically. They tend to be about whether to do or not to do, not about the struggle with psychologically incompatible ideas.

That the process I am describing is radically different from thought and the expression or reception of thoughts in communicative language might seem inconsistent with the fact that psychotic persons are usually quite capable of talking and writing, albeit sometimes in ways that are strange and idiosyncratic. Although such persons have learned language and aspects of culture in their formal or literal sense, for example vocabulary and grammar, language is employed concretely as objects that exert force or pressure, both expressively and receptively, rather than abstractly as representations or parts of thought. Grammar and syntax are normal; there are changes in morphology (neologisms), semantics and pragmatics.

The psychoses comprise a spectrum of illness ranging from milder forms (the serious personality disorders) to severe forms (schizophrenia, manic-depressive and traumatic psychoses). There are four basic factors that produce psychosis and determine its severity. To begin with, the affective-relational template from the attachment phase that forms the implicit or procedural knowledge on which PMA draws is disturbed. Second, there is a relative preponderance of PMA over thought. Of most importance, thirdly, there is a dissociation or absence of integration between PMA and whatever capacity for thought exists; so that PMA is not disciplined and used adaptively with regard to time, place and function. And finally, PMA is used maladaptively with regard to the socio-cultural context in which the person is expected to function, leading to immaturity.

Examples of PMA in psychosis

Lisabeth's problems were at the less severe end of the psychotic continuum. She was very successful in a professional career because her ability to think was entirely devoted to projecting a false self, keeping an emotional distance from people, and hiding her deep distress and disturbance which was based on lack of a separate sense of self and a somatically based conviction she was literally excrement. Outside of the workplace she functioned almost entirely in PMA. Two vignettes taken from the latter stages of a lengthy and successful psychoanalytically based therapeutic process illustrate problems experiencing herself as a separate autonomous person and conceptualizing, bearing and sustaining her own thoughts and feelings.

We had missed a couple of sessions because I was out of town for a few days, and when we reconvened she seemed somewhat disorganized and quite anxious. After some discussion she became aware she felt angry. Associations gradually linked her anger to our separation which she proceeded to talk about more directly and concretely. She recounted having driven around the community in which we both lived and gradually realizing that an amorphous sense of distress was related to the realization that I was not there. As she could not actually see me she had felt empty. After she told me this I suggested we discuss where I "am" for her; specifically whether that depends on immediate concrete sensory-perceptual experience or whether she might keep in mind caring feelings and feelings of sadness related to missing me. As we talked she began to experience such feelings and she said she felt better.

During another hour soon thereafter, following a long weekend separation, she first remarked that she was feeling distressed. Then she said she believed that her chair was a couple inches further away from mine than usual. In fact it might have been. In any case she immediately proceeded to try to move it closer. I asked her to stop the action and consider whether her feelings about me were far away or close and she soon realized that she had managed to eliminate feelings of caring about me and missing me. Immediately she felt better and moving the chair was no longer an issue.

In the later stages of her therapy Lisabeth wrote an essay in which she described her mental state prior to therapy (Robbins, 2011, pp. 150–159). She writes: "I was not able to reflect upon or indentify what feelings (e.g. loss, rage, love) might be driving my actions, nor did I even know what feelings were. To me feelings were a global state where I felt either hopeless, helpless, and anxious (often expressed somatically), or 'better'." And, "Given my inability to understand, develop and sustain emotional connections without concrete contact, any separations from Dr. Robbins were agony, especially summer vacations." Finally, "As therapy progressed I began to develop the capacity to have and reflect upon identifiable feelings and thoughts. I developed a deeper interest in words and their nuance, wrote increasingly lengthy reflections on my now more tolerable feelings."

Caroline had many hospitalizations and a variety of unsuccessful treatments before entering therapy with me, during which it was clear she satisfied the DSM criteria for schizophrenia. In the earlier stages of a psychoanalytically based therapy Caroline's conversation was usually bizarre, with little evidence of constructive realistic thinking. She manifested amorphous global states of self-pity and of blame of others based on the belief she was a victim of unfair treatment. At other times she was wooden in posture and expression and her voice lacked affective modulation. Though she manifested diffuse rages she had no conception she was angry. She so thoroughly narcotized herself by creating a delusional world that she was unaware of a need to bear the emotions appropriate to her objectively pathetic state as a young woman who was unable or unwilling to take the most basic care of herself, to do any productive work or form any close relationships. She believed she did not need to take care of herself and did not need to work to form relationships because she was already the special consort of one or another of the doctors who cared for her. After a several day coma following a massive overdose of medication stolen from the nurse's station on the ward where she was hospitalized she formed the conviction that she was the special love-interest of the emergency room doctor who had saved her life, and that they had some sort of mystical union while she lay naked on the emergency room gurney. The frightened helpless needy state that should have been associated with her situation was not within her emotional awareness. Somatic binging whether involving pills, food or sex, and purging whether involving vomiting, rageful blaming of others, or using words as concrete objects, were present where emotions might otherwise have been.

Here is an example of how she rid herself of anything troublesome and believed others were taking care of her, from a period of therapy long after the time when she had ceased concretely using food to binge and purge. She was addicted to regular mass-mailing inappropriate and bizarre recitations of her personal business to a large group of persons, with many of whom she had had no contact for years. She informed me she was "wording" them; forcing her literal mind-body self into their "mailboxes" (their persons) so they would have to take care of her. "Wording" and "mailboxes" were not symbols but concrete objects of assault.

Her delusional system based on affect-driven somatization and concrete action magically believed to alter reality made it seem unnecessary for her to learn to think and to identify emotional responses to differentiated people and events. In the course of discussing her unwillingness to take basic responsibility for her life, I made what seemed to me an obvious logical connection between her impulsive spending of money in order to gratify wishes, which she seemed to do so that she would not need to experience any emotion related to wants, needs and deprivation, and her very limited resources. I expressed a worried concern she would soon run out of funds and I wondered what would become of her. She responded in a matter-of-fact way, bypassing the need to experience fear, shame or other emotions, and saying, "I'm going to buy a $100 pair of desert boots because they keep my feet warm so I won't be so distressed in the next few months."

When I began to experience some success motivating Caroline to think about painful issues and identity feelings rather than act on the basis of delusion beliefs about herself and the world, she would often make a facial expression I mistakenly construed as a yawn. On one such occasion I asked her to tell me what this was about and she replied, "I'm opening my mouth because I want you to go in and find my feelings."

In addition to expressing herself in PMA Caroline learned with it in a literal way. She came to a session in a blaming rage directed at a man who had concluded a conversation with her with what seemed to me to be an innocuous typically American farewell remark, "take care." She saw nothing out of the ordinary about her enraged response, for she believed he was concretely forcing her to take responsibility for herself, and she was unable to maturely conceptualize her anger related to having to take care of herself and its relationship to her anger that as a child of two psychotic parents she had not adequately been taken care of.

Findings from neuroscience

The advent of research, both neuroscientific and infant observation, has furnished us with information not available to Freud, Klein and even Bion. There is an accumulation of neuroscientific evidence (summarized in Robbins, 2004, 2008, 2010, 2011) supporting the qualitative distinction between the neural circuitry underlying PMA and that of thought. It suggests that similar neural processes underlie dreaming (Solms, 1997; Solms and Turnbull, 2002), the immature brain of early life, and more suggestively the phenomenology of schizophrenia. Each of these phenomena are driven by the centers in the limbic system responsible for diffuse global psychosomatic affect rather than those in the prefrontal cortex that identify and process specific emotions. Each of these phenomena use parts of the brain responsible for holistic processes that do not differentiate the person from the world and the other. Both dreaming and schizophrenic delusions and hallucinations involve preferential activation of the temporal and occipital cortices that produce sensory-perceptual experiences. In dreaming and schizophrenia there seems to be a pattern of relative activation and quiescence within the parietal lobes related to functions of self-object differentiation that would account for the inaccurate perception of the locus of action as external rather than internal. The limbic and paralimbic structures that should be activated when a person is expected to perform cognitive tasks are not active in schizophrenics or in dreamers. The disconnection of limbic-paralimbic functioning with the prefrontal cortex and the general absence of activity in the prefrontal cortex would seem to underlie the absent capacity in schizophrenia to integrate experiences and related affects with a conscious reflective sense of self, and the inability to represent and be aware of feelings that is characteristic of PMA. None of these conditions make much use of the areas of prefrontal cortex necessary for symbolic reflective thought, a condition that when discussing schizophrenia Andreasen *et al.* (1992) called hypofrontality.

Rapid eye movement (REM) activity, that underlies dreaming, has been detected *in utero* suggesting that the neural circuitry responsible for PMA seems to be fully formed and operative at birth whereas studies of myelination of the brain support the observation that the capacity for logical realistic thought and thought-related language develops gradually over the first decade of life.

Development and shaping of psychosis: the family environment

How and why does a mental activity that is normal in infancy and early childhood become the mental foundation of adult psychosis? PMA is the normal way the mind works in the first several years of life because its particular neural circuitry involving subcortical limbic projections to the right hemisphere is more or less fully developed at birth, whereas myelination, the left brain and prefrontal cortical circuitry responsible for thought, matures slowly over the first decade or so of life (Paus *et al.*, 1999). PMA has superior adaptive value at a time when thinking is rudimentary and communicative language has yet to develop because its peremptory affect-inducing quality conveys states of need and distress and influences caregivers immediately and deeply in a way that a thoughtful request might not. It is difficult for anyone to ignore the cries and bodily expressions of an infant. While Klein believed this is a defense mechanism against instinctual rage – splitting and projective identification – neuropsychoanalytic attachment theorists look at the non-verbal communication between infant and caregiver that includes equally reflexive response of caregiving adults using baby talk, making noises, faces, mirroring expressions, in general behaving in such a way that the parent may be surprised to discover he or she is capable of. Such communication involves a complementary or mirroring PMA response in the adult. Reciprocally, the deep impressive or introjective quality of PMA makes it a powerful learning vehicle for the infant. Whereas PMA is the exclusive or nearly exclusive modality of infancy and early childhood, the parental expression of PMA is controlled and regulated as to time, place and purpose by the thoughtful adult mind so that it is a constructive aspect of parenting. Adults who function predominantly in PMA without such thoughtful regulation may not be good parents because they may be driven by "negative" affects – destructive, anxious, dysphoric, depressive – leading to behaviors toward the infant that distort the affective substrate of infant attachment in ways that have already been noted.

The capacity for thought and thought-related language matures slowly over the first decade of life. It does not evolve out of PMA nor does the capacity for PMA disappear; thought develops from separate neurological circuitry. It comes to predominate as the mental activity of choice, as it has superior socio-cultural adaptive value for the growing child and eventually the adult. The discipline that is an aspect of thought ordinarily enables development of control over the times, places and purposes for which PMA will be employed in addition to dreaming; usually ones that are sanctioned by the community.

In the instance of psychosis, for example schizophrenia, PMA persists as the preferred mental activity beyond the time when it is adaptive outside the family, and it draws on disturbed implicit affective leaning. In such instances development of thought is usually rudimentary and what thoughtful mind exists is dissociated from manifestations of PMA so that the circumstances and uses of PMA are not constructively regulated. Many people, starting with Sullivan (1953), and including an extensive family therapy literature of the 1950s and 1960s, have described pathogenic family configurations that distort the initial affective-relational attachment process, reward disabled or infantile behavior that is based on PMA and discourage development of thought, personal autonomy and separation from the family. Those who believe that schizophrenia is an illness of adolescence and early adulthood have not taken into account the tendency of such families to deny; not to perceive abnormality. Such denial keeps the disturbance from the attention of the outside world until the adolescent or young adult clearly fails to meet ordinary developmental milestones and creates social disruption in the process. For the child entrapped in such a stressful and confusing dependent situation there is no adaptive value to learn to think, bear and cope with painful thoughts and feelings, and primary mental expression becomes the modus operandi long after it becomes maladaptive in the larger culture into which the growing person must move. This we call psychosis.

References

Andreasen, N., Rezai, K., Alliger, R., Swayze, V., Flaum, M. and Kirchner, P. (1992) Hypofrontality in neuroleptic-naïve patients and patients with chronic schizophrenia: assessment with xenon 135 single photon-emission computed tomography and the Tower of London, *Archives of General Psychiatry* 49: 943–958.

Ainsworth, M.D.S., Blehar, M.C., Waters, E. and Wall, S. (1978) *Patterns of Attachment: A Psychological Study of the Strange Situation*, Hillsdale, NJ: Lawrence Erlbaum Associates, Inc.

Bion, W.R. (1957) Differentiation of the psychotic from the non-psychotic personalities, *International Journal of Psycho-Analysis* 38: 266–275.

Bion, W.R. (1959) Attacks on linking, *International Journal of Psycho-Analysis* 40: 308–315.

Bion, W.R. (1962) *Learning from Experience*, London: Tavistock.

Bion, W.R. (1967) *Second Thoughts*, London: Heinemann.

Bollas, C. (1987) *The Shadow of the Object: Psychoanalysis of the Unthought Known*, London: Free Association Books.

Bowlby, J. (1969) *Attachment and Loss, Vol. I: Attachment*, London: Hogarth Press.

Bucci, W. (2000) Pathways of emotional communication, *Psychoanalytic Inquiry* 21: 40–70.

Clyman, R. (1991) The procedural organization of emotions: a contribution from cognitive science to the psychoanalytic theory of therapeutic action, *Journal of the American Psychoanalytic Association* 39: 349–382.

Darwin, C. (1872) *The Expression of Emotion in Man and Animals*, Chicago: University of Chicago Press, 1965.

Dimberg, U. *et al.* (2000) Unconscious facial reactions to emotional facial expressions, *Psychological Science* 2: 86–89.

Emde, R. (1983) The prerepresentational self and its affective core, *Psychoanalytic Study of the Child*, 38: 165–192.

Freud, S. (1900) The interpretation of dreams, in J. Strachey (ed.) *Standard Edition*, Vols 4 and 5, London: Hogarth Press, 1962.

Gallese, L., Fadiga, L., Fogassi, L. and Rizzolatti, G. (1996) Action recognition in the premotor cortex, *Brain* 119: 593–609.

Grigsby, J. and Hartlaub, G. (1994) Procedural learning and the development and stability of character, *Perceptual and Motor Skills* 79: 355–370.

Klein, M. (1930) The importance of symbol-formation in the development of the ego, in *The Writings of Melanie Klein, Vol.1: Love, Guilt and Reparation and Other Works 1921–1945*, London: Hogarth Press, 1975, 219–232.

Klein, M. (1935) A contribution to the psychogenesis of manic-depressive states, in *The Writings of Melanie Klein, Vol.1: Love, Guilt and Reparation and Other Works 1921–1945*, London: Hogarth Press, 1975, 262–289.

Klein, M. (1937) Love, guilt and reparation, in *The Writings of Melanie Klein, Vol. 1: Love, Guilt and Reparation and Other Works 1921–1945*, London: Hogarth Press, 1975, 306–343.

Klein, M. (1946) Notes on some schizoid mechanisms, in *The Writings of Melanie Klein, Vol. 3: Envy and Gratitude and Other Works 1946–1963*, London: Hogarth Press, 1975, 1–24.

Lorberbaum, J.P., Newman, J.D., Horwitz, A.R., Dubno, J.R., Lydiard, R.B., Hamner, M.B., Bohning, D.E. and George, M.S. (2002) A potential role for thalamocingulate circuitry in human maternal behavior, *Biological Psychiatry* 51: 431–445.

Lyons-Ruth, K. (1999) The two-person unconscious: intersubjective dialogue, enactive relational representation, and the emergence of new forms of relational organization, *Psychoanalytic Inquiry* 19: 576–617.

Lyons-Ruth, K. (2003) Dissociation and the parent–infant dialogue: a longitudinal perspective from attachment research, *Journal of the American Psychoanalytic Association* 51: 883–911.

Manning, J.T., Trivers, R.L., Thornhill, R., Singh, D., Denman, J., Eklo, M.H. and Anderton, R.H. (1997) Ear asymmetry and left-side cradling, *Evolution and Human Behavior* 18: 327–340.

Meltzer, D. (1976) Dream-narrative and dream-continuity, *Contemporary Psychoanalysis* 12: 423–432.

Molnar-Szaracs, I., Gallese, V., Buccino, G. and Mazziotta, J.C. (2005) Grasping the intentions of others with one's own motor neuron system, *PLoS Biology* 3: 79.

Pally, R. (2007) The predicting brain: unconscious repetition, conscious reflection and therapeutic change, *International Journal of Psycho-Analysis* 88: 861–888.

Panksepp, J. (1998) *Affective Neuroscience: The Foundations of Human and Animal Emotions*, New York: Oxford University Press.

Paus, T., Zijdembos, A., Worsele, K., Collins, L., Blumenthal, J., Geidd, J., Rapoport, J., Evans, A., *et al.* (1999) Structural maturation of neural pathways in children and adolescents: in vivo study, *Science* 283: 1908–1911.
Robbins, M. (2004) Another look at dreaming: disentangling Freud's primary and secondary process theories, *Journal of the American Psychoanalytic Association* 52: 55–384.
Robbins, M. (2008) Primary mental expression: Freud, Klein and beyond, *Journal of the American Psychoanalytic Association* 56: 177–202.
Robbins, M. (2010) The primordial mind and psychosis, *Korean Journal of Schizophrenia Research* 13: 1–4.
Robbins, M. (2011) *The primordial mind in health and illness: A cross cultural perspective.* London: Routledge.
Robertson, J. and Robertson, J. (1971) Young children in brief separation—a fresh look, *Psychoanalytic Study of the Child* 26: 264–315.
Schore, A. (2003) *Affect Disregulation and Disorders of the Self*, New York: Norton.
Schore, A. (2005) A neuropsychoanalytic viewpoint: commentary on paper by Steven H. Knoblauch, *Psychoanalytic Dialogues* 15: 829–854.
Segal, H. (1957) Notes on symbol formation, *International Journal of Psychoanalysis* 38: 39–45.
Sifneos, P.E. (1975) Problems of psychotherapy of patients with alexithymic characteristics and physical disease, *Psychotherapy and Psychosomatics* 26: 65–70.
Solms, M. (1997) *The Neuropsychology of Dreams: A Clinico-Anatomical Study*, Mahwah, NJ: Lawrence Erlbaum Associates, Inc.
Solms, M. and Turnbull, O. (2002) *The Brain and the Inner World*, New York: Other Press.
Squire, L. (1986) Mechanisms of memory, *Science* 232: 1612–1619.
Stern, D.B. (1989) The analyst's unformulated experience of the patient, *Contemporary Psychoanalysis* 25: 1–33.
Stern, D.N. (1985) *The Interpersonal World of the Infant*, New York: Basic Books.
Stern, D.N., Sander, L.W., Nahum, J.P., Harrison, A.M., Lyons-Ruth, K., Morgan, A.C., Bruschweilerstern, N. and Tronick, E.Z. (1998) Non-interpretive mechanisms in psychoanalytic therapy: the "something more" than interpretation, *International Journal of Psycho-Analysis* 79: 903–921.
Sullivan, H. (1953) *Schizophrenia as a Human Process*, New York: Norton.
Tomasello, M. (1999) *The Cultural Origins of Human Cognition*, Cambridge, MA: Harvard University Press.
Trevarthen, C. (1980) The foundations of intersubjectivity: development of interpersonal and cooperative understanding in infants, in D. Olson (ed.) *The Social Foundation of Language and Thought*, New York: Norton, 316–342.

Chapter 12

Subordination, submission and the evolution of depression after psychosis

Andrew Gumley and Max Birchwood

> It is a total psychological experience. There is no strategies you can make. You just have to sit there and experience – abuse. And, the most important thing, and I said this to my psychiatrist, is my illness has my entire back catalogue <laughs>. It has my entire diary, so it can pick things that have happened years ago, show a symbol of it, show a picture of it, and it's a horrible experience because you begin to relive those experiences. You don't have to relive them because they are generally bad experiences, of my schizophrenia, a lot of embarrassment, a lot of humiliation, and the reasons why they are so bad is that virtually every time I have an attack, the illness goes through them and makes you relive them to a certain extent.

Introduction

Quality of life is increasingly regarded as a key dimension of outcome in complex mental health problems reflecting the importance of the individual's subjective evaluation of their experience, their autonomy in determining valued outcomes for themselves and the wider interpersonal, societal and cultural context of their recovery. It is now becoming clear that the experience of depression is one of the major factors which contribute to poorer quality of life amongst individuals with psychotic disorders generally (Saarni *et al.*, 2010) and in those diagnosed with schizophrenia specifically (Narvaez *et al.*, 2008; Meijer *et al.*, 2009). These latter studies show no association between quality of life and positive, negative and disorganisation symptoms. Although methods of assessing quality of life in people with psychosis and mental health problems more generally have been criticised (Brazier, 2010) it remains clear that depression in schizophrenia is linked to a number of problematic outcomes and poorer overall recovery. In this chapter we will explore the correlates and mechanisms underpinning the experience of depression amongst those individuals recovering from psychosis. We will present a psychological understanding of depression derived from evolutionary psychology, which focuses on the crucial role of shame and threats to self-identity in the evolution and expression of depression in the context of psychosis. Finally, we will illustrate the psychotherapeutic implications of this understanding for recovery after psychosis.

Post-psychotic depression (PPD)

It has been estimated that around 6 per cent of individuals with a diagnosis of schizophrenia will complete suicide during their lifetime (Palmer *et al.*, 2005). The National Institute of Mental Health Longitudinal Study of Chronic Schizophrenia found that over a six-year period, 38 per cent had at least one suicide attempt and 57 per cent were admitted to hospital with suicidal thinking (Roy and Pompili, 2009). Suicide and attempted suicide have been most strongly linked to hallucinations, depression, social isolation, substance misuse, longer duration of untreated psychosis and demoralisation (Pinikahana *et al.*, 2003; Bertelsen *et al.*, 2007; Falcone *et al.*, 2010). Depression is a major marker for risk of suicide and prevalence rates of depression in those with a diagnosis of schizophrenia suggest that between 33 per cent and 50 per cent of individuals also meet criteria for major depression (Whitehead *et al.*, 2002). Depression is a common antecedent of first episode psychosis (Hafner *et al.*, 2005) and of relapse (Birchwood *et al.*, 1989) as well as being prevalent in the acute phase.

It has also been shown that depression emerges following the acute phase and is independent of positive symptom severity, relapse and negative symptoms. This has given rise to the concept of post-psychotic depression. PPD is a relatively common clinical state emerging in the aftermath of acute psychotic symptoms with prevalence rates reaching around 50 per cent (McGlashan and Carpenter, 1976; Birchwood *et al.*, 2000). Attempts to describe the course pattern of PPD suggest that its onset occurs concurrently with psychosis but becomes clinically prominent only after psychotic symptoms subside (McGlashan and Carpenter, 1976). It is in the context of PPD that the hopelessness and suicidal thinking unfolds. Depression has been associated with poorer adherence to treatment (Conley *et al.*, 2007), longer duration of untreated psychosis (Drake *et al.*, 2003), greater problems in family relationships (Rocca *et al.*, 2005), poorer interpersonal functioning (Rocca *et al.*, 2005), early life trauma and stressful life events (Ventura *et al.*, 2000; Scheller-Gilkey *et al.*, 2002) and greater experiences of stigma (Angermeyer *et al.*, 2004). Most consistently, in a meta-analysis of 40 studies greater depression has been linked to greater insight (Minz *et al.*, 2003). Insight is also linked to suicidal behaviour (Amador *et al.*, 1996; Crumlish *et al.*, 2005). Whilst good insight in itself is linked to improved adherence and engagement, where this insight is accompanied by feelings of stigma, the relationship between insight and depression is strong (Staring *et al.*, 2009).

Shame and depression

Internalised stigma and shame are key features of depression in schizophrenia (Gumley *et al.*, 2010). Acute psychosis and its sequelae can be understood as a stressful life event, which evokes feelings of loss and threatens an individual's social identity, rank, value and/or acceptance by others. Individuals who develop depression and suicidal thinking following psychosis appraise this life event as representing a humiliating threat to their future status leading to the loss of a sense of personal value in various social roles (Birchwood *et al.*, 2000, 2006). Birchwood *et al.* (1993) showed that depression following an acute episode of psychosis was associated with individuals' perception of being unable to prevent or control relapse (e.g. 'I am powerless to influence or control my illness') or the fear of psychosis itself (e.g. 'My illness frightens me'). Rooke and Birchwood (1998) followed up this group of patients 2 and a half years later. Levels of depression were persistent over time, as were appraisals of entrapment (inability to control or escape from psychosis), loss of social role and self-blame. Individuals who were depressed felt greater entrapment and loss in relation to their psychosis. In addition there was evidence that these appraisals were consistent with participants' personal experiences of psychosis. For example, participants with depression were more likely to have experienced more compulsory admissions and the loss of or drop in employment status. Theoretical perspectives derived from evolutionary psychology as exemplified by social ranking theory (Gilbert, 1992) have provided a theoretical framework to explain these findings. A person's perception of their social attractiveness and acceptability to others confirm their sense of rank, importance and place within their social, cultural and interpersonal environment. Therefore life events that evoke feelings of loss (e.g. loss or disruption in important attachments or friendships) or events that threaten an individual's social ranking or importance (e.g. feeling humiliated by an episode of psychosis) are depressogenic via threats to social identity leading to the lowering of perceived self-esteem, social status and the triggering of self-criticism (e.g. 'My illness means I'm defective'). In this context self-criticism is understood as a coping strategy aimed at correcting perceived signs of stigmatised status thus countering threats to social identity. However, self-criticism may ultimately play a key role in confirming negative expectations and driving demoralisation and disengagement from valued activities and roles.

In relation to people with a diagnosis of schizophrenia, these processes can be observed in two important studies. Birchwood *et al.* (2000) found that, in a sample of 105 individuals, a proportion of 36 per cent developed post-psychotic depression (PPD) without any associated changes in positive and negative symptoms. Participants who developed PPD were more likely than their non-PPD counterparts to attribute the cause of psychosis to themselves (self-blame), perceive greater loss of autonomy and valued role, and perceive themselves as entrapped and humiliated by their illness. In addition, individuals with and without PPD aspired to similar social and vocational roles. However, consistent with the predictions of social ranking theory, those who developed PPD saw their future status as lower. These participants also had greater insight into having a psychotic illness. Individuals who developed depression following psychosis appraised this life event as representing a humiliating threat to their future status, leading to the loss of valued social roles, from which escape was blocked due to actual or feared relapse, or indeed persistent symptoms. Gumley and Schwannauer (2006) in a prospective one-year follow-up compared individuals who experienced a relapse versus those who remained well. Those experiencing a relapse reported significantly increased feelings of self-blame and shame over time. In addition (although we did not observe differences between these two groups in terms of positive and negative symptoms, negative appraisals of illness and psychological distress at the outset of the study), 12-months later relapsers had significantly more psychological distress including somatisation, obsessive compulsive symptoms, interpersonal sensitivity, depression and anxiety. In addition, we found that relapsers had significantly greater feelings of self-blame and loss, and lower self-esteem (Gumley and Schwannauer, 2006). We have also found that feelings of entrapment and low self-esteem characterise social anxiety in persons diagnosed with schizophrenia (Gumley *et al.*, 2004) and that feelings of entrapment predict the presence of both anxiety and depressive disorders which co-occur with schizophrenia (Karatzias *et al.*, 2007) and hopelessness (White *et al.*, 2007).

Shame and social anxiety

Michail and Birchwood (2009) found that amongst individuals recovering from a first episode psychosis who were also experiencing social anxiety, levels of depression were also significantly higher. Indeed, in their group there was a significant overlap in levels of depression so that over half of their sample who were depressed were also socially anxious, whereas amongst those individuals who did not meet criteria for depression, only 12 per cent were experiencing social anxiety. In this sense depression and social anxiety in the context of psychosis may go hand in hand and reflect a common core underlying psychological mechanisms.

Extending our analysis of shame in PPD, there is considerable evidence that shame also underpins the experience of social anxiety amongst individuals with psychosis (Gumley *et al.*, 2004). Although there is evidence that social anxiety is a precursor to the development of psychosis (Johnstone *et al.*, 2005), there is also evidence that social anxiety emerges in the recovery period after psychosis (Pallanti *et al.*, 2004). In an important study of social anxiety and shame in first episode psychosis, Birchwood and colleagues (2006) and Michail and Birchwood (2009) found that social anxiety was not linked to the symptoms of psychosis particularly to severity of persecutory delusions and levels of suspiciousness, therefore underlining the case that social anxiety was not merely a byproduct of psychotic symptoms. Neither did Birchwood and colleagues find that social anxiety was related to premorbid social and interpersonal functioning, suggesting that social anxiety in their sample was unlikely to reflect longstanding premorbid anxiety difficulties. Taking into account levels of depression in their sample, feelings of shame about psychosis were the most significant predictor of social anxiety. Those individuals meeting criteria for social anxiety disorder (SAD; 29 per cent of sample) felt more entrapped by their psychosis and perceived greater social loss arising from their psychosis. This group of individuals were also more depressed underlining the significant component of mood in the context of social anxiety. These results suggest that acceptance of a new social ('schizophrenic') identity emerges as a key dimension of self-identity that unfolds in social interactions. This was further reflected in these individuals seeing themselves as having a lower rank and attractiveness compared to others and thus adopting a subordinate social status. In addition, Michail and Birchwood (2009) found that individuals with social anxiety are more likely to appraise individuals in their environment as threatening and are more likely to rate the threat arising from these individuals as awful. In a further analysis of these data (Michail and Birchwood, under review) individuals with social anxiety experience greater shame proneness and perceived their social rank as lower, alongside greater feelings of entrapment, loss of status and social role. From an evolutionary, social ranking theory perspective, subordination and submission can be understood as coping strategies aimed at the avoidance of rejection and attack from more powerful others.

Understanding emotional adaptation as a response to social identity threat and stigma

A key dimension by which we can develop an understanding of individuals' adaptation and recovery from psychosis is through understanding the nature of threats arising from these experiences and their sequelae. In the studies discussed above those individuals with lower levels of depression and/or social anxiety also reported greater denial and minimisation of psychosis. Furthermore, Lysaker and colleagues (2008) showed that higher levels of self-awareness in combination with lower levels of internalised stigma (or shame about psychosis) were linked to more enriched and coherent self and recovery narratives. In this sense greater internal stigma acts as a block to the development of individuals' capacity to narrate and make sense of their experiences. Lysaker and colleagues (2005) also found that greater self-reflexivity was associated with greater depression. This is likely to be linked to the perception of shame and stigma as demonstrated by Birchwood and colleagues' (2000) findings that those with greater depression and social anxiety report greater insight into and awareness of their experiences.

One key threat facing individuals recovering from psychosis is the presence of external societal stigma (Major and O'Brien, 2005). Major and O'Brien (2005) conceptualise stigma as a threat to social identity. Goffman (1963) defined stigma as having 'an attribute that is deeply discrediting' (p. 3). Thus stigma related to how the individual is held in the eyes of others and not solely arising from self-perceptions. According to Goffman, stigmatisation represents a process whereby an individual who possesses a 'deviant attribute' is globally devalued. Stigma arises during a social interaction when an individual's actual social identity does not meet normative societal expectations of the attributes the individual should possess. Thus, the individual's social identity is spoiled, and he or she is assumed to be incapable of fulfilling the role requirements within their social, cultural and interpersonal context. Schizophrenia is highly stigmatised in our society (Haghighat, 2001) and is often associated with perceptions of unattractiveness, exclusion from work and relationships, homelessness and violence. Importantly, actual increased social distance appears to be associated with a diagnosis of schizophrenia but not with depression (Angermeyer *et al.*, 2004). Kurzban and Leary (2001) have argued that stigmatization occurs:

> when a shared characteristic of a category of people becomes consensually regarded as a basis for disassociating from (that is, avoiding, excluding, ostracizing, or otherwise minimizing interaction with) individuals who are perceived to be members of that category.
>
> (Leary and Schreindorfer, 1998, p. 15)

Specifically, Kurzban and Leary (2001) argued that stigmatisation has emerged through evolution to ensure reproductive success, reciprocal co-operation and social cohesion. Thus individuals or other groups perceived to threaten group security become subject to stigma and exclusion. Social rank theory suggests that some forms of social competition (for acceptance and status in social groups, access to resources, allies and sexual partners) are linked to the ability to be attractive to others, to be chosen and/or included. Those deemed unattractive, for whatever reason, are at risk of being either passively avoided (not chosen or included) or actively rejected (Gilbert, 2002). Therefore, social anxiety reflects a focus on (a) a belief that one has to compete for one's own social place, e.g. for friendships, sexual partners, that is impress others; but (b) in attempting to do this one will be seen as boring and/or incompetent, that is rendered unattractive in some way and thus will be passively ignored or avoided, or actively rejected (Gilbert and Trower, 2001). Depression is focused on (a) actual and perceived losses in valued roles and life goals; and (b) a sense of shame, humiliation and social marginalisation. When combined with a sense of entrapment or blocked escape from persisting symptoms, relapse or encapsulation in psychiatric services this results in the emergence of a new socially flawed and defective self-identity. These common shared underlying mechanisms linked to both depression and social anxiety provide a basis to understand the evolution of negative affect observed following first episode psychosis.

Within the fields of sociology, anthropology, political science and psychology issues of social power, social control, subordination and submissiveness have been central areas of study (e.g. Scott, 1990). The dynamics of power, rank and subordination are linked closely to the expression of cultural, social/group and self-identity and interconnectedness (see Gilbert, 2000 for a review). Furthermore, problems related to behaving overly submissively have been strongly associated with psychological problems, especially depression and social anxiety. Submissive behaviours can be viewed as stable strategies, which have unfolded through our evolutionary history to provide a series of defences against aggression and interpersonal conflict, social threats (including loss of status and social standing), separation from sources of security and attachment, and exclusion or rejection from social groups. Submissive strategies are designed to modify or change the mental states of others who are in positions of greater social power and rank. Submissive strategies orientate individuals to adopt certain behaviours to attenuate, minimise and/or eliminate threats coming from other individuals or the group. First, they are linked to increasing attention to and vigilance for signals of social threat. This may therefore include ruminative preoccupation with the mental states of others. In keeping with this analysis preoccupied attachment organisation is associated with greater, hyperactive (but thwarted) efforts to mentalise (Fonagy *et al.*, 1998). Second, submissive strategies are linked to moderating or curtailing behaviour in order to avoid eliciting attacks from others; for example, this might involve active avoidance of interpersonal situations or the inhibition or avoidance of one's own emotional needs, beliefs and autonomy in favour of those of others. Third, the avoidance of conflicts and rejections may be achieved by submitting quickly or by being overly compliant with others' wishes, needs, intentions and desires. This might involve compliance with antipsychotic medication, seeking reassurance and expressions of neediness, or the internalisation of externally held threats to the self. Therefore externally held stigmatising beliefs and behaviours become internalised as self-stigmatising and self-attacking/shaming beliefs and behaviours. Therefore, we can understand sensitivity to threat including heightened attention to others' mental states, subordinated and submissive behaviour, and disengagement from valued social roles and goals as part of a social mentality designed to manage social, interpersonal and group threats to the multiple aspects of selfhood (Gilbert and Liotti, 2011).

Psychological problems as unintended consequences of coping

A social mentalities analysis of social identity threat detection, appraisal and coping provides an evolutionary based perspective to consider the utility of submissive/subordinated strategies. Whilst subordination, submission and self-criticism are designed as survival-based safety-seeking strategies, they bring with them costs or unintended consequences that often define the nature of problems experienced by individuals. In this way emotional problems observed during the processes of recovery after psychosis can be understood as an expression of individuals' best efforts to adapt to and cope with the stressful experiences arising from psychosis. A key aspect of this model is that it offers a dynamic understanding of the unfolding of affect, coping and symptom expression over time. Therefore, in this sense affect regulation (e.g. avoidance of negative emotions) influences the direct expression of affect (e.g. downplaying the significance of experiences) but also the responses of others (e.g. misunderstanding a person's primary concerns), which in turn influences emotional experience (e.g. feelings of frustration and loneliness) and so on. In this sense affect and coping sit within a wider interpersonal, group and cultural frame, which shapes the evolution of adaptation and recovery (Gumley and Schwannauer, 2006). Table 12.1 describes the relationship between threat, types of submissive strategy and unintended consequences.

In the context of emotional recovery after psychosis submissive/subordinated strategies inadvertently magnify the expression and experience of painful affect. Increased vigilance towards social threats, stigma, shame and fear of recurrence increases anxiety and fearfulness via more availability of threat-related information and greater preoccupation with self or other mental states. Avoidance is linked to increased feelings of shame, loss and disconnection from valued roles and social relationships. Subordination and compliance are linked to feelings of powerlessness, lack of control, shame, need for reassurance and others taking a more dominant stance in relation to self. This can give rise to feelings of resentment and being misunderstood, thus amplifying feelings of loss, loneliness and defeat associated with the development of depression.

Key tasks in promoting emotional recovery

One of the key implications of our analysis is an understanding of the relational and interpersonal context of recovery beginning with an examination of our own ways of relating to the person and their context in recovery. Therefore, given our preceding analysis, therapeutic strategies that focus on compliance with medication and other treatments can unintentionally reinforce subordinate or submissive coping. Similarly educational strategies emphasising a unidimensional illness-based understanding of the person's experiences place the provider of the education and treatment in a position of expertise and power, thus replicating the dynamics of dominance and subordination.

Valuing the person, their experiences, beliefs, values and their autonomy and exploration lies at the heart of recovery. A key means to achieving this is

Table 12.1 Social identity threat, defence and unintended consequences

Sources of social threat	*Social defensive (submissive) strategies*	*Unintended consequences*
e.g. Disapproval by others	Increasing attention to and vigilance for threat	Increased availability of threat related information. Anxiety and fearfulness. Preoccupation/rumination with others' mental states. Preoccupation/rumination with own mental state and behaviour.
e.g. Social rejection	Avoidance	Narrowing social supports. Increasing sense of shame. Loneliness and isolation. Feeling misunderstood. Loss of role and friendships. Disengagement from goals. Others failing to understand or respond accurately to person's needs.
e.g. Fear of recurrence	Subordination, submission and compliance	Increased feelings of powerlessness. Greater internalised stigma and shame. Feelings of anger and resentment. Others adopting a more dominant stance. Feeling out of control. Needing reassurance. Feelings of entrapment, defeat, hopelessness and depression.

through the building of a collaborative relationship, which acts as the overarching principle governing cognitive therapy. This collaborative stance requires: (a) unconditional acceptance; (b) an accurate attunement to the person's internal reality; (c) working within the person's zone of proximal development (see Chadwick, 2006); (d) development of exploration, choice and autonomy as well as a secure base to encourage help seeking, expression and clarification of meaning and affect (see Gumley and Schwannauer, 2006). Key to the approach that we have outlined is the development of a shared understanding of individuals' attempts to cope with threats to self-identity. Our approach brings with it an opportunity to validate how individuals respond to threatening events and experiences by understanding the utility (or advantages) of coping strategies (e.g. self-criticism, withdrawal and avoidance, adoption of a defective 'illness' identity). This is best understood by placing individuals' coping in the context of a timeline enabling the exploration of experiences, availability of social support, utilisation of social supports and the unfolding of affect and quality of life over time. Such a focus on developing an understanding of the interplay between experience, support, coping and affect provides a framework to develop alternative coping strategies (or strengthen existing coping) in a way that minimises unintended negative consequences. A focus on coping strategies aligned to individuals' values and goals is key to enabling the individual to re-engage in valued activities and relationships. This can be supported by enabling the development of skills in tolerating distress and also in responding non-judgementally and compassionately to feelings of threat, shame and humiliation.

Whilst this kind of work can take place on an individual (White *et al.*, 2011) or group basis (Braehler *et al.*, 2012), it is also important to consider the service context of recovery. In particular, strategies for engagement that emphasise compliance and psychiatric insight may interact in an unhelpful way with submissive, subordinated or self-critical strategies, leading to passive engagement and lack of empowerment of service users, increased dependence on services, acceptance of a defective social identity and loss of autonomy and valued goals and activities. The framework outlined here provides a potentially useful context for service providers to think about how their response to recovery after psychosis can shape individuals' adaptation in a dynamic way.

References

Amador, X.F., Friedman, J.H., Kasapis, C., Yale, S.A., Flaum, M. and Gorman, J.M. (1996) Suicidal behavior in schizophrenia and its relationship to awareness of illness, *American Journal of Psychiatry* 153: 1185–1188.

Angermeyer, M.C., Matschinger, H. and Corrigan, P.W. (2004) Familiarity with mental illness and social distance from people with schizophrenia and major depression: testing a model using data from a representative population survey, *Schizophrenia Research* 69: 175–182.

Bertelsen, M., Jeppesen, P., Petersen, L., Thorup, A., Ohlenschlaeger, J., Quach, P., Ostergaard, T., Krarup, G., Jorgensen, P. and Nordentoft, M. (2007) Suicidal behaviour and mortality in first episode psychosis: the OPUS trial, *British Journal of Psychiatry* 191: 140–146.

Birchwood, M., Smith, J., MacMillan, F., Hogg, B., Prasad, R., Harvey, C. and Bering, S. (1989) Predicting relapse in schizophrenia: the development and implementation of an early signs monitoring system using patients and families as observers: a preliminary investigation, *Psychological Medicine* 19: 649–656.

Birchwood, M., Mason, R., Macmillan, F. and Healey, J. (1993) Depression, demoralisation and control over psychotic illness, *Psychological Medicine* 23: 387–395.

Birchwood, M., Iqbal, Z., Chadwick, P. and Trower, P. (2000) Cognitive approach to depression and suicidal thinking in psychosis I. Ontogeny of post-psychotic depression, *British Journal of Psychiatry* 177: 516–521.

Birchwood, M., Trower, P., Brunet, K., Gilbert, P., Iqbal, Z. and Jackson, C. (2006) Social anxiety and shame of psychosis: a study in first episode psychosis, *Behaviour Research and Therapy* 45: 1025–1037.

Braehler, C., Gumley, A., Harper, J., Wallace, S. and Gilbert, P. (2012) Compassion focused group therapy for recovery after psychosis: results from a pilot randomized controlled trial, *British Journal of Clinical Psychology* DOI: 10.111/bjc.12009

Brazier, J. (2010) Is the EQ-5D fit for purpose in mental health?, *British Journal of Psychiatry* 197: 348–349.

Chadwick, P. (2006) *Person-based Cognitive Therapy for Distressing Psychosis*, Chichester: Wiley.

Conley, R.R., Ascher-Svanum, H., Zhu, B., Faries, D. and Kinon, B.J. (2007) The burden of depressive symptoms in the long-term treatment of patients with schizophrenia, *Schizophrenia Research* 90: 186–197.

Crumlish, N., Whitty, P., Kamali, M., Clarke, M., Browne, S., McTique, O., Lane, A., Kinsella, A., Larkin, C. and O'Callaghan, E. (2005) Early insight predicts depression and attempted suicide after 4 years in first episode schizophrenia and schizophreniform disorder, *Acta Psychiatrica Scandinavica* 112: 449–455.

Drake, R.J., Pickles, A., Nentall, R., Kinderman, P., Haddock, G., Tarrier, N. and Lewis, S.W. (2003) The evolution of insight, paranoia and depression during early schizophrenia, *Psychological Medicine* 34: 285–292.

Falcone, T., Mishra, L., Carlton, E., Lee, C., Butler, R.S., Janigro, D., Simon, B. and Franco, K. (2010) Suicidal behaviour in adolescents with first episode psychosis, *Clinical Schizophrenia and Related Psychoses* 4: 34–40.

Fonagy, P., Target, M., Steele, H. and Steele, M. (1998) Reflective functioning manual (Version 5) for application with the adult attachment interview. Unpublished manuscript.

Gilbert, P. (1992) *Depression: The Evolution of Powerlessness*, Hove, UK: Lawrence Erlbaum Associates, Inc.

Gilbert, P. (2000) Varieties of submissive behaviour as forms of social defense: their evolution and role in depression, in L. Sloman and P. Gilbert (eds) *Subordination and Defeat: An Evolutionary Approach to Mood Disorders and their Therapy*, Hove, UK: Lawrence Erlbaum Associates Ltd.

Gilbert, P. (2002) Body shame: a biopsychosocial conceptualisation and overview, with treatment implications, in P. Gilbert and J. Miles (eds) *Body Shame: Conceptualisation, Research and Treatment*, London: Brunner-Routledge.

Gilbert, P. and Trower, P. (2001) Evolution and process in social anxiety, in W.R. Crozier and L.E. Alden (eds) *International Handbook of Social Anxiety*, Chichester: Wiley, 259–280.

Gilbert, P. and Liotti, I. (2011) Mentalizing, motivation, and social mentalities: theoretical considerations and implications for psychotherapy, *Psychology and Psychotherapy: Theory, Research and Practice* 84: 9–25.

Goffman, I. (1963) *Stigma: Notes on the Management of Spoiled Identity*, Englewood Cliffs, NJ: Prentice Hall.

Gumley, A. and Schwannauer, M. (2006) *Staying Well After Psychosis: A Cognitive Interpersonal Approach to Emotional Recovery and Relapse Prevention*, Chichester: Wiley.

Gumley, A., O'Grady, M., Power, K.G. and Schwannauer, M. (2004) Negative beliefs about illness and self-esteem: a comparison of socially anxious and non-socially anxious individuals with psychosis, *New Zealand and Australia Journal of Psychiatry* 38(11–12): 960–964.

Gumley, A., Braehler, C., Laithwaite, H., Macbeth, A. and Gilbert, P. (2010) A compassion focused model of recovery after psychosis, *International Journal of Cognitive Psychotherapy* 3(2): 186–201.

Hafner, H., Maurer, K., Trendler, G., van der Heiden, W. and Schmidt, M. (2005) The early course of schizophrenia and depression, *European Archives of Psychiatry and Clinical Neuroscience* 255: 163–173.

Haghighat, R. (2001) A unitary theory of stigmatization—pursuit of self-interest and routes to destigmatisation, *British Journal of Psychiatry* 178: 207–215.

Johnstone, E.C., Ebmeier, K.P., Miller, P., Owens, D.G.C. and Lawrie, S.M. (2005) Predicting schizophrenia: findings from the Edinburgh high-risk study, *British Journal of Psychiatry* 186: 18–25.

Karatzias, T., Gumley, A.I., Power, K.G. and O'Grady, M. (2007) Illness appraisals and self-esteem as correlates of anxiety and affective co-morbid disorders in schizophrenia, *Comprehensive Psychiatry* 48(4): 371–375.

Kurzban, R. and Leary, M. (2001) Evolutionary origins of stigmatization: the functions of social exclusion, *Psychological Bulletin* 127: 187–208.

Leary, M.R. and Schreindorfer, L.S. (1998) The stigmatization of fflV and AIDS: rubbing salt in the wound, in V.J. Derlega and A.P. Barbee (eds) *HIV and Social Interaction,* Thousand Oaks, CA: Sage, 12–29.

Lysaker, P.H., Carcione, A., Dimaggio, G., Johannesen, J.K., Nicolo, G., Procacci, M. and Semerari, A. (2005) Metacognition amidst narratives of self and illness in schizophrenia: associations with neurocognition, symptoms, insight and quality of life, *Acta Psychiatrica Scandinavica* 112: 64–71.

Lysaker, P.H., Buck, K.D., Taylor, A.C. and Roe, D. (2008) Associations of metacognition and internalized stigma with quantitive assessments of self experience in narratives of schizophrenia, *Psychiatry Research* 157: 31–38.

McGlashan, T.H. and Carpenter, W.T. (1976) An investigation of the postpsychotic depressive syndrome, *American Journal of Psychiatry* 133: 14–19.

Major, B. and O'Brien, L.T. (2005) The social psychology of stigma, *Annual Review Psychology* 56: 393–421.

Meijer, C.J., Koeter, M.W., Sprangers, M.A. and Schene, A.H. (2009) Predictors of general quality of life and the mediating role of health related quality of life in patients with schizophrenia, *Social Psychiatry Psychiatric Epidemiology* 44: 361–368.

Michail, M. and Birchwood, M. (2009) Social anxiety disorder in first episode psychosis: incidence, phenomenology and relationship with paranoia, *British Journal of Psychiatry* 195: 234–241.

Michail, M. and Birchwood, M. (under review) Social anxiety and shame cognitions in psychosis.

Minz, A.R., Dobson, K.S. and Romney, D.M. (2003) Insight in schizophrenia: a meta-analysis, *Schizophrenia Research* 61: 75–88.

Narvaez, J.M., Twamley, E.W., McKibbin, C.L., Heaton, R.K. and Patterson, T.L. (2008) Subjective and objective quality of life in schizophrenia, *Schizophrenia Research* 98: 201–208.

Pallanti, S., Quercioli, L. and Hollander, E. (2004) Social anxiety in outpatients with schizophrenia: a relevant cause of disability, *American Journal of Psychiatry* 161: 53–58.

Palmer, B.A., Pankratz, V.S. and Bostwick, J.M. (2005) The lifetime risk of suicide in schizophrenia: a reexamination, *Archives of General Psychiatry* 62: 247–253.

Pinikahana, J., Happell, B. and Keks, N.A. (2003) Suicide and schizophrenia: a review of literature for the decade (1990–1999) and implications for mental health nursing, *Issues in Mental Health Nursing* 24: 27–43.

Rocca, P., Bellino, S., Calvarese, P., Marchiaro, L., Patria, L., Rasetti, R. and Bogetto, F. (2005) Depressive and negative symptoms in schizophrenia: different effects on clinical features, *Comprehensive Psychiatry* 46: 304–310.

Rooke, O. and Birchwood, M. (1998) Loss, humiliation and entrapment as appraisals of schizophrenia in a prospective study of depressed and non-depressed patients, *British Journal of Clinical Psychology* 37: 259–268.

Roy, A. and Pompili, M. (2009) Management of schizophrenia with suicide risk, *Psychiatric Clinics of North America* 32: 863–883.

Saarni, S.I., Viertio, S., Perala, J., Koskinen, S., Lonnqvist, J. and Suvisaari, J. (2010) Quality of life of people with schizophrenia, bipolar disorder and other psychotic disorders, *British Journal of Psychiatry* 197: 386–394.

Scheller-Gilkey, G., Thomas, S.M., Wooline, B.J. and Miller, A.H. (2002) Symptoms in patients with co-morbid substance use and schizophrenia, *Schizophrenia Bulletin* 28: 223–231.

Scott, J.C. (1990) *Domination and the Arts of Resistance: Hidden Transcripts*, New Haven, CT: Yale University Press.

Staring, A.B.P., van der Gaag, M., van den Berge, M., Dulvenvoorden, H.J. and Mulder, C.L. (2009) Stigma moderates the associations of insight with depressed mood, low self esteem, and low quality of life in patients with schizophrenia spectrum disorders, *Schizophrenia Research* 115: 363–369.

Ventura, J., Neuchterlein, K.H., Subotnik, K.L., Hardesty, J.P. and Mintz, J. (2000) Life events can trigger depressive exacerbation in the early course of schizophrenia, *Journal of Abnormal Psychology* 109: 139–144.

White, R., McCreery, M., Gumley, A.I. and Mulholland, C. (2007) Hopelessness in schizophrenia: the impact of symptoms and beliefs about illness, *Journal of Nervous and Mental Disease* 195(12): 968–975.

White, R., Gumley, A., McTaggart, J., Rattrie, L., McConville, D., Cleare, S. and Mitchell, G. (2011) A feasibility study of acceptance and commitment therapy for emotional adaptation following psychosis, *Behaviour Research and Therapy* 49(12): 901–907.

Whitehead, C., Moss, S., Cardno, A., Lewis, G. and Furtado, V.A. (2002) Antidepressants for people with both schizophrenia and depression, *Cochrane Database of Systematic Reviews* Issue 2, Art. No: CD002305.

Chapter 13

Negative symptoms in schizophrenia

The role of social defeat

Ross White, Heather Laithwaite and Paul Gilbert

Negative symptoms account for much of the long-term morbidity and poor functional outcome of patients with schizophrenia (Kurtz *et al.*, 2005). To date, the etiological mechanisms underlying negative symptoms remain poorly understood and there has been comparatively little work done on developing effective treatments for negative symptoms. Building on themes from evolutionary psychology, we propose that the experience of social defeat and the brain systems evolved to cope with defeats play important roles in the emergence of negative symptoms. In support of these claims, the chapter will integrate research findings relating to psychological, biochemical and neuro-imaging correlates of negative symptoms to help further understanding about the emergence and persistence of negative symptoms. A clinical vignette will be used to illustrate how the experience of social defeat can be used to help formulate the development of negative symptoms. The chapter will conclude by discussing how a social defeat model of negative symptoms may lead to innovative psychosocial interventions being developed to ameliorate negative symptoms.

Phenomenology of negative symptoms

The use of the word 'negative' in the term 'negative symptoms' reflects the way in which these symptoms have traditionally been considered abnormal not because they are present but because they are absent. Negative symptoms are, by definition, deficient from normal functioning (e.g. reduced emotional responsiveness). Strauss *et al.* (1974) were the first to coin the term 'negative symptoms' when investigating predictors of outcome in schizophrenia. However, the types of deficit to which the term now applies had been noted much earlier. Emile Kraepelin (1971) described the weakening of the well-springs of volition as one of the two groups of maladies of dementia praecox. Bleuler (1950) noted that the restriction in emotional experience and expression in patients with schizophrenia could not be considered secondary to what they described as the 'dissociative pathology', e.g. delusions and hallucinations. Rado (1956) and Meehl (1962) gave special emphasis to the reduced hedonic capacity observed in patients with schizophrenia. Following the introduction of the term, contention emerged about what precisely qualified as a 'negative symptom'. Crow (1985) proposed that negative symptoms have two principal manifestations: a poverty of speech and flat affect. However, Andreasen (1985) used a much broader definition of negative symptoms that included flat affect, poverty of speech, avolition-apathy and anhedonia-asociality. Negative symptoms of psychosis are most commonly assessed using standardised interviewer rated measures including the Positive and Negative Syndrome Scale (PANSS; Kay *et al.*, 1987) and the Scale for Assessment of Negative Symptoms (SANS; Andreasen, 1981). Mueser *et al.* (1994) reported a factor analysis study of the SANS which resulted in three factors: (1) affective flattening/blunting; (2) avolition/apathy and anhedonia/asociality; and (3) alogia and inattention.

Arango *et al.* (2004) proposed that the inclusion of pathological phenomena that are actually distinct from negative symptoms has detracted from the construct validity of negative symptoms. Arango *et al.* (2004) noted that symptoms associated with the disorganisation of thought aspect of psychosis (e.g. impaired attention, inappropriate affect, poor concentration and stereotyped movements) can be confused clinically with negative symptoms. Problems with differentiating negative symptoms from impairments in individuals' functioning were also highlighted. For example, poor hygiene or limited social activities may be the result of negative symptoms, but these functional impairments can also be a consequence of reality distortion, adverse medication effects or stigmatising reactions from others (Arango *et al.*, 2004). Carpenter *et al.* (1985) had previously made a distinction between negative symptoms that are *Primary* (i.e. symptoms are said to arise directly from the pathophysiology of psychosis), and those that are *Secondary* (i.e. caused by something other than psychosis, e.g. side effects of drugs, depression and understimulation). To help distinguish between Primary and Secondary negative symptoms, Kirkpatrick *et al.* (1989) developed the Schedule for Deficit Syndrome which draws a contrast between individuals with schizophrenia and primary negative symptoms (i.e. *deficit* schizophrenia) and those without primary negative symptoms (*non-deficit* schizophrenia). Buchanan *et al.* (2007) proposed that approximately 15 to 20 per cent of individuals diagnosed with schizophrenia had deficit syndrome. As yet however, no specific etiopathophysiologic pathway has been identified that distinguishes deficit from non-deficit schizophrenia. As such the validity and reliability of this distinction remains questionable.

Correlates of negative symptoms

Negative symptoms have been shown to be strongly associated with poor insight in schizophrenia (Mutsatsa *et al.*, 2006). Mintz *et al.* (2004) proposed that this association between negative symptoms and impaired insight may serve to reduce patients' ability to be aware of the negative social consequences of the disorder. Deficits in social functioning are highly correlated with negative symptom levels in individuals with first episode psychosis (Milev *et al.*, 2005) and in individuals with chronic schizophrenia (Wittorf *et al.*, 2008). Some have argued that social impairments in the initial stages of illness predict the emergence of high levels of negative symptoms in the future (Meng *et al.*, 2006). However, others have proposed that negative symptoms are prominent predictors of the prospective development of impaired social functioning (Weinberg *et al.*, 2009). Research evidence has also raised the possibility that negative symptoms actually mediate associations between neurocognitive deficits and social functioning in schizophrenia (Addington and Addington, 2000; Milev *et al.*, 2005). Research evidence has consistently demonstrated strong associations between negative symptoms and neurocognitive deficits. The MATRICS consensus on designing clinical trials for neurocognitive medications for schizophrenia (see Buchanan *et al.*, 2005) proposed that there are six distinct neurocognitive domains: reasoning and problem solving; speed of processing; attention/vigilance; working memory (verbal); verbal learning and memory; and visual learning and memory. Dominguez *et al.* (2009) conducted a systematic review of research investigating associations between these neurocognitive domains and psychotic psychopathology. On the basis of evidence from previous meta-analyses, the authors also included research findings relating to three additional neurocognitive domains: IQ, verbal fluency and executive control. Dominguez *et al.* (2009) found that negative symptoms were modestly but meaningfully associated with impairments in the majority of neurocognitive domains. Associations were in the expected direction and the largest effect sizes were obtained for verbal fluency, verbal learning/memory and IQ.

Grant and Beck (2009) have proposed that the relationship between neurocognitive impairment and negative symptoms may be indirect; that emerging neurocognitive impairments increase the likelihood of discouraging life events, leading to the development of negative expectancies and defeatist beliefs. Defeatist beliefs were shown to mediate the relationship between neurocognitive impairment and negative symptoms – even when the effects of depression and positive symptom levels were controlled for (Grant and Beck, 2009). The cognitive model of negative symptoms proposes that 'negative symptoms represent, in part, a compensatory pattern of disengagement in response to threatening delusional beliefs, perceived social threat, and anticipated failure in tasks and social activities' (Rector *et al.*, 2005, p. 247). This theory builds on previous claims made by Strauss *et al.* (1989) that negative symptoms can be understood as a mechanism of defence against conflicts with the surroundings. Defeatist beliefs may therefore play an important role in the maintenance and/or potential exacerbation of negative symptoms. Social mentality theory (Gilbert, 2001, 2005) highlights the important implications that defeat experiences can have on understanding human psychopathology.

We believe that social mentality theory can be useful in helping to enhance understanding about the biopsychosocial mechanisms underlying the emergence and persistence of negative symptoms in psychosis.

Social mentality theory and negative symptoms

Biological and psychological systems evolve because they solve challenges to survival and genetic replication (Gilbert, 1989). The way in which different individuals relate to each other is an important determinant of the survival of animal species. Relationships between individuals can take a variety of different forms (e.g. competitive-conflictual, dominant-subordinate, caring-nurturing) that will have different implications for the survival of particular individuals. Social mentality theory (Gilbert, 2001, 2005) proposes that evolutionary derived systems lead to the interplay between emotional, motivational, cognitive and behavioural processes that shape relationships between the self and others. Social mentalities are context dependent. For example, the toning down of positive emotion, confidence and explorative behaviour (depression) may be adaptive when suffering a major defeat or loss of attachment, but not under other circumstances. In humans, however, the stimulators of social mentalities can also be internally regulated through individuals' capacity to reflect on the mental states of self and others, and to anticipate and plan for particular outcomes. It is suggested that social mentalities play a critical role in appraising threat, enhancing safeness, and in regulating the affect associated with these evolutionary challenges (MacBeth *et al.*, 2008). Building on the work of Panksepp (1998), Depue and Morrone-Strupinsky (2005) and others, Gilbert (2009) has proposed that three interacting systems are responsible for regulating emotions:

1 *The threat system*: associated with threat detection and defensive responses.
2 *The drive system*: linked to reward seeking. Dopamine has been highlighted as an important neurotransmitter for the regulation of drive.
3 *The soothing/affiliative system*: the action of opiates and oxytocin appears to be important for the experience of soothing.

Early experiences and attachment history appear to play an important role in the maturation, organisation and preferential use of social mentalities (Gilbert, 2005). Children who experience primary caregivers as available, accessible and affectionate tend to develop secure attachment styles (Chaffin *et al.*, 2006). Through relational experiences they construct working models of others as safe, helpful and supportive. This enables the individual to experience themselves as lovable and able to internalise self-soothing and compassionate behaviours (Gillath *et al.*, 2005). In times of managing distress, these individuals are more likely to turn to others for help and have an improved capacity to self-soothe. This capacity towards caring for distress he/she or others have experienced is referred to as the *caring social mentality*. In contrast, children who experience the parent as abusive, neglectful or unable to respond to their initiations will be subject to different emotional, motivational, cognitive and behavioural processes. Fewer experiences of soothing and calming in interpersonal relationships will lead to the formation of internal working models of others as either not available or as potentially serious threats. This raises the possibility that one of the primary sources of regulation of threat processing (i.e. through affiliation) becomes unavailable to these individuals (Gilbert, 2010). Consequently the caring social mentality may be poorly developed. In its place a social mentality better suited for dealing with social threats (i.e. the *social rank mentality*) takes precedence and focuses individuals' attention on the potential power of others. When the social rank mentality is activated, 'we turn our attention to our social position in a social hierarchy, to think about our relationships in terms of hierarchies and social comparisons . . . and to behave in ways appropriate to hierarchies' (Gilbert, 2009, p. 108).

We propose that the social rank mentality and the impact this exerts on affect regulation systems has important implications for understanding the emergence of negative symptoms. First, the phenomenology of negative symptoms appears consistent with a collapse in the drive system and the associated loss of motivation to pursue rewards. Second, there seems to be a marked reduction in the ability to experience safeness through affiliation. We believe that negative symptoms can therefore be explained in terms of individuals' experience of social defeat and the impact that this has on affect regulation. Research has been conducted into biological and psychological processes associated with the experience of social defeat. We will now discuss the implications that this research has for understanding the proposed role of social defeat in the emergence and maintenance of negative symptoms.

Role of social defeat and negative symptoms

Laboratory studies on rodents have shown that repeated experiences of social defeat reliably result in physiological and behavioural changes including: a decrease in offensive aggression (Lagerspetz and Sandnabba, 1982); an increase in defensive responses (Kulling *et al.*, 1987); decreases in subsequent exploratory behaviour and increases in 'freezing' (Raab *et al.*, 1986); weight loss (Adams and Boice, 1983); reduction of appetitive behaviours (van de Poll *et al.*, 1982); and disruption of escape learning (Williams and Lierle, 1988). The activity of the neurotransmitter dopamine appears to be important for the experience of social relationships (Cozolino, 2007). Grant *et al.* (1998) found lower D_2 dopamine receptors among subordinate monkeys, hypothesising that the stress of subordination produced a down regulation of D_2 dopamine receptors in monkeys. Defeats seem to be associated with animals losing interest in their environments and in resource acquisition (Willner, 1993a, 1993b). This may be adaptive in the sense that a 'loss of interest' would mean that animals are not motivated to pursue resources in a social environment where to do so might elicit injurious down rank attacks. Voruganti and Awad (2006) have shown that alphamethyl paratyrosine (AMPT) induced dopamine depletion leads to blunted pleasure responsivity, clouded thinking, loss of motivation and lowered vigilance in humans. This is a profile of changes that overlaps with the phenomenology of negative symptoms. Significant inverse correlations have been observed between negative symptom levels and plasma levels of the dopamine metabolite homovanillic acid (HVA) (Steinberg *et al.*, 1993). Wolf *et al.* (2008) proposed that ventral striatum hypofunction plays a role in the initiation, maintenance or progression of negative symptoms, and represents an intermediate phenotype for future study.

Dopamine release in the ventral striatum is positively associated with serum cortisol levels (Wand *et al.*, 2007). We have found that negative symptoms are negatively correlated with serum cortisol levels in individuals diagnosed with schizophrenia (White *et al.*, 2010a). The association between cortisol and negative symptoms highlights the potential importance of the hypothalamic–pituitary–adrenal axis in the emergence of negative symptoms. A meta-analysis by Dickerson and Kemeny (2004) of studies that recruited healthy people concluded that the greatest activation of the HPA axis was produced by laboratory stressors that included social-evaluative components. Socially threatening acute and chronic stressors are associated with a declining sensitivity to glucocorticoids (Miller *et al.*, 2002). Social evaluative threat (especially of being subordinated by powerful others) can be a key feature of the experience of schizophrenia, e.g. in the experience of paranoia (Freeman and Garety, 2004), feelings of external/internal shame (Birchwood *et al.*, 2007) and hallucinatory voices (Birchwood *et al.*, 2000). In support of an association between social evaluative threat and negative symptoms, we have recently found that negative symptoms are correlated with the extent to which hallucinatory voices are perceived as malevolent and appraisals which individuals make about the level of social support they receive from others (White *et al.*, 2010b). In a major meta-analysis of subordinate stress in monkeys, Abbott *et al.* (2003) found that cortisol levels in subordinates were predicted by two key variables: first, the rates of conflicts and stressors experienced; second, subordinate opportunities for affiliative kin and supportive interactions. This is important because affiliative interactions may stimulate positive affect systems and the release of oxytocin which can inhibit cortisol and reduce stress (Depue and Morrone-Strupinsky, 2005). This highlights the potential benefit that activating people's ability to feel safe in social relationships and experience affiliative interactions might have for alleviating negative symptoms.

Towards an integrated understanding of the emergence of negative symptoms

We propose that negative symptoms represent a particular organisation of the different systems used to regulate affect. These systems can be specified in terms of threat, reward/drive and soothing/affiliation systems. Social relationships are key to the regulation of these systems. There is increasing evidence that poor experiences of affiliation serve to shift processing towards more threat and social rank based mechanisms. Within this context, dopamine systems are highly sensitive to experiences such as defeat which can cause a major collapse in drive and affiliation. We propose that understanding the complex links between people's experiences of relationships in the past, genetic vulnerability, ongoing experiences of self in relationship to others and finding ways of reactivating the dopamine drive system are key to furthering understanding about negative symptoms and developing effective treatments.

We propose that experiences of interpersonal threat and social defeat predating the emergence of the psychosis are important factors in the emergence of negative symptoms. Research has highlighted links between negative symptoms and premorbid functioning. Asociality prior to hospital admission has been found to be significantly predictive of negative symptoms during illness phases and predicted longer term functional outcomes (Carpenter and Strauss, 1991; Buchanan and Carpenter, 1994). Fenton and McGlashan (1994) found that alogia, avolition, anhedonia and impaired attention were all significantly related to premorbid adjustment. Similarly, Kelley *et al.* (1992) reported that alogia and attentional impairment were significantly correlated with poor premorbid adjustment in early and late adolescence. However, in addition to premorbid factors, the experience of psychosis itself and factors associated with interpersonal defeat (malevolent positive symptoms, negative beliefs about illness, stigmatising reactions from others, etc.) can serve to compound the shift in processing towards more threat and social rank based mechanisms. For example, White *et al.* (2007) found significant associations between the level of negative symptoms and the extent to which individuals felt they had lost control over their illness (entrapment) and the extent to which they felt the schizophrenia had impacted on their capacity for independence (loss of autonomy). Consistent with Gilbert and Allan's (1998) finding that the experience of defeat was associated with hopelessness, White *et al.* (2007) also found that individuals with schizophrenia who were hopeless had significantly higher levels of negative symptoms than those who were not hopeless. We propose that the experience of psychosis leads to an even greater collapse in the affiliation and drive systems, which accentuates the levels of negative symptoms still further. The precise nature of the development of negative symptoms will vary from individual to individual depending on their premorbid functioning, interpersonal history and the nature of the psychosis that they have experienced. This highlights the importance of using a person-based approach to conceptualising and formulating negative symptoms. The following clinical vignette will be used to demonstrate how a person-based approach can be used to formulate negative symptoms.

Formulating negative symptoms

Sally was a 38-year-old lady with a diagnosis of schizophrenia. She had one younger brother. Sally had a largely unremarkable upbringing. Her father was a GP and her mother worked in a bank. Sally described a close relationship with her mum when she was growing up. She described her as warm and loving. However, Sally's father was very keen for her to do well academically and he could be critical of her academic performance at school. This led to many arguments between Sally and her father. Sally remembers being quite anxious during childhood. After Sally left school, she trained to be a primary school teacher. However, she found it difficult to cope with school placements and failed to complete the course. Over the last 16 years Sally had experienced three episodes of psychosis. Her last episode of psychosis occurred 15 months previously. She had spent most of the time since the last episode in hospital. She was originally hospitalised because of grandiose delusions and persistent auditory hallucinations. She believed that Jesus was speaking to her and instructing her to heal the sick.

Since Sally's last admission there had been a marked reduction in her social functioning. Her verbal exchanges were limited to three- or four-word utterances and she rarely initiates conversation. Sally did not report feeling depressed or anxious. Her verbal communication was generally limited to one or two words, and she rarely initiated conversation. Her facial expression rarely varied. Sally attended a Life Skills group run by occupational therapy staff for patients on the ward. She found it difficult to spontaneously engage in activities; nonetheless, she would complete a task when requested. Sally had limited social networks and seemed to lack any drive to engage in social activity. Sally did not complain about being bored and did not report feeling lonely. Although she spent much of her free time watching DVDs, she did not seem to get much enjoyment from this and found it difficult to recall the detail of what she had been watching. Over the last 15 months, Sally's presentation had remained largely unchanged irrespective of whether she has been medication-free, or treated with conventional or newer atypical antipsychotic medication.

Conceptualising Sally's negative symptoms

It is possible that the unrelenting standards that Sally's father had relating to Sally's academic performance led to the activation of the social rank mentality. As Sally grew up this would have exerted a powerful influence on the internal working models that she formed about how she should relate to other people. Her concerns about her father being critical of her were generalised to other people. This impacted on her ability to form close bonds with her peers. Her initial episode of psychosis occurred in the context of her becoming increasingly stressed by the workload at teaching college. This stress was in part compounded by the unrelenting standards that she had for herself. Her perceived inability to reach these standards led to a persisting sense of threat and defeat and feelings of being down-ranked. The two relapses that Sally experienced over the following years served to accentuate her sense of defeat. This helped create a context in which there was persistent activation of the threat emotional regulation system, which led to a mutual inhibition of the reward/incentive seeking emotion regulation system. The grandiose positive symptoms that she experienced could be understood as a defence against this under-activation of the reward system. It seems that her experiences had taught her that other people are critical of her, and that engaging in social contact was not associated with rewarding experiences. She was therefore less inclined to seek out affiliative contact with others. It is in this context that Sally's negative symptoms (flat affect, loss of motivation, lack of social engagement) emerged.

Psychological interventions for negative symptoms

To date psychological interventions for psychosis have mainly focused on reducing the level of positive symptoms or more generally attempting to prevent relapse. However, the recent development of a cognitive model of negative symptoms (Rector *et al.*, 2005; Beck *et al.*, 2009) has provided a rationale for structuring interventions aimed at specifically targeting negative symptoms. The cognitive model of negative symptoms postulates that the behaviours and attitudes which are operationalised as negative symptoms likely reflect, at least in part, negative self-beliefs (e.g. 'Nothing will ever work out for me', 'I am no good at anything'). It is suggested that negative symptoms can be addressed through cognitive behavioural therapy (CBT) by targeting negative self-beliefs. Rector *et al.* (2003) designed a CBT package for negative symptoms that included behavioural self-monitoring; activity scheduling; mastery and pleasure ratings; graded task assignments; and assertiveness training methods. Cognitive strategies included: eliciting patients' reasons for inactivity and testing these beliefs directly with behavioural experiments; direct attempts to stimulate interests (either new interests or a reactivation of previously held interests); and identifying, challenging and changing self-critical automatic thoughts. At 12-month follow-up there was significant and large effect size for this CBT package versus enhanced treatment as usual for a reduction in negative symptoms. Although promising, further research of this type is required before firm conclusions can be drawn about the efficacy of CBT for negative symptoms. The proposed development and evaluation of CBT interventions for negative symptoms is consistent with a growing awareness that CBT for psychosis should focus on particular types of symptoms rather than being more broadly aimed at relapse prevention (Wykes *et al.*, 2008). We believe that associations highlighted in this chapter between social defeats and negative symptoms provide an important opportunity to reflect on how CBT interventions for negative symptoms can be refined further.

Over the course of the chapter we have proposed that negative symptoms are the emotional, cognitive and behavioural consequences of chronic defeat states. Evidence has been presented that highlights the overlap between negative symptoms and the behavioural changes associated with social defeat experiences. In particular, the dopaminergic and opiate systems seem to be implicated in the experience of social defeat and the experience of affiliation respectively. As an extension of our *Social Defeat Model of Negative Symptoms* theory we propose that psychological interventions for negative symptoms should focus on alleviating these defeat states. One therapeutic approach that has been specifically developed to help promote affiliative experiences is *compassion focused therapy* (CFT; Gilbert 2005, 2009, 2010). CFT employs compassionate imagery and compassion-focused exercises to tone down threat processing by preferentially activating the soothing/affiliative emotion regulation system. There are a number of early indicators that suggest that compassion-focused interventions lead to the activation of positive affect and greater social connectedness (Fredrickson *et al.*, 2008; Hutcherson *et al.*, 2008). In terms of applying compassion work with psychosis, case studies have evidenced an effect of CFT on individuals who experience malevolent hallucinatory voices (Mayhew and Gilbert, 2008); auditory hallucinations became less malevolent, less persecuting and more reassuring. As yet, however, no research has been conducted to investigate whether CFT may be effective at alleviating negative symptoms in individuals diagnosed with psychosis. We propose that cognitive behavioural interventions which focus on enhancing positive expectations, whilst simultaneously incorporating compassion-focused strategies aimed at reducing social defeat and associated feelings of shame, will be effective at treating negative symptoms. We would encourage researchers to investigate this hypothesis. We believe that in designing compassion-focused interventions for negative symptoms it will be important to explore opportunities to employ multimodal inputs aimed at activating physiological systems implicated in positive affect – e.g. through massage, affiliative group work, affiliative meditative practices, etc. It is hoped that innovative approaches of this kind will help progress psychological interventions for negative symptoms.

References

Abbott, D.H., Keverne, E.B., Bercovitch, F.B., Shively, C.A., Mendoza, S.P., Saltzman, W., Snowdon, C.T., Ziegler, T.E., Beanjevic, M., Garland Jr, T. and

Sapolsky, R.M. (2003) Are subordinates always stressed? A comparative analysis of rank differences in cortisol levels among primates, *Hormones and Behaviour* 43: 67–82.

Adams, N. and Boice, R. (1983) A longitudinal study of dominance in an outdoor colony of domestic rats, *Journal of Comparative Psychology* 97: 24–33.

Addington, J. and Addington, D. (2000) Neurocognitive and social functioning in schizophrenia: a 2.5 year follow-up study, *Schizophrenia Research* 44: 47–56.

Andreasen, N.C. (1981) *Scale for the Assessment of Negative Symptoms (SANS)*, Iowa City: University of Iowa.

Andreasen, N.C. (1985) Positive versus negative schizophrenia: a critical evaluation, *Schizophrenia Bulletin* 11: 380–389.

Arango, C., Buchanan, R.W., Kirkpatrick, B. and Carpenter, W.T. (2004) The deficit syndrome in schizophrenia: implications for the treatment of negative symptoms, *European Psychiatry* 19: 21–26.

Beck, A.T., Rector, N.A., Stolar, N. and Grant, P. (2009) *Schizophrenia: Cognitive Theory, Research and Therapy*, New York: Guilford Press.

Bleuler, E. (1950) *Dementia Praecox or the Group of Schizophrenias* (Trans. J. Zinken), New York: International Universities Press. (Original work published in 1911.)

Birchwood, M., Meaden, A., Trower, P., Gilbert, P. and Plaistow, J. (2000) The power and omnipotence of voices: subordination and entrapment by voices and significant others, *Psychological Medicine* 30: 337–344.

Birchwood, M., Trower, P., Brunet, K., *et al.* (2007) Social anxiety and the shame of psychosis: a study in first episode psychosis, *Behaviour Research Therapy* 45: 1025–1037.

Buchanan, R.W. and Carpenter, W.T. (1994) Domains of psychopathology: an approach for the reduction of heterogeneity in schizophrenia, *Journal of Nervous and Mental Disease* 182: 193–204.

Buchanan, R.W., Davis, M., Goff, D., Green, M.F., Keefe, R.S., Leon, A.C., *et al.* (2005) A summary of the FDA-NIMH-MATRICS workshop on clinical trial design for neurocognitive drugs for schizophrenia, *Schizophrenia Bulletin* 31: 5–19.

Buchanan, R.W., Freedman, R., Javitt, D.C., Abi-Dargham, A. and Lieberman, J.A. (2007) Recent advances in the development of novel pharmacological agents for the treatment of cognitive impairments in schizophrenia, *Schizophrenia Bulletin* 33: 1120–1130.

Carpenter, W.T. and Strauss, J.S. (1991) The prediction of outcome in schizophrenia: IV. Eleven-year follow-up of the Washington IPSS cohort, *Journal of Nervous and Mental Disease* 179: 517–525.

Carpenter, W.T., Heinrichs, D.W. and Alphs, L.D. (1985) Treatment of negative symptoms, *Schizophrenia Bulletin* 11: 440–452.

Chaffin, M., Hanson, R., Saunders, B.E., Nichols, T., Barnett, D., Zeanah, C., *et al.* (2006) Report of the APSAC task force on attachment therapy, reactive attachment disorder, and attachment problems, *Child Maltreatment* 11: 76–89.

Cozolino, L. (2007) *The Neuroscience of Human Relationships: Attachment and the Developing Brain*, New York: Norton.

Crow, T. (1985) The two-syndrome concept. Origins and current status, *Schizophrenia Bulletin* 11: 471–485.

Depue, R.A. and Morrone-Strupinsky, J.V. (2005) A neurobehavioral model of affiliative bonding, *Behavioral and Brain Sciences* 28: 313–395.

Dickerson, S.S. and Kemeny, M.E. (2004) Acute stressors and cortisol responses: a theoretical integration and synthesis of laboratory research, *Psychological Bulletin* 130: 355–391.

Dominguez, M., Viechtbauer, W., Simons, C.J.P., van Os, J. and Krabbendam, L. (2009) Are psychotic psychopathology and neurocognition orthogonal? A systematic review of their associations, *Psychological Bulletin* 135: 157–171.

Fenton, W.S. and McGlashan, T.H. (1994) Antecedents, symptom progression, and long-term outcome of the deficit syndrome in schizophrenia, *American Journal of Psychiatry* 151: 351–356.

Fredrickson, B.L., Cohn, M.A., Coffey, K.A., Pek, J. and Finkel, S.M. (2008) Open hearts build lives: positive emotions, induced through loving-kindness meditation, build consequential personal resources, *Journal of Personality and Social Psychology* 95: 1045–1062.

Freeman, D. and Garety, P.A. (2004) Bats amongst birds: the psychology of persecutory delusions, *The Psychologist* 17: 642–645.

Gilbert, P. (1989) *Human Nature and Suffering*, Hove, UK: Lawrence Erlbaum Associates Ltd.

Gilbert, P. (2001) Evolutionary approaches to psychopathology: the role of natural defences, *Australian and New Zealand Journal of Psychiatry* 35: 17–27.

Gilbert, P. (2005) Compassion and cruelty: a biopsychosocial approach, in P. Gilbert (ed.) *Compassion: Conceptualisations, Research and Use in Psychotherapy*, Hove, UK: Brunner-Routledge, 9–74.

Gilbert, P. (2009) *The Compassionate Mind*, London: Constable.

Gilbert, P. (2010) *Compassion Focused Therapy*, London: Routledge.

Gilbert, P. and Allan, S. (1998) The role of defeat and entrapment (arrested flight) in depression: an exploration of an evolutionary view, *Psychological Medicine* 28: 584–597.

Gillath, O., Shaver, P.R. and Mikulincer, M. (2005) An attachment-theoretical approach to compassion and altruism, in P. Gilbert (ed.) *Compassion: Conceptualisations, Research and Use in Psychotherapy*, London: Routledge, 121–147.

Grant, K.A., Shively, C.A., Nader, M.S., Ehrenkaufer, R.L., Line, S.W., Morton, T.E., Gage, H.D. and Mach, R.H. (1998) Effects of social status on striatal dopamine D_2 receptor binding characteristics in cynomolgus monkeys assesses with positron emission tomography, *Synapse* 29: 80–83.

Grant, P.M. and Beck, A.T. (2009) Defeatist beliefs as a mediator of cognitive impairment, negative symptoms and functioning in schizophrenia, *Schizophrenia Bulletin* 35: 798–806.

Hutcherson, C.A., Seppala, E.M. and Gross, J.J. (2008) Loving-kindness meditation increases social connectedness, *Emotion* 8: 720–724.

Kay, S.R., Fiszbein, A. and Opler, L.A. (1987) The Positive and Negative Syndrome Scale (PANSS) for schizophrenia, *Schizophrenia Bulletin* 13: 261.

Kelley, M.E., Gilbertson, M., Mouton, A. and van Kammen, D.P. (1992) Deterioration of premorbid functioning in schizophrenia: a developmental model of negative symptoms in drug-free patients, *American Journal of Psychiatry* 149: 543–1548.

Kirkpatrick, B., Buchanan, R.W., McKenney, P.D., Alphs, L.D. and Carpenter Jr, W.T. (1989) The Schedule for the Deficit Syndrome: an instrument for research in schizophrenia, *Psychiatry Research* 30: 119–123.

Kraepelin, E. (1971) *Dementia Praecox and Paraphrenia* (Trans. R.M. Barclay), Huntington, NY: Robert E. Krieger. Facsimile of 1919 edn.

Kulling, P., Frischknecht, H.R., Pasi, A., Waser, P.G. and Siegfried, B. (1987) Effects of repeated as compared to single aggressive confrontation on nociception and defense behaviour in C57BL/6 and DBA/2 mice, *Physiology and Behaviour* 39: 599–605.

Kurtz, M.M., Moberg, J.P., Ragland, J.D., Gur, R.C. and Gur, R.E. (2005) Symptoms versus neurocognitive test performance as predictors of psychosocial status in schizophrenia: a 1- and 4-year prospective study, *Schizophrenia Bulletin* 31: 167–174.

Lagerspetz, K.M.J. and Sandnabba, K. (1982) The decline of aggressiveness in male mice during group caging as determined by punishment delivered by the cage mates, *Aggressive Behaviour* 8: 319–328.

MacBeth, A., Schwannauer, M. and Gumley, A.I. (2008) Attachment style, social mentalities and paranoid ideation: an analogue study, *Psychology and Psychotherapy: Theory, Research and Practice* 81: 79–93.

Mayhew, S. and Gilbert, P. (2008) Compassionate mind training with people who hear malevolent voices: a case series report, *Clinical Psychology and Psychotherapy* 15: 113–138.

Meehl, P.E. (1962) Schizotaxia, schizotypy, and schizophrenia, *American Psychologist* 17: 827–838.

Meng, H., Schimmelmann, B.G., Mohler, B., Lambert, M., Branik, E., Koch, E., Karle, M., Strauss, M., Preuss, U., Amsler, F., Riedesser, P., Resch, F. and Burgin, D. (2006) Pretreatment social functioning predicts 1-year outcome in early onset psychosis, *Acta Psychiatrica Scandinavica* 114: 249–256.

Milev, P., Ho, B.-C., Arndt, S. and Andreasen, N.C. (2005) Predictive values of neurocognition and negative symptoms on functional outcome in schizophrenia: a longitudinal first-episode study with 7-year follow-up, *American Journal of Psychiatry* 162: 495–506.

Miller, G.E., Cohen, S. and Ritchey, A.K. (2002) Chronic psychological stress and the regulation of pro-inflammatory cytokines: a glucocorticoid-resistance model, *Health Psychology* 21: 531–541.

Mintz, A.R., Addington, J. and Addington, D. (2004) Insight in early psychosis: a 1-year follow-up, *Schizophrenia Research* 67: 213–217.

Mueser, K.T., Sayers, S.L., Schooler, N.R., Mance, R.M. and Haas, G.L. (1994) A multisite investigation of the reliability of the scale for the assessment of negative symptoms, *American Journal of Psychiatry* 151: 1453–1462.

Mutsatsa, S.H., Joyce, E.M., Hutton, S.B., *et al.* (2006) Relationship between insight, cognitive function, social function and symptomatology in schizophrenia: the West London first episode study, *European Archives of Psychiatry and Clinical Neuroscience* 256: 356–363.

Panksepp, J. (1998) *Affective Neuroscience*, New York: Oxford University Press.

Raab, A., Dantzer, R., Michaud, B., Mormede, P., Taghzouti, K., Simon, H. and LeMoal, M. (1986) Behavioural, physiological and immunological consequences of social status and aggression in chronically co-existing resident–intruder dyads of male rats, *Physiology and Behaviour* 36: 223–228.

Rado, S. (1956) *Psychoanalysis of Behavior*, New York: Grune and Stratton.

Rector, N.A., Seeman, M.V. and Segal, Z.V. (2003) Cognitive therapy of schizophrenia: a preliminary randomized controlled trial, *Schizophrenia Research* 63: 1–11.

Rector, N.A., Beck, A.T. and Stolar, N.M. (2005) The negative symptoms of schizophrenia: a cognitive perspective, *Canadian Journal of Psychiatry* 50: 247–257.

Steinberg, J.L., Garver, D.L., Moeller, F.G., *et al.* (1993) Serum homovanillic acid levels in schizophrenic patients and normal control subjects, *Psychiatry Research* 48: 93–106.

Strauss, J., Carpenter Jr, W.T. and Bartko, J. (1974) The diagnosis and understanding of schizophrenia: Part III. Speculations on the processes that underlie schizophrenic symptoms and signs, *Schizophrenia Bulletin* 1: 61–69.

Strauss, J.S., Rakfeldt, J., Harding, C.M. and Lieberman, P. (1989) Psychological and social aspects of negative symptoms, *British Journal of Psychiatry* 155: 128–132.

van de Poll, N.E., Smeets, J., van Oyen, H.G. and van de Zwan, S.M. (1982) Behavioural consequences of agonistic experiences in rats: sex differences and effects of testosterone, *Journal of Comparative and Physiological Psychology* 96: 893–903.

Voruganti, L.N. and Awad, A.G. (2006) Subjective and behavioural consequences of striatal dopamine depletion in schizophrenia—findings from an in vivo SPECT study, *Schizophrenia Research* 88: 179–186.

Wand, G.S., Oswald, L.M., McCaul, M.E., *et al.* (2007) Association of amphetamine induced striatal dopamine release and cortisol responses to psychological stress, *Neuropsychopharmacology* 32: 2310–2320.

Weinberg, D., Shahar, G., Davidson, L., McGlashan, T.H. and Fennig, S. (2009) Longitudinal associations between negative symptoms and social functioning in schizophrenia: the moderating role of employment status and setting, *Psychiatry* 72: 370–381.

White, R.G., McCleery, M., Gumley, A.I. and Mulholland, C. (2007) Hopelessness in schizophrenia: the impact of symptoms and beliefs about illness, *Journal of Nervous and Mental Disease* 195: 968–975.

White, R.G., McCleery, M., Gumley, A.I. and Mulholland, C. (2010a) Deficit syndrome: associations with plasma cortisol levels and appraisals about illness, *Psychiatry Research*, in submission.

White, R.G., McCleery, M., Gumley, A.I. and Mulholland, C. (2010b) Associations between hallucinatory experiences and appraisals about social support, *Schizophrenia Research*, in submission.

Williams, J.L. and Lierle, D.M. (1988) Effects of repeated defeat by a dominant conspecific on subsequent pain sensitivity, open-field activity, and escape learning, *Animal Learning and Behavior* 16: 477–485.

Willner, P. (1993a) Animal models of stress: an overview, in C. Stanford and P. Salmon (eds) *Stress: From Synapse to Syndrome*, London: Academic Press, Harcourt Brace and Co., 145–165.

Willner, P. (1993b) Anhedonia, in C.G. Costello (ed.) *Symptoms of Depression*, New York: Wiley, 63–84.

Wittorf, A., Wiedemann, G., Buchkremer, G. and Klingberg, S. (2008) Prediction of community outcome in schizophrenia 1 year after discharge from inpatient treatment, *European Archives of Psychiatry and Clinical Neuroscience* 258: 48–58.

Wolf, I.M., Heitzer, M.D., Grubisha, M. and DeFranco, D.B. (2008) Coactivators and nuclear receptor transactivation, *Journal of Cellular Biochemistry* 104: 1580–1586.

Wykes, T., Steel, C., Everitt, B. and Tarrier, N. (2008) Cognitive behavior therapy for schizophrenia: effect sizes, clinical models, and methodological rigor, *Schizophrenia Bulletin*, 34: 523–537.

Index

Note: Only those individuals who have been mentioned in some detail have been indexed (omitting passing reference). Footnotes are indicated by the letter n as in '18n'.